"We Are Coming"

"We Are Coming"

The
Persuasive Discourse
of Nineteenth-Century
Black Women

Shirley Wilson Logan

SOUTHERN ILLINOIS UNIVERSITY PRESS

Carbondale and Edwardsville

02 01 00 99 4 3 2 1

Library of Congress Cataloging-in-Publication Data

Logan, Shirley W. (Shirley Wilson), [DATE]
We are coming : the persuasive discourse of nineteenth-century black women /
Shirley Wilson Logan.
    p.   cm.
Includes bibliographical references and index.
    1. Afro-American women—Political activity—History—19th century. 2. Afro-
American women—Language. 3. Afro-American women—Intellectual life. 4.
Persuasion (Rhetoric)—History—19th century. 5. Afro-American intellectuals—
History—19th century. 6. Women intellectuals—United States—History—19th
century. I. Title.
E185.86.L57 1999
973.5′082—DC21
ISBN 0-8093-2192-0 (cloth : alk. paper)   98-35109
ISBN 0-8093-2193-9 (pbk. : alk. paper)   CIP

The paper used in this publication meets the minimum requirements of American
National Standard for Information Sciences—Permanence of Paper for Printed Library
Materials, ANSI Z39.48-1984. ♾

Dedicated to the memory of
Susan Marie Oswald (1961–1995),
a friend sorely missed

Contents

Appendixes

Illustrations

Preface

This book examines the public persuasive discourse of nineteenth-century black women intellectuals. With the exception of the texts by Maria W. Miller Stewart and some of Frances Ellen Watkins Harper's early speeches and essays, it was all produced during the last decade of the century, in the midst of a period described by Rayford Logan as the "nadir" of black American history. This period is usually dated from the Hayes-Tilden Compromise of 1877—when representatives of then presidential candidate Rutherford B. Hayes and representatives of the South confirmed an agreement leading to his election and the withdrawal of federal troops from the South—to 1915, around the time of the migration of large numbers of blacks to the North when America was preparing to enter World War I. During this period, white supremacy in the South and general black oppression were consolidated. Emigration and subsequent colonization initiatives escalated. Blacks in some southern states moved west and later north to the major industrial centers. Booker T. Washington delivered his "Atlanta Compromise Address," implying acceptance of an inferior status for blacks. With the *Plessy* v. *Ferguson* decision, the U.S. Supreme Court upheld the doctrine of separate but equal. Jim Crow laws and "grandfather clauses" were enacted to deny blacks voting rights and to limit access to public facilities. The number of reported lynchings and the number of race riots increased sharply. At the same time and partially in response to these events, two major periodicals—the *AME Church Review* and the *Woman's Era*—were established. Black women's clubs merged to form the National Association of Colored Women. The American National Baptist Convention was formed. The National Association for the Advancement of Colored People (NAACP) was founded. Black regiments fought in the Spanish-American War. Chicago's Provident Hospital opened the first school for black nurses, and a number of black colleges were established in the South.

It was within this context that most of the speeches under consideration here were produced. Yet they were produced by the more prominent "race women" of the time who left extant texts. Charles Nero suggests that an "inherent class bias" constrains the study of black oratory since the speeches of "working-class or poor people" are seldom recorded (271). As a result, we are left to study the oratory of a relative elite. Certainly, the discursive practices of all black women, long overlooked, need critical consideration, but they deserve a scrutiny that only careful partitioning allows. Further, as well known as the women under consideration may have been during their time, the names of few are recognized today outside of the community of nineteenth-century black history and literary scholars.

A related concern, of course, is the availability of extant nineteenth-century texts to analyze. The rhetorical activities of many prominent black women can be addressed only in general terms. Even less survives of the impromptu addresses delivered on informal occasions where no reporters were present and no proceedings were recorded. Another consideration is that while most of these women belonged to a relatively educated and social elite, their messages addressed the concerns of all classes. As Dorothy Sterling points out in her introduction to *We Are Your Sisters*, "in the mobile society of black nineteenth-century America, the working-class woman and the superachiever often encountered the same problems" (ix). Historian Evelyn Brooks Higginbotham notes the paradox that the motto of the National Association of Colored Women, "Lifting As We Climb," expressed "belief in black womanhood's common cause and recognition of differential values and socioeconomic positions" ("Metalanguage" 271). Frances Smith Foster also acknowledges that it would be "naive and insulting" to ignore differences in the literature produced by various classes of African American women, but she rejects, at the same time, the assumption that formal published materials, such as speeches, novels, and essays, are less authentic expressions of nineteenth-century African American struggle than oral literature and artifacts from ordinary women. Foster argues that

[t]o assert that those who adopted forms and techniques of western literature and addressed their remarks to an audience not confined to the African American community were really writing just to convince white people that they, too, could sing America is also an ingenuous and ignoble conclusion. It devalues the relationships between black writers and black readers and it disregards the vitality and versatility of African American culture. . . . I suggest that the extant literature from 1746 to 1896, . . . proves that African American women, like African American men, deliberately chose to participate in the public discourse despite considerable Anglo-American resistance to their doing

so. They appropriated the English literary tradition to reveal, to interpret, to challenge, and to change perceptions of themselves and the world in which they found themselves. (*Written* 15–16)

Although Foster refers here to all types of literature, the statement can be applied in particular to the extant literature of public address because that literature gave the authors direct and immediate access to those empowered to bring about change.

In this work I consider the speeches in my collection, *With Pen and Voice: A Critical Anthology of Nineteenth-Century African-American Women* (1995), but also examine additional texts and other women. While none were preachers, they all came from a church tradition that, according to C. Eric Lincoln and Lawrence Mamiya, "made possible prominent roles in religion for women both in Africa and on American plantations" (277). They recall that in some African religious cultures women played major roles as priestesses, queens, and diviners. The prominent if constrained participation of African American women in religious discourse represents one manifestation of this tradition. While most historians of nineteenth-century black women focus on the National Association of Colored Women and the secular club movement, the training ground for developing organizational and—I would add—speaking skills was the black church. Higgenbotham points out that black women made up two-thirds of the black Baptist convention movement in the last decades of the century, forming their own Woman's Convention in 1900, only five years after the creation of the male-dominated National Baptist Convention and adds that many churches also held (and still hold) annual Women's Day programs that "offered black women a forum wherein to articulate a public discourse critical of women's subordination" (*Righteous* 6–8, 10).

Also considered is the public discourse of Mary Ann Shadd Cary, pioneer journalist and outspoken advocate of Canadian emigration, affiliated with the American Missionary Association (AMA). The Association was founded in 1846 by staunch Christian abolitionists who believed in evangelizing through good works and supported the emigration of blacks to Canada. One other important source has been the *Black Abolitionist Papers*, with the persuasive discourse of black abolitionist women, including Mary Ann Shadd Cary, Mary E. Bibb, Sarah Parker Remond, Sojourner Truth, and Frances Harper.

This work seeks to identify "distinctive and recurring patterns of rhetorical practice" in the public persuasive discourse of historical nineteenth-century black women. "Distinctive and recurring patterns of rhetorical practice" is Herbert Simons's definition of a rhetorical genre. He defines "rhetorical practice" as any discourse or symbolic act designed to influence others" (50). Simons offers a scientifically quantifiable approach to what he calls "genre-alizing" about rhetoric. According to his system, a pattern must have specific identifiable features before it may be classified as representative of a rhetorical genre, features that meet a set of criteria designed to ensure genre validity and reliability. Although I borrow Simons's term, "distinctive and recurring patterns of rhetorical practice," it is not my intention here to argue for a genre called "black women's rhetoric" based on the patterns I identify or to apply a scientifically verifiable approach to identifying them. So while I look for recurrences, I do not claim that they constitute a genre. Instead, my focus is both singular and collective in that I consider individual speakers and the occasions surrounding particular rhetorical acts but with an eye toward the features of that act that are shared by other rhetorical acts arising from similar but not identical rhetorical situations. As Campbell and Jamieson suggest, this approach of "studying bodies of rhetoric" illustrates the "development, fruition, and degeneration of rhetorical forms and strategies" (13–14). Thus rather than argue for genres, I identify common practices across rhetorical acts that were molded and constrained by prevailing conventions and traditions. Such an approach can also provide what these authors refer to as "a venture into intellectual history through public address" (13), in this instance the intellectual history of nineteenth-century black women. As Perelman and Olbrechts-Tyteca point out, we can learn a great deal about past cultures by studying the speeches addressed to it (21). One could argue that it is more useful to focus on distinctive features across common rhetorical situations than on features common among speakers who share the same ethnic origins and are identified as members of the same racialized group. However, for these nineteenth-century African American orators, identity and situation converge into one seamless exigence.

I concentrate on public discourse produced during the last two decades of the century, particularly the work of club women, church women, and educators, with many women active in all three groups. Following the overview of chapter 1, "Black Women on the Speaker's Platform, 1832–1900," each subsequent chapter develops around features of their public address as best exemplified in the oratory of particular women speakers of the era. Chapter 2, "African Origins/American Appropriations: Maria Stewart and 'Ethiopia Rising,'" explores early nineteenth-century prophetic oratory with its allusions to Ethiopian retribution. As most likely the first American-born woman to speak publicly on political matters, Stewart mounted the platform during an earlier decade, from 1832 to 1833; however, examining her speeches exposes a background against which to consider later oratory. Her pioneering oratorical performances cleared the way for the more polished performances of subsequent speakers. Chapter 3, "'We Are All Bound Up Together': Frances Harper's Converging Communities of Interest," drawing on Perlman and Olbrechts-Tyteca's discussion of argumentative dissociations, examines the strategic shifts from "a part of" to "apart from" in Harper's persuasive discourse, as she argues for common communities of interest among varying combinations of auditors. Also informed by concepts from *The New Rhetoric*, chapter 4, "'Out of Their Own Mouths': Ida Wells and the Presence of Lynching," considers her use of presence to argue against mob violence, demonstrating the effect of description to persuade audiences geographically and emotionally removed from the circumstances to which they were being asked to respond. The central role of audience adaptation emerges in chapter 5, "'Women of a Common Country, with Common Interests': Fannie Barrier Williams, Anna Julia Cooper, Identification and Arrangement," as well. With Williams's 1893 speech titled "The Intellectual Progress of the Colored Women of the United States" as a springboard, this chapter examines ways in which she and her contemporaries engaged a form of Burkean identification as a strategy for persuading auditors from whom, in many respects, they were divided. Anna Cooper's tactics of arrangement in lecturing to black men on the needs of black women highlight accommodations to gender differences. Chapter 6, "'To Embalm Her Memory in Song and Story': Victoria Earle Matthews and Situated Sisterhood," applies a Bitzerian analysis of the manner in which Matthews's discourse responded to the exigences of tightly constrained rhetorical situations and constituted fitting responses to them. Finally, chapter 7, "'Can Woman Do This Work?': The Discourse of Racial Uplift," discusses how the discourse of racial uplift induced social action by representing it as work. This representation is particularly salient in speeches presented at conferences and church conventions convened in the late 1880s and the 1890s to tackle problems facing blacks in the nadir.

I define persuasive discourse as verbal communication directed toward a particular audience to obtain what Perelman and Olbrechts-Tyteca call "the adherence of minds." It is the kind of communication nineteenth-century black women engaged in to address the pressing needs of people of African descent. I consider how the language of this discourse worked to achieve their communicative aims. While most of the analyzed texts are speeches, I also draw from editorials, essays, and letters, for example, in the case of Mary Ann Shadd Cary, by all accounts a prolific and powerful speaker, for whom we have no extant speeches other than a few brief excerpts quoted in newspapers. Since rhetorical analysis requires an understanding of the formal features of a text in conjunction with its historical context, I consider pertinent historical details—biographical, social, political, and cultural. Moving from the historical, I address various characteristics of a chosen text in the light of these details. The selection of characteristics is informed by classical rhetoric and its twentieth-century reconstructions. My hope is that these discussions might also add to a clearer understanding of nineteenth-century culture and of the ways in which the persuasive discourse of nineteenth-century black women adapted itself to its multiple audiences and multilayered exigences. These strategies were grounded always in African origins but adapted to rhetorical situations requiring both identification with and dissociation from those whose adherence they sought. Thus it was a discourse revealing unity in diversity.

The texts that comprise the appendixes—seven speeches and one journal article—are those discussed in chapter 7, " 'Can Woman Do This Work?' " With the exception of the recent reprinting of Mary V. Cook's speech, all appear here for the first time since their original publication. I have edited conservatively. Obvious typographical errors, for example, missing quotation marks or periods, have been silently emended. Paragraphing and section divisions are as in the original texts. I have added the explanatory notes.

Acknowledgments

Portions of chapter 1 are excerpts from my chapter, "Black Women on the Speaker's Platform (1832–1899)," in *Listening to Their Voices: The Rhetorical Activities of Historical Women*, edited by Molly Meijer Wertheimer. Reprinted by permission of University of South Carolina Press. Portions of chapter 4 are an excerpt from an earlier version published in *SAGE: A Scholarly Journal on Black Women*, 8.1, 1991, Copyright 1991 by *SAGE*. Reprinted by permission of Sage Women's Educational Press, Inc.

A substantial amount of this book was written during a twelve-month sabbatical granted me by the Department of English and the College of Arts and Humanities of the University of Maryland. I express special gratitude to the many sister scholars and feminist rhetoricians who provided moral and intellectual support and extend specific thanks to Cheryl Glenn, Andrea Lunsford, Joyce Irene Middleton, and Jacqueline Royster. I am indebted to the university and to my colleagues in the Professional Writing Program who encouraged me and carried on during my absence. I am particularly grateful to Bob Coogan, who served as interim director of the program and gently nudged me away from the office; to Jean Johnson, who assisted with proofreading; and to Rosalie Lynn, who took on the tedious task of retyping from old copies the texts included in the appendixes. I thank Terry Sayler, Hubert Steward, and other members of the McKeldin Interlibrary Loan staff of the University of Maryland for their persistence in locating material. I am grateful to copyeditor Marie Maes and to the editorial staff at Southern Illinois University Press, including former acquisitions editor Tracey J. Sobol and managing editor Carol A. Burns. I appreciate as always the support of my family—Mother, Thelma, Melva, Junior, Mac, Enid, Malcolm, Monica, and John—for whom I say a silent prayer of thanks daily. The immeasurable assistance of others not cited here is no less appreciated.

I thank God who has promised a future with hope.

"We Are Coming"

I

✧

Black Women on the Speaker's Platform, 1832–1900
An Overview

Our progress depends in the united strength of both men and women—
the women alone nor the men alone cannot do the work. We have so fully
realized that fact by witnessing the work of our men with the women in
the rear. This is indeed the women's era, and we are coming.

—Rosetta Douglass-Sprague, July 20, 1896

Nineteenth-century African American women were full participants
in the verbal warfare for human dignity. Describing the women and
the times, Rosetta Douglass-Sprague, daughter of Anna Murray
Douglass and Frederick Douglass, proclaimed at the first Annual Convention
of the National Federation of Afro-American Women, July 20–22, 1896, "This
is indeed the women's era, and we are coming" (*History* 37). During the three-
day conference, the footsteps of advancing black women resonated in the
speeches and remarks of such forward-thinking intellectuals as Ida B. Wells,
Victoria Earle Matthews, Alice Ruth Moore, and Frances Ellen Watkins
Harper. They echoed, as well, in the poem "We Are Coming," which "little
Margaret Tate" recited at the closing session (*History* 57).[1] The participants at
this convention, held at the Nineteenth Street Baptist Church in Washington,
D.C., united with the other national black women's organization, the National
League of Colored Women, to form the National Association of Colored
Women (NACW).[2] Representing a milestone rather than a beginning, the
merger provided a larger forum for public expression. Black women addressed
women's organizations, church groups, antislavery associations, and temperance

unions. They spoke in all sections of the United States, in Canada, and in the British Isles. They spoke to black audiences, white audiences, and mixed audiences on the panoply of issues challenging peoples of African descent throughout America at the time. In addition to the oppressive defining issue of slavery, these concerns included employment, civil rights, women's rights, emigration, and self-improvement. After the Civil War, mob violence, racial uplift, and support for the Southern black woman were added to the list.

Not limiting themselves to being mere participants in public forums, black women also created, organized, and publicized a large number of them. Maria W. Stewart, the first American woman to speak publicly to a mixed group of women and men and to leave extant texts, was such a woman. She delivered her first address in 1832, six years before Angelina Grimké's appearance at Pennsylvania Hall, and her speeches were published in Garrison's *Liberator*. Mary Ann Shadd Cary, after considerable discussion, was reluctantly seated at the 1855 Colored National Convention in Philadelphia, becoming the first woman to address that body by a vote of 38 yeas and 23 nays (*Minutes* 10). An article in the October 26, 1855, edition of *Frederick Douglass' Paper* describes that performance:

She at first had ten minutes granted her as had the other members. At their expiration, ten more were granted, and by this time came the hour of adjournment; but so interested was the House, that it granted additional time to her to finish, at the commencement of the afternoon session; and the House was crowded and breathless in its attention to her masterly exposition of our present condition, and the advantages open to colored men of enterprise. (Sterling, *Sisters* 171)

Frances Harper was employed as a lecturer for the Maine Anti-Slavery Society in 1854, becoming possibly the first black woman to earn a living as a traveling lecturer. She was certainly the most prolific. The black women's club movement was also a site of extensive issue-oriented public discussion, as any edition of the *Woman's Era* demonstrates. The pages of this periodical, published by the Woman's Era Club of Boston, from 1894 to 1897, were filled with reports from the various black women's clubs around the country relating their very public presence in current affairs. For example, the April 1895 issue carried an article by Mary Church Terrell, editor of the Washington, D.C., column, in which she condemned T. Thomas Fortune, editor of the *New York Age*, for criticizing "the race with which he is identified for whining" (3). Fortune had complained that blacks needed to become more self-sufficient and to stifle their demands for rights. In the same issue, the column from Georgia, edited by Alice Woodby McKane, reports on the club's interest in the emigration of two hundred blacks to Liberia. In the June 1, 1894, issue, Ednah Cheney, white Boston reformer, commends the *Woman's Era* for its involvement in opening the medical profession to women. Later issues teem with support for a national gathering of women, which did occur in 1895, providing another opportunity for black women to address publicly urgent race concerns. Although this volume develops around the rhetorical accomplishments of individual nineteenth-century black women, in this overview chapter, I consider those rhetors within the larger sociohistorical context. This context was shaped by the following broad and necessarily overlapping issues: the abolition of slavery, women's rights, mob violence, and racial uplift.

Abolition of Slavery

It should be clear that the abolition of slavery dominated discourse among black women during the first half of the century. Of the 750,000 blacks living in the United States at the time of the census of 1790, approximately 92 percent or 691,000 were enslaved, and most lived in the South Atlantic states. In 1808, legislation finally made the African slave trade illegal, although it continued underground for many years. In the 1790 census, Boston was the only city that listed no slaves, with approximately 27,000 free blacks living in the North and 32,000 free blacks in the South (Franklin and Moss 80–81).

One can best appreciate the range of black women's abolitionist rhetoric by considering the careers of three speakers who migrated to new locales, delivering their antislavery messages to audiences in England, Canada, and across the United States. Sarah Parker Remond, a member of a prominent abolitionist family in Massachusetts, lectured in England and Scotland. Mary Ann Shadd Cary, whose father was a leader in the Underground Railroad movement in Delaware, fled with her family to Canada to avoid the consequences of the Fugitive Slave Act of 1850 and developed into an outspoken presence in the antislavery movement there. Frances Harper, whose uncle William Watkins was active in the abolitionist movement, left Baltimore about 1850, also in response to the Fugitive Slave Act, eventually traveling across the country with her antislavery message.

Although slavery was abolished in the British Empire in 1833, antislavery activities against its American version continued throughout the first half of the century, when a number of black abolitionists, including Sarah Remond (1815–1894), traveled to the British Isles to generate support for their cause. Sarah Remond's family was part of the abolitionist society of Salem, Massachusetts. In 1856 Remond was appointed agent for the American Anti-Slavery Society and, as an affiliate of William Lloyd Garrison, became one of the first black women to lecture regularly before antislavery audiences. Initially a reluctant speaker, Remond toured throughout New England, New York, and Ohio between 1856 and 1858 and developed into an accomplished orator. From 1859 to 1861, she delivered more than forty-five lectures in eighteen cities in England, three cities in Scotland, and four cities in Ireland (Wesley 974). She was received enthusiastically wherever she spoke. In 1866 she returned to the United States and applied her oratorical skills to the task of racial uplift, in the manner of her brother Charles Remond and of Frederick Douglass. In 1867 she traveled again to England and subsequently settled in Florence, Italy, to practice medicine. It was said that she spoke in a "well-toned" and "pleasing style" and "demonstrated an unerring sensitivity to the political and social concerns of her listeners—particularly women reform activists" (Ripley, vol. 1, 441).

Unlike most male lecturers, Remond did not hesitate to speak about the exploitation of enslaved black women. In an hour-and-fifteen-minute lecture delivered to an overflow crowd at the Music Hall in Warrington, England, January 24, 1859, Remond relentlessly detailed the treatment of the enslaved black woman, using as a case in point the story of Kentucky slave mother Margaret Garner. Garner, who "had suffered in her own person the degradation that a woman could not mention," escaped with her husband and four children across the Ohio River into Cincinnati in 1856. Under the Fugitive Slave Law of 1850, escapees could be recaptured in free states and returned to captivity. To prevent this, when Garner realized that they would be overcome by a large posse, she killed her three-year-old daughter but was prevented from killing the others.[3] Remond stated that "above all sufferers in America, American women who were slaves lived in the most pitiable condition. They could not protect themselves from the licentiousness which met them on every hand—they could not protect their honour from the tyrant" (Remond, "Music Hall" 437). She also criticized the Dred Scott Decision of 1857, denying blacks the right to citizenship, and the heinous Fugitive Slave Act, which sent many blacks fleeing to abolitionist communities within northern states, Canada, and the British Isles.

Remond drew support for her arguments from contemporary events. She chronicled current and widely publicized incidents with significant impact on American slavery, showing how such events, like the trial of Margaret Garner and the Dred Scott Decision, mirror the sad conditions of a slave society. Stressing the hypocrisy of the Christian church, in this same speech Remond cited the shooting of a black man for insubordination by a clergyman in Louisiana and the dismissal of a minister in Philadelphia after he preached an antislavery sermon. From her English audiences she wanted public outcry. In a September 14, 1859, speech delivered at the Athenaeum in Manchester, England, she asked them to exert their influence to abolish slavery in America:

Give us the power of your public opinion, it has great weight in America. Words spoken here are read there as no words written in America are read. . . . I ask you, raise the moral public opinion until its voice reaches the American shores. Aid us thus until the shackles of the American slave melt like dew before the morning sun. (Remond, "Athenaeum" 459)

Mary Ann Shadd Cary (1823–1893), the first black female newspaper editor, published the *Provincial Freeman*, a weekly Canadian newspaper for fugitive slaves and others who had fled to Canada in the wake of the Fugitive Slave Act during the 1850s. From 1852 to 1853, she was the only black missionary in the field for the American Missionary Association (AMA), the largest abolitionist organization in America (DeBoer xi). Cary taught fugitive slaves recently arrived, who, in her view, lacked motivation and self-discipline. Along with Samuel Ward and Alexander McArthur, Cary established the *Provincial Freeman* in March of 1853, after the AMA informed her that it would no longer support her school. The *Freeman* soon became Cary's vehicle for promoting industry among former slaves and exposing the misconduct of unscrupulous antislavery agents. In her historic 1855 address to the Colored National Convention, mentioned above, she advocated for the emigration of blacks to Canada and for their total integration into Canadian society. Cary's intense speaking style left its impression, as noted by the eye witness quoted above and here:

Miss Shadd's eyes are small and penetrating and fairly flush when she is speaking. Her ideas seem to flow so fast that she, at times hesitates for words; yet she overcomes any apparent imperfections in her speaking by the earnestness of her manner and the quality of her thoughts. She is a superior woman; and it is useless to deny it; however much we may differ with her on the subject of emigration. (Sterling, *Sisters* 170–71)

All accounts of the works and days of the strong-willed Cary suggest that she rarely held her tongue or backed down from a position. Offering Cary as an example of the many mid-century "literary and professional colored men and women," Martin R. Delany, in his book titled *The Condition, Elevation, Emigration, and Destiny of the Colored People of the United States*, described her as "intelligent" and "peculiarly eccentric" (131).[4] She opposed the growing popularity of evangelical, better-life-in-the-afterworld preachers who neglected contemporary issues, with "their gross ignorance and insolent bearing, together with their sanctimonious garb," who "hang tenaciously to exploded customs," giving some the impression that "money, and not the good of the people" motivates them (Letter 32–33). One biographer describes her style as follows:

By nineteenth-century norms, Cary's caustic, jolting language seemed ill-suited to a woman. She used phrases such as "gall and wormwood," "moral pest," "petty despot," "superannuated minister," "nest of unclean birds," "moral monsters," and "priest-ridden people," in order to keep her ideas before the public. (Calloway-Thomas 225)

Most of Cary's extant writings are letters and scathing editorials from the pages of *Provincial Freeman* railing against intemperance, those who have "addled the brains of our young people," and any number of other displeasing states of affairs (DeBoer 175). Texts of her speeches are scarce, but the following excerpt, reprinted with limited editorial intervention, comes from a sermon "apparently delivered before a Chatham [Canada West] audience on 6 April 1858" (Ripley 2: 388) and suggests the fervor of her biblically based and feminist antislavery rhetoric:

We cannot successfully Evade duty because the Suffering fellow . . . is only a woman! She too is a neighbor. The good Samaritan of this generation must not take for their Exemplars the priest and the Levite when a fellow woman is among thieves—neither will they find excuse in the custom as barbarous and anti-Christian as any promulgated by pious Brahmin that . . . they may be only females. The spirit of true philanthropy knows no sex. (Cary, Sermon 389)

As William Still's history of the Underground Railroad documents, Frances Ellen Watkins Harper (1825–1911) joined the abolitionist movement largely because of an incident that occurred in the slave state of Maryland, her home state. In 1853 a law was passed prohibiting free blacks from entering Maryland. When a man unintentionally violated that law, he was arrested and sent to Georgia as a slave. He escaped but was recaptured and soon died. Hearing of this sequence of events, Harper remarked, "Upon that grave I pledge myself to the Anti-Slavery cause" (Still 758). In 1854, Harper, gave up teaching to become a lecturer for the Maine Anti-Slavery Society.

Harper delivered what was probably her first antislavery speech at a meeting in New Bedford, Massachusetts, in 1854, possibly titled the "Education and Elevation of the Colored Race" (Still 758). She continued to speak out against slavery and its consequences, traveling throughout New England, southern Canada, and west to Michigan and Ohio. During one six-week period in 1854, she gave at least thirty-three lectures in twenty-one New England towns (Foster, *Brighter* 13).

Because of her articulate and reserved manner, many who heard her found it difficult to believe that she was of African descent. Grace Greenwood, a journalist, labeled her "the bronze muse," bemoaning the fact that a woman of such stature could possibly have been a slave, as if to suggest that slavery was more acceptable for the unwashed. For such observers, she was considered a fascinating aberration, as this account by a Maine abolitionist suggests: "Miss W.[atkins] is slightly tinged with African blood, but the color only serves to add a charm to the occasion which nothing else could give, while at the same time it disarms the fastidious of that so common prejudice which denies to white ladies the right to give public lectures" (Sterling, *Sisters* 161). This commentary also highlights the perception that white women were different and that while they were yet denied the right to give public lectures, anomalous black women were not always frowned upon in this role.

Harper frequently focused on the economic aspects of slavery and the irony of owning "property that can walk." In a lecture, "Could We Trace the Record of Every Human Heart," delivered during the 1857 meeting of the New York City Anti-Slavery Society, she argued that slavery's financial benefits would make its abolishment more difficult:

A hundred thousand new-born babes are annually added to the victims of slavery; twenty thousand lives are annually sacrificed on the plantations of the South. Such a sight should send a thrill of horror through the nerves of civilization and impel the heart of humanity to lofty deeds. So it might, if men had not found a fearful alchemy by which this blood can be transformed into gold. Instead of listening to the cry of agony, they listen to the ring of dollars and stoop down to pick up the coin. (n. pag.)

Her commitment to the abolition of slavery led her to do more than lecture. Harper was active in the Philadelphia Underground Railroad, giving time, money, and talents to its efforts. She never refused an opportunity to engage in activities designed to promote emancipation. Without exception, those who reviewed Harper's lectures commented as much on her platform presence, her ethos, as upon the content of her speeches. Such phrases as "splendid articulation," "pure language," "pleasant voice," "thought flowed in eloquent and poetic expression," "never assuming, never theatrical," "spoke feelingly and eloquently," and "a nature most femininely sensitive" characterize the lasting impression she left on her audiences. Even her contemporary, Mary Ann Shadd Cary, acknowledged Harper's superiority as an orator. In an 1858 letter to her husband, Cary writes, "She is the greatest female speaker ever was here, so wisdom obliges me to keep out of the way as with her prepared lectures there would just be no chance of a favorable comparison" (Sterling, *Sisters* 174). These reactions add credence to the claim that a speaker's personality may be her most persuasive appeal.

Harper's magnetic personality should not, however, overshadow the powerful substance of her antislavery messages. One of her strongest messages, "Our Greatest Want," appeared in an 1859 issue of the *Anglo-African Magazine*, addressed not to whites but to Northern blacks, in response to a growing interest in material wealth: "The respect that is bought by gold is not worth much. It is no honor to shake hands politically with men who whip women and steal babies. If this government has no call for our services, no aim for your children, we have the greater need of them to build up a true manhood and womanhood for ourselves (103).

Women's Rights

Prominent black women abolitionists like Remond and Cary, as well as Maria W. Stewart and Sojourner Truth, frequently combined antislavery discussions with discussions of feminist issues, framing their antislavery arguments in feminist terms. By the same token, white free antislavery feminists, as Yellin puts it, conflated the oppression of enslaved and free women by equating the literal enslavement of black women to their own figurative enslavement. Yellin goes on to point out, however, that the speeches of black women testify to no confusion between the two experiences. She writes:

Nor did they confuse the free women's struggle for self-liberation from a metaphorical slavery with their own struggle for self-liberation from slavery. For them, the discourse of antislavery feminism became not liberating but confining when it colored the self-liberated Woman and Sister white and reassigned the role of the passive victim, which the patriarchy traditionally had reserved for white women, to women who were black. (78–79)

Remond often cited the abuses of enslaved black women to bolster her abolitionist appeals. In her 1859 speech in Manchester, she made a special appeal to the women of England, pointing out that "women are the worst victims of the slave power" ("Athenaeum" 459). Cary, in addition to her abolitionist activities in Canada, addressed groups in behalf of woman's rights, assigning the emancipation of slaves and the liberation of women equal importance. In her 1858 Chatham sermon, quoted from above, she makes appeals for "the Slave mother as well as the Slave father" and places in the same "pit" the "colored people of this country" and "the women of the land," invoking Christ as supreme example of one who implied "an Equal inheritance" for the sexes (Sermon 388–90). When in 1869, Cary, under pressure from black women delegates, was allowed to address the National Colored Labor Union, she spoke on woman's rights and suffrage. As a result, the union voted to include women workers in its organizations (Giddings 69).

Black women had been defending their rights well before these and other more organized events occurred. A religious abolitionist who justified social activism with biblical scriptures, Maria W. Stewart (1803–1879), addressed the Afric-American Female Intelligence Society of Boston in 1832, exhorting the women to exert their influence: "O woman, woman! Your example is powerful, your influence great; it extends over your husbands and your children, and throughout the circle of your acquaintance" (55). In a speech at Franklin Hall she commented on the lack of employment opportunities for young black women in Boston as a consequence of "the powerful force of prejudice," a force that prevented them from becoming more than domestic workers (46).

Born Maria Miller in Hartford, Connecticut, Stewart moved to Boston and married James W. Stewart, a ship's outfitter, in 1826. They were members of Boston's black middle class and friends of David Walker, the fiery outspoken abolitionist and author of *Walker's Appeal, in Four Articles, Together With a Preamble, to The Coloured Citizens of the World, But in Particular And Very Expressly, To Those of the United States of America.* In this pamphlet, written in 1829, Walker urged the slaves to revolt, slay their masters, if necessary, and escape to freedom. Incorporating much of Walker's style, Stewart delivered her Franklin Hall address in 1832, shortly after her husband's death. Stewart spoke on several other occasions between 1832 and 1833, but because of strong criticism, she retired from public speaking, delivering her farewell address on September 21, 1833. In her 1833 farewell address, Stewart lamented the fact that she was not well received as a public speaker, declaring:

I am about to leave you, perhaps never more to return. For I find it is no use for me as an individual to try to make myself useful among my color in this city. It was contempt for my moral and religious opinions in private that drove me thus before a public. Had experience more plainly shown me that it was the nature of man to crush his fellow, I should not have thought it so hard. (70)

Marilyn Richardson points out the irony that although Stewart's speeches call for the liberation of all men and women, when published in William Lloyd Garrison's abolitionist newspaper, the *Liberator*, they were "for the sake of editorial propriety" relegated to the "Ladies' Department" (11).

After leaving slavery, Sojourner Truth (1797–1883) moved to New York City, became a domestic worker, and joined a religious commune. In 1843, at that time about forty-six years old, Isabella Baumfree declared herself to be Sojourner Truth, called by God to travel and preach. In this manner she began her career as a lecturer. She told her story across Long Island and entered Connecticut and then Massachusetts, where she joined the Northampton Association of Education and Industry. While in Massachusetts, she met some of the leading abolitionists, including William Lloyd Garrison, Frederick Douglass, David Ruggles, Parker Pillsbury, and Wendell Phillips. It was during her affiliation with the association that she sharpened her speaking skills.

At the Akron, Ohio, Woman's Rights Convention in 1851, legend has it that Sojourner Truth publicly validated all women when she contradicted previous speakers who had claimed women weak and helpless and, after observing convention proceedings for one day, asked for and was granted permission to speak, even though many of the women feared that Truth's appearance would damage their cause by association with the slavery issue. It was on this occasion that she delivered her well-known—if misnamed—"Ar'n't I a Woman" speech. One of the many ironies associated with this—her most famous—address is that although it has continuing appeal among women's activists today, it received little attention at the time it was delivered. It was not even mentioned in the official conference proceedings (Painter, "Life and Memory" 7). Further, the rendering most frequently anthologized today was recorded by Frances Gage twelve years after the event in an inconsistent Southern dialect.[5] In this speech she pointed to contradictions exemplified in her ability to perform physical tasks as well as any man and reminded her audience that Jesus was the product of God and a woman, without the help of a man. Several years later, at the May 9, 1867, meeting of the American Equal Rights Association (AERA), Truth entered the debate over the proposed Fifteenth Amendment to grant black men but not women the right to vote. There she estimated the consequence of such a change on black women in particular:

There is a great stir about colored men getting their rights, but not a word about the colored woman; and if colored men get their rights, and not colored women get theirs, you see the colored men will be masters over the women, and it will be just as bad as it was before. . . . I want women to have their rights. In the courts women have no right, no voice; nobody speaks for them. I wish woman to have her voice there among the pettifoggers. If it is not a fit place for women, it is unfit for me to be there. ("American Equal Rights Association" 28)

Black women intellectuals like Frances Harper and, later, Ida B. Wells, while clearly supporters of women's rights, considered it more important to align themselves with racial concerns than with cross-racial gender issues.[6] To a greater extent than any of the other black women activists discussed here, Truth, female and formerly enslaved, embodied the arguments she made in support of abolition and women. She spoke not of weakness but of power, "the lack of power that men ascribe to womankind and the presence of her own power and the power of all women" (Yellin 80). Yet Truth provided white women a substitute for the patriarchal domination they sought to escape. Instead of finding inspiration in Truth's independence, they shifted to this imposing figure the responsibility for their liberation. Frances Gage's description of the effect of Truth's speech articulated this transference: "Amid roars of applause, she turned to her corner, leaving more than one of us with streaming eyes and hearts beating with gratitude. She had taken us up in her strong arms and carried us safely over the slough of difficulty, turning the whole tide in our favor" (Truth, *Narrative* 135). It is not clear to what extent Truth actually advanced the white women's cause. She was so different from them in physical appearance and background it would have been easier to dissociate her from the "true women" in the audience than to identify her with them. She may have been viewed more as a curiosity than as an authentic outspoken feminist. Those women who, according to Gage, objected to her being allowed to speak at the 1851 Akron Conference ("Don't let her speak, Mrs. Gage, it will ruin us.") must have understood this.

After emancipation, black women speakers concentrated on the newly freed women in the South who needed training and protection. They addressed women's rights conventions and church conferences and organized their own gatherings to defend their honor and claim their place in public life. Frances Harper continued to lecture on convergence in the plights of black and white women. In her 1866 address to the Eleventh National Woman's Right's Convention, "We Are All Bound Up Together," she described her shabby treatment by the state of Ohio two years earlier upon the death of her husband Fenton Harper. She acknowledged that "justice is not fulfilled so long as woman is unequal before the law." Later in that same speech, however, she expressed doubt that all white women could be counted on to look out for the best interests of black women: "I think that like men they [white women] may be divided into three classes, the good, the bad, and the indifferent," indicating black women's awareness that although there were common interests among black and white women, there were also major differences (46).

The black church provided a number of rhetorical opportunities for black preaching women and black women advocates of such secular causes as woman's rights and abolitionism. As Lincoln and Mamiya point out, "many of these community service and political activities stemmed from a moral concern to uplift the race that was deeply rooted in religious motivation" (281). In fact, nearly all the women discussed here were active members of black churches. It is not surprising then that much of the discourse on women's rights emerged from church women like those associated with the Black Baptist Convention.

Lucy Wilmot Smith (1861–1890) spoke of black women's needs to a largely male audience at the 1886 meeting of the American National Baptist Convention. At the time of her address, she was historian of the association and, along with two other Baptist church women, Mary Cook and Virginia Broughton, led the challenge against this predominantly male organization (Higginbotham, *Righteous* 135). Smith opened her address, "The Future Colored Girl," by decrying the lack of adequate professional training for all women through the ages and closed by describing in particular the black woman's condition. She catalogued employment options for black women, among them raising poultry, small fruit, or flowers; bee farming; dairying; lecturing; newspaper work; photography; medicine; teaching; and practicing elocution. Her point was that black women needed to explore a range of work opportunities in order to move beyond domestic labor toward some independence:

It is one of the evils of the day that from babyhood girls are taught to look forward to the time when they will be supported by a father, a brother or somebody's [*sic*] else brother. In teaching her that in whatever field of labor she enters she will abandon after a few years is teaching her to despise the true dignity of labor. The boy is taught to fill this life with as many hard strokes as possible. The girl should receive the same lesson. (L. Smith 74)

She spoke uncompromisingly of the lack of training and employment opportunities for black women. In her eulogy, Mary Cook characterized Smith as a woman dedicated to church work and racial uplift. Cook, in an 1890 essay, "The Work for Baptist Women," prepared for the *Negro Baptist Pulpit: A Collection of Sermons and Papers*, also encouraged the church to give women more responsibilities for "the salvation of the world" and to enlist them "to labor by the side of the men" so that "it will not be many years before a revolution will be felt all over this broad land, and the heathen will no longer walk in darkness, but will praise God, the light of their salvation" (285).

In the 1890s, black women organized themselves nationally, in part, as a result of the powerful rhetorical activities of Ida B. Wells. In 1895 Josephine St. Pierre Ruffin, a Boston woman's activist, issued a call for a conference of black women. One concern was an open letter from John W. Jacks, president of the Missouri Press Association. The letter attacked Wells's character and by implication the morality of all black women in an attempt to rebut Ida Wells's accounts of Southern lynching. As a result of Ruffin's call, the First Congress of

Colored Women convened July 29, 1895, in Boston. On the program at the 1895 conference were the names of several prominent black women who spoke on issues affecting black women.

One of the most provocative addresses, "The Value of Race Literature," was delivered by Victoria Earle Matthews (1861–1907). Matthews, born in Fort Valley, Georgia, moved to New York in 1873. She became a journalist and helped to organize the Women's Loyal Union of New York and Brooklyn. In the speech, Matthews paraded before her elite audience the range of stereotypical black characters portrayed in literature by whites and called for those present to take the lead in creating more literature of their own. But the speech that more specifically focused on women's rights was "The Awakening of the Afro-American Woman," delivered in 1897 at the San Francisco meeting of the Society of Christian Endeavor. A former slave, Matthews recalled slavery's past horrors: "As I stand here to-day clothed in the garments of Christian womanhood, the horrible days of slavery, out of which I came, seem as a dream that is told', some horror incredible. Indeed, could they have been, and are not?" (150). Matthews also protested the laws forbidding mixed marriages, laws that, she claimed, disgraced black women most: "As long as the affections are controlled by legislation in defiance of Christian law, making infamous the union of black and white, we shall have unions without the sanction of the law, and children without legal parentage, to the degradation of black womanhood and the disgrace of white manhood" (154).

Fannie Barrier Williams, with a solid reputation as a speaker and well known in Chicago women's circles, presented one of the major addresses, "The Intellectual Progress of the Colored Women of the United States since the Emancipation Proclamation," at the World's Congress of Representative Women. The congress was part of the Columbian Exposition, held from May 15 to May 22, 1893, in Chicago. Williams (1855–1944) was born to a prominent New York family and attended the Collegiate Institute of Brockport, the New England Conservatory of Music, and the School of Fine Arts in Washington, D.C., where she taught for almost ten years. In her speech to the congress, Williams wisely emphasized similarities rather than differences. She argued that many black women were rapidly becoming social and intellectual equals to white women and that those who were not, needed their support. Such support, she claimed, would be in their best interest: "If it be the high purpose of these deliberations to lessen the resistance to woman's progress, you can not fail to be interested in our struggles against the many oppositions that harass us (710).

Anna Julia Cooper (1858–1964), present at both the National Conference of Colored Women and the Congress of Representative Women, delivered her most challenging defense of black women at the 1886 Convocation of Colored Clergy in Washington, D.C. She criticized the clergy and the Episcopalian Church for discriminating against women. Cooper taught at Wilberforce College in Xenia, Ohio, from 1884 to 1885, then returned to St. Augustine's College, where she began her education, and remained there until 1887. Cooper then moved to Washington, D.C., where she held several teaching positions. She was also in the vanguard of the black women's club movement, helping to organize the Washington Colored Women's League.

In her speech, "Womanhood A Vital Element in the Regeneration and Progress of a Race," she rehearses the history of women in general and the future prospects for the Southern black woman in particular. Like Frances Harper twenty years earlier, Cooper employed the "same but different" argument directed to audiences throughout the century. Appealing, on the one hand, to a common womanhood, Cooper highlighted, on the other, those difference resulting from slavery and color prejudice: "With all the wrongs and neglects of her past, with all the weakness, the debasement, the moral thralldom of her present, the black woman of to-day stands mute and wondering at the Herculean task devolving upon her. But the cycles wait for her. No other hand can move the lever. She must be loosed from her bands and set to work" (28).

Antilynching Campaign

That the entry "antilynching movement" in *Black Women in America: An Historical Encyclopedia* is essentially an article about Ida Wells indicates clearly the extent of her crusade against mob violence. Although most of the speakers discussed here spoke out against lynching, none did it more effectively and more consistently than Ida B. Wells (1862–1931). Further, most turn-of-the-century antilynching activities revolved around the efforts of Ida Wells. The national black women's club movement received its strongest push from Wells's rhetoric against mob violence. Thus, discussion of antilynching discourse centers on this forceful speaker.

In manner of speaking and reputation, Wells can be compared with Cary.

Both were bold, straightforward, and hard hitting. She also attended the 1893 World's Congress of Representative Women, but unlike her contemporaries, Frances Harper and Fannie Barrier Williams, Wells had no official slot on the program of speakers. Instead, she positioned herself near the Haitian Pavilion, where Frederick Douglass was presiding, and distributed copies of an eighty-one-page protest pamphlet titled *The Reason Why the Colored American Is Not in the World's Columbian Exposition.* The pamphlet contained pieces by Douglass; Ferdinand Barnett, a prominent Chicago attorney who later married Wells; I. Garland Penn, a newspaperman; and Wells herself. Over ten thousand copies were circulated during the fair. But this was only one of many causes Wells espoused. Wells the social activist spoke out over a period of almost forty years, until her death in 1931, against the denial of women's rights, against racism generally, and, of course, against the practice of lynching.

Ida B. Wells, born in Holly Springs, Mississippi, was the child of former slaves. Both parents died of yellow fever in 1878, leaving Wells, at sixteen the oldest, in charge of five siblings. Taking two sisters with her, she eventually moved to Memphis to teach but soon discovered that she did not adapt well to the profession's constraints, confessing, in her autobiography, "I never cared for teaching" (Wells, *Crusade* 31). In 1889 Wells became editor and part owner of the Memphis *Free Speech and Headlight.* Her editorials protested racial injustice in education, voting rights, and public transportation. Eager to get her newspaper into the homes of those who could not read, Wells printed several editions on easily identified pink paper. Not until 1892, after three of her friends were lynched in Memphis and her newspaper office was burned down by an angry mob, did Wells launch a verbal war against lynching that continued into the twentieth century. In response to the events in Memphis, a group of prominent black women from New York and Brooklyn organized a testimonial in her honor at Lyric Hall on October 5, 1892. On this occasion Wells delivered her first public speech, "Southern Horrors: Lynch Law in All Its Phases," in which she proposed corrective action against lynching: "Nothing is more definitely settled than [that] he must act for himself. I have shown how he may employ the boycott, emigration, and the press, and I feel that by a combination of all these agencies can be effectually stamped out lynch law, that last relic of barbarism and slavery" (24). Many prominent blacks, including Wells, had convinced themselves that those being lynched were indeed guilty and deserved to die. But after incidents like the one in Memphis, they began to recognize lynching as an attempt to suppress black progress. Wells stresses this point in this—her first—public speech.

Not limiting herself to this country, she took her antilynching campaign to Europe and found favor there, in the face of disparagement by the Southern press in the United States. Wells traveled to England and Scotland in April of 1893 to deliver a series of antilynching lectures. She returned to England for a six-month stay in 1894, serving as paid correspondent for the Chicago *Inter-Ocean*. On February 13, 1893, before leaving for her first tour of England, Wells addressed the Boston Monday Lectureship. In this speech, "Lynch Law in All Its Phases," Wells rehearsed in detail the Memphis incident and appealed to her audience with gruesome details of a lynching in Paris, Texas, only two weeks earlier. She appealed to this predominantly white audience for public outcry, advancing her belief that their failure to act was a result of ignorance rather than apathy and drawing on their concern for America's reputation:

I am before the American people to-day . . . because of a deep-seated conviction that the country at large does not know the extent to which lynch law prevails in parts of the Republic, nor the conditions which force into exile those who speak the truth. I cannot believe that the apathy and indifference which so largely obtains regarding mob rule is other than the result of ignorance of the true situation. . . . Repeated attacks on the life, liberty and happiness of any citizen or class of citizens are attacks on distinctive American institutions; such attacks imperiling as they do the foundation of government, law and order, merit the thoughtful consideration of far-sighted Americans; not from a standpoint of sentiment, not even so much from a standpoint of justice to a weak race, as from a desire to preserve our institutions. (333)

Concern about discriminatory punishment of offenders was raised again in the May 1, 1894, *Woman's Era*. In an unsigned article, "How to Stop Lynching," the writer took exception to a proposal advanced by Albion Tourgée that the jurisdiction in which lynchings occur be required to compensate the families of the victims and questioned the inequality of hanging murderers of whites and only exacting a fine for the murder of blacks. This article was followed by another defending Tourgée, perhaps the period's most vocal white supporter of blacks rights, and calling for the recognition of "the futility of mere talk in the vindication of his [the previous writer's] race manhood" (8). Wells continued to publish pamphlets and articles documenting the injustice of mob violence, including *A Red Record: Tabulated Statistics and Alleged Causes of Lynching in the*

United States, *1892–1893–1894* (1895), *Lynch Law in Georgia* (1899), *Mob Rule in New Orleans: Robert Charles and His Fight to the Death* (1900).

Racial Uplift

In the midst of the struggle for freedom and equality, black women pressed their people toward self-help, self-improvement, and racial uplift. They emphasized racial uplift from two perspectives: encouraging those who were in need to take initiative and challenging those who had accomplished to "lift" those who had not. In addition, then, to public address focused specifically on improving the working and living conditions of black women, much public discourse presented arguments for general assistance to Southern blacks after the Civil War under the banner of racial uplift. Three activist educators, Harper, Edmonia Highgate, and Lucy Laney, were prominent advocates of this concept. Frances Harper made a point of addressing directly those in need of social and emotional uplift in the post–Civil War South. Edmonia G. Highgate spent her brief life teaching the newly freed in the South and lecturing for financial support in the North. Lucy Craft Laney in 1893 organized a day and boarding school in Augusta, Georgia, developed the city's first kindergarten, and stressed in her speeches to educated blacks their crucial role in the work of racial advancement.

Frances Harper, who spoke on all the issues discussed in this chapter, adopted the first perspective—encouraging self-help. She availed herself of every opportunity to speak directly to the people for whom she fought, traveling throughout the Midwest before the war and in the Deep South after the war. In his biographical sketch of Harper, William Still writes, "For the best part of several years, since the war, she has traveled very extensively through the Southern States, going on the plantations and amongst the lowly, as well as to the cities and towns, addressing schools, Churches, meetings in Court Houses, Legislative Halls, &c., and, sometimes, under the most trying and hazardous circumstances" (767). According to one story, during an appearance in Darlington, South Carolina, instead of standing in the pulpit of the church where she spoke, she stood near the door, where those outside as well as those inside could hear.

In a September 21, 1860, letter to Jane E. Hitchcock Jones, a Quaker abolitionist from Ohio, she expresses her view that such lectures among free and formerly enslaved blacks help to lift morale and develop self-esteem:

There are a number of colored settlements in the West, where a few words of advice and encouragement among our people might act as a stimulant and charm; and if they would change the public opinion of the country, they should not find it, I hope, a useless work to strive to elevate the character of the colored people, not merely by influencing the public *around* them but *among* them; for after all, this prejudice of which such complaint has been made, if I understand it aright, is simply a great protest of human minds rising up against slavery, and so hating it for themselves that they learn not only to despise it, but the people that submit to it, and those identified with them by race. (82)

Harper must have recognized the opportunity for instruction that public speaking afforded to those who did not read and did not subscribe to newspapers. She also wrote of giving lectures privately to women at no charge. Her speeches to such audiences were usually impromptu, and generally journalists were not present; consequently, no extant texts of these spontaneous orations remain.

Born to former slaves in Syracuse, New York, Edmonia Highgate (1844–1870) lived for only twenty-six years, but during those years, she did all she could for racial uplift, alternately teaching the newly freed in the South and lecturing for their support in the North. At the age of twenty, Highgate was sent by the AMA to Norfolk, Virginia, to teach. After three months of intense work, she had a mental breakdown and returned to Syracuse. Shortly after her return, Highgate addressed the 1864 National Convention of Colored Men, held in Syracuse. Highgate and Frances Harper were the only women to address the exclusively male organization. When Frederick Douglass introduced her he said: "You have your Anna Dickinsons; and we have ours. We wish to meet you at every point" (*Minutes* 14). Douglass was referring here to Anna Dickinson, the orator, who had achieved fame after her 1861 Philadelphia address, at the age of nineteen, on "The Rights and Wrongs of Women." Although the Convention minutes do not include the text of Highgate's speech, a summary in the October 26, 1864, *New Orleans Tribune* demonstrates the tenor of her political activism and astuteness:

Miss Highgate said she would not be quite in her place, perhaps, if a girl as she is, she [*sic*] should tell the Convention what they ought to do; but she had, with others *thought* about what had been proposed and those thoughts she would tell them. Miss Highgate was evidently a strong *Lincoln* MAN; so much so, that she felt that Gen. Fremont ought not to be a candidate. . . . Miss Highgate urged the Convention to press on, to not abate hope until the glorious time spoken of to-night, shall come. (Sterling, *Sisters* 296; emphasis in original)

While back in New York, Highgate lectured to raise funds for freedmen's relief. She returned South in 1865, teaching for a while in Maryland, Louisiana, and Mississippi. After four years, she again returned and resumed lecturing in New York, New England, and Canada. In February of 1879, she spoke at the Thirty-sixth Annual Meeting of the Massachusetts Anti-Slavery Society. Following a lengthy address by John M. Langston, a prominent black activist from Ohio, Highgate warned against hasty optimism. A paraphrase in the *National Anti-Slavery Standard* states the following:

Miss Highgate said that, after laboring five years as a teacher in the South, it was perhaps appropriate for her to give a report on the state of things there. In her opinion, even if the Fifteenth Amendment should now be ratified, it would be only a paper ratification. Even in the instruction given to the ignorant there lacks some of the main essentials of right instruction. The teachers sent out by the evangelical organizations do very little to remove caste-prejudice, the twin sister of slavery. . . . President Lincoln was accustomed to take credit to himself for moving forward no faster than the people demanded. The Republicans in the South do no better. We need *Anti-Slavery* teachers there; teachers who will show that it is safe to do right. The Anti-Slavery Society must not disband, because its work in the South is not yet half done; and if not now thoroughly done, it will have to be done over again. (n. pag.; emphasis in original)

In June of 1870 in a letter to abolitionists Gerrit and Ann Smith, Highgate mentions the advice of Theodore Tilton, famous speaker and friend, who, impressed with her speaking skills, urged her "to write a lecture to interest the general public, deliver it as other lecturers do and you will then be on your way to secure the funds necessary to aid the cause to which you are so devoted" (Sterling, *Sisters* 301). Highgate implied in the letter that she might like to visit the Smiths to gain the privacy needed to write such a lecture. But she never did so. A month later, she requested instead that the AMA send her South again to Jackson, Mississippi, for another teaching tour. She never returned South, however. Edmonia Highgate died in Syracuse in October of 1870.

As the title of Lucy Laney's "The Burden of the Educated Colored

Woman" indicates, her 1899 speech centered on racial uplift. During the post-Reconstruction period, those who had acquired education and prosperity felt a duty to educate those less fortunate. This education extended to morality and economy as well as reading and writing. As Giddings, at one point quoting Laney, writes: "Whatever their views about social sanctions, one reason for the emphasis on morality was that lack of it could be impoverishing. . . . a good part of the philosophy of racial uplift had to do with lifting the burdens of 'ignorance and immorality' with 'true culture and character, linked with—cash' " (102). Although Laney called this challenge a "burden," she was not resentful but despairing that the times had created this triple burden of "shame and crime and prejudice." The "shame" Laney saw as a consequence of nonlegalized slave marriages, poor parenting skills, and ignorance of hygiene. The large numbers of young men and women incarcerated provided evidence of the "crime." The "prejudice" came from those in power, who made it difficult to overcome the other two burdens. This speech was delivered in 1899 at the third Hampton Negro Conference on the campus of one of the black schools formed after the Civil War, Hampton University, in Hampton, Virginia. At these annual conferences, Hampton graduates and other prominent race leaders discussed strategies toward racial improvement. As was the case at many such conferences, the men and women met separately, under the unfortunate assumption that women operated in a separate sphere and had no need to address issues that were, in fact, of collective importance.

Lucy Craft Laney (1854–1933) was born in Macon, Georgia, to free, literate parents. Her father, an ordained Presbyterian minister, earned enough money while enslaved to purchase himself and his wife. Laney was graduated from the Normal School division of Atlanta University in 1873, a member of the first graduating class. After teaching for ten years, Laney established a school in Augusta, Georgia; the school eventually became the Haines Normal and Industrial Institute. Laney, one of several black women near the end of the century who founded their own schools, offered a curriculum in liberal arts as well as vocational training and was especially interested in the education of girls. By the time she spoke to the Hampton Negro Conference in 1899, Laney's school was on its way to becoming an established success. In "The Burden of the Educated Colored Woman," she called specifically on "the educated Negro woman" not only to teach but to speak. Laney argued that "as a public lecturer she may give advice, helpful suggestions, and important knowledge that will change a whole community and start its people on the upward way." She cited, along with four other women, the example of Frances Harper. She closed her speech with a story about a group of male laborers who successfully lifted "a heavy piece of timber to the top of a building" only when they asked the women to help them, reinforcing her message that women as well as men were needed to ensure successful racial uplift: "Today not only the men on top call, but a needy race,—the whole world, calls loudly to the cultured Negro women to come to the rescue. Do they hear? Are they coming? Will they push?" (344).

The rhetorical activities of numerous other nineteenth-century black women speakers have not been mentioned here. They spoke their minds from platform and pulpit and went to work correcting the wrongs they saw before them. They left no records, wrote no books, organized no conferences, but they helped to establish a tradition of political activism among black women. The activities of the women discussed merely illustrate the range of issues brought to public attention by women using oratory to effect change. The general response of white audiences to the very presence of intelligent, articulate black women was often much stronger than their response to anything the women had to say. These speakers were the embodiment of their message—whether the message was the abolishment of slavery, support for black women, or recognition of racial autonomy. They authenticated their arguments; the messenger was the message. African American women of the nineteenth century participated in history largely through their rhetorical activities. As we shall see, the pages of the *Woman's Era* provide ample evidence of their participation in the public political discourse of their time. The Woman's Era Club chose as its motto a phrase from the last message of woman's rights activist Lucy Stone, memorialized on the front page of the *Era's* inaugural issue. Throughout the nineteenth century, ordinary black women—unknown and well known—spoke simply to "make the world better."

Frances E. W. Harper. Records of the Universal Peace Union, Swarthmore College Peace Collection.

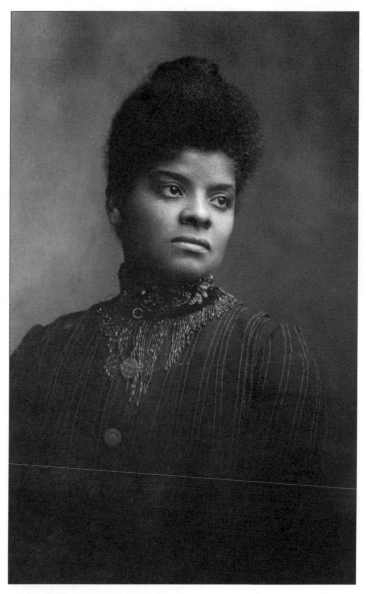

Ida B. Wells. Department of Special Collections,
University of Chicago Library.

Fannie Barrier Williams. Moorland-Spingarn
Research Center, Howard University.

Anna Julia Cooper. Oberlin College Archives, Oberlin, Ohio.

Albaugh's Opera House, Washington, D.C., site of the first triennial meeting of the National Council of Women, where Frances E. W. Harper challenged the characterization of blacks as a "dependent race." Library of Congress.

Third Building, Erected 1881, Burned 1894

Tremont Temple, Boston, where Ida B. Wells in 1893 gave her speech "Lynch Law in All Its Phases." Boston Athenaeum.

Victoria Earle Matthews. Photographs and Prints Division,
Schomburg Center for Research in Black Culture, The New York
Public Library, Astor, Lenox, and Tilden Foundation.

Berkeley Hall housed in Odd Fellows' Hall, Boston, where the First Congress of Colored Women was held in 1895. *King's Handbook of Boston.* Boston Athenaeum.

2

ॐ

African Origins/American Appropriations
Maria Stewart and "Ethiopia Rising"

> The day-star from on high is beginning to dawn upon us, and Ethiopia
> will soon stretch forth her hands unto God. These Anti-slavery societies,
> in my opinion, will soon cause many grateful tears to flow, and many de-
> sponding hearts to bound and leap for joy.
>
> —Maria W. Stewart, "Cause for Encouragement," 1832

Nineteenth-century black speakers frequently invoked the spiritual and
political prophecy from the Old Testament Psalm 68:31: "Princes shall
come out of Egypt, and Ethiopia shall soon stretch out her hands to
God"—alluding, in some instances, to future international dominance of African people. It has been characterized as "the most quoted verse in black religious history" (Raboteau 42). Although most explicit references to Ethiopia or
to an African connectedness are found in speeches by nineteenth-century black
men—no doubt because they had more opportunities to engage in such political activities as speaking—black women's discourse evoked Africa's spirit as
well. This chapter considers allusions to Ethiopian retribution and to African
origins in the persuasive speeches and essays of Maria W. Stewart, whose first
essay appeared in 1831. Stewart's allusions are discussed particularly in the context of similar references by her contemporaries, predecessors, and successors. I
also trace the evolution and variations in meanings of the term "Ethiopia."

Discussion of these allusions is informed by Perelman and Olbrechts-
Tyteca's classification in *The New Rhetoric* of the rhetorical figures of choice,
figures of presence, and figures of communion, according to their argumentative effect rather than their structure (172–77). Figures of choice have to do with
selective interpretations of meaning that point to one particular characteristic

of a term to the exclusion of others. Figures of presence operate to bring the subject of the discourse more clearly into mental focus for the auditors. Figures of communion bring about increased audience identity through references to a common past, tradition, or culture. Allusion, as employed by Stewart in reference to an African past, functions as such a figure. Kwame Gyekye's discussion of communalism among African peoples also provides a useful frame of reference. The group identity that Stewart's figures of communion help to promote could well be rooted in this African cultural tradition of communalism, perhaps the one "characteristic [that] defines Africaness." While acknowledging the diversities of African traditions, Gyekye argues that horizontal relationships across cultures produce an array of common cultural elements and ideas. Communalism, defined as the "doctrine that the group constitutes the main focus of the lives of the individual members of that group, and that the extent of the individual's involvement in the interests, aspirations, and welfare of the group is the measure of that individual's worth," emerges as the most pervasive of these elements (Gyekye 208). Stewart, with her frequent allusions to African origins and to Ethiopian retribution, may at the same time have reawakened latent feelings of group unity or communalism. These allusions in Stewart's prose demonstrate a strong sense of African origins and a prevailing respect for the power of the word to effect change among a displaced people who needed to recall a proud heritage.

One manifestation of this heritage was appreciation for the power of the word or *nommo*. In Marcel Griaule's *Conversations with Ogotemmêli*, the concept *nommo* is introduced and explicated through a series of discussions with the Dogon hunter and priest Ogotemmêli.[1] In his summary of these conversations, Janheinz Jahn notes that the Dogon people of Mali, one of the oldest West African empires, designated *nommo* the "word-seed," essential to the development of all significant human actions. He adds that "all the activities of men, and all the movement in nature, rest on the word, on the productive power of the word, which is water and heat and seed and Nommo, that is, life force itself" (125–26). The spoken word was considered an integral part in creation. Conjurations accompanied the administering of medicine, rendering it effective, and even in the Western practice of medicine, the persuasiveness of the physician has been acknowledged as a crucial element of healing. According to the tradition of *nommo*, sowing alone is not sufficient to produce crops. Sowing must be accompanied by speech, "for it is the words that make the grasses ger-

minate, the fruits grow, the cows go in calf and give milk" (125). Speaking transforms "thing-forces" into "forces of meaning," even in the case of a newborn
child who becomes a complete human being only when the father gives her a
name and pronounces it (125, 151). The illocutionary force of such speech acts,
the actions that are performed by saying the words, brings to awareness the
understanding that language can have, at the same time, perlocutionary power,
the power to persuade, the rhetorical effect achieved by stating the words.[2]

   This belief in the power of the word manifested itself in early African
American society as a recognition of the power of literacy, legally forbidden to
the enslaved and valued among both free and enslaved. Their rhetorical practices combined African foundations syncretically with appropriated Western
practices of literacy to produce a discourse of liberation. Frederick Douglass, in
an 1891 tribute to the Reverend John Wesley Edward Bowen, eloquently summarized this prevailing view that language had the power to effect change. In
his welcoming remarks to Reverend Bowen, minister of the Asbury Methodist
Episcopal Church in Washington, D.C. from 1890 to 1892, Douglass said the
following:

It is often asked, by ignorance what have such men as Garnet, Ward, Remond and others done for the colored race? and ignorance has answered its own question: They have
only talked; but talk itself is a power. . . . Great is the miracle of human speech—by it
nations are enlightened and reformed; by it the cause of justice and liberty is defended,
by it evils are exposed, ignorance dispelled, the path of duty made plain, and by it those
that live to-day are put into the possession of the wisdom of ages gone by. ("Great"
476–77)

In 1995, bell hooks depicts this appropriation of English by Africans in
America:

I imagine, then, Africans first hearing English as "the oppressor's language" and then
re-hearing it as a potential site of resistance. Learning English, learning to speak the
alien tongue, was one way enslaved Africans began to reclaim their personal power
within a context of domination. Possessing a shared language, black folks could find
again a way to make community, and a means to create the political solidarity necessary
to resist. (170)

   Identifying with certainty specific features of speeches by African Americans with African roots is difficult. First, there was hardly a unified African

culture directly transferred across the Atlantic to a unified black American culture. Wilson Moses, in a thought-provoking chapter of *Black Messiahs and Uncle Toms,* "A Search for African Roots of the Tradition," identifies some of the inconsistencies in such an assumption. Speaking in particular of religious practices, he cautions:

It is probably correct to say that there is a Pan-African religion, but it is no more correct than to say that religiosity seems to be a universal human experience and that there are similarities in the way that it manifests itself among all peoples. The religion of black slaves in the United States was similar to both that of West Africans and that of Europeans. These similarities may be attributed to African retentions, syncretic tendencies, and spontaneous parallel evolution. (28)

Carla Peterson also points to the complexity associated with attempts to identify "Africanisms in nineteenth-century African-American cultural life." Drawing on Sterling Stuckey's work on slave culture, which implicates blending of cultures during and after Middle Passage, Peterson concludes that such connections "to a certain extent, must remain speculative" (242n62). Perhaps the same caution should be heeded in the search for African origins in certain rhetorical practices. It has been pointed out that the word "African," not indigenous to Africa, has Latin roots and that those living in what we now call Africa did not necessarily think of themselves as a collective but rather as members of particular cultural groups: "Only when the Europeans arrived on the scene in great numbers did these diverse peoples begin to think of themselves as 'Africans'" (Wilson 23–24). However, in *An Essay on African Philosophical Thought,* Gyekye has countered, "If it makes sense to talk of Western or Eastern philosophy, would it not make sense to talk of African philosophy too?" (189). This perspective enables as well a discussion of both an African rhetoric and distinct African discursive practices. Thus, while the exact nature and scope of such African cultural influences are difficult to document, it is clear that enslaved Africans brought with them traditions of literacy. As Frances Foster writes:

The slave trade was an equal opportunity employer. It did not discriminate in regards to religion, ethnicity, or educational level. Consequently, some of those kidnapped slaves included priests and holy women, business people, students, griots, and poets. . . . In the northern colonies and states, black Americans compared favorably with white Americans in their abilities to make their marks. (*Written* xxi)

These traditions of literacy influenced rhetorical practices. Within the context of the fact that North American blacks have their origins in Africa and inevitably retained much of their various cultures, the pull toward an African connectedness justifiably persists. According to Molefi Asante: "Africa is at the heart of *all* African-American behavior. Communication styles are reflective of the internal mythic clock, the epic memory, the psychic stain of Africa in our spirits" (48).

Further, parallel rhetorical practices have been identified. Among West African societies, proverbs are commonly used to validate judicial arguments by affirming that the rhetor's position finds support in well-established truths. One study of proverb rhetoric among the largest ethnic group in Ghana, the Akan, stresses that proverb use varies according to the speaker's intent and is most effective when used in conjunction with valid evidence (Yankah 288). In other words, Yankah cautions that the proverb in African rhetoric is generally perceived as a tool in the service of other discursive strategies and has limited persuasive effect on its own. William Piersen, historian of eighteenth-century New England African American subculture, suggests that the practice among enslaved blacks in eighteenth-century New England of invoking proverbs to support arguments against slavery should be understood as a continuation of this West African tradition, albeit a less effective tactic of support in a culture that privileged written documents over communal wisdom.

Ethiopia as Concept

Belief in united community action—what hooks calls "political solidarity"—carries over from African cultural traditions. The assumption that the group constitutes the main focus of individual members undergirds the explicit call to African communalism in the passage from the Old Testament Psalms. The passage, "Princes shall come out of Egypt, and Ethiopia shall soon stretch out her hands to God," is often understood by many as a nineteenth-century prefiguring of the 1960s civil rights movement's slogan "We shall overcome." But this prophecy of Ethiopia, as it was used by nineteenth-century orators, meant much more than future political empowerment in America. It alluded to the messianic destiny of African peoples internationally. Eric Sundquist points out that the expression, usually with the first clause dropped, changes in meaning from context to context, but the ideology of Ethiopianism portrays a "colonized Africa or enslaved Africans in the diaspora as prepared for providential delivery from bondage" (553). As invoked by nineteenth-century Pan-Africanists, this passage is more radically interpreted as a prophesy of "a black millennium, a violent seizure of freedom through acts of revolt sanctioned by God and led, literally or figuratively, by a black redeemer from within Africa, or in some interpretations, from America" (553).

William Leo Hansberry, pioneer Africanist, wrote that the earliest references to the term are found in the *Iliad* and the *Odyssey*, around the ninth century B.C.E.. He adds that the term comes from a Greek word meaning, approximately, "a man with a (sun) burned or black face" (5–6). Hansberry reminds us that the term and its earliest designations are essentially European:

> Since the name Ethiopia seems to have been a distinctively European or Greek product and therefore a relatively late creation so far as Nilotic history is concerned, it need hardly be urged that the term had little if any currency among the peoples native to the area. Indeed, so far as we know, the ancient Ethiopians, as odd as it may seem, never called themselves "Ethiopians" or their land "Ethiopia." (7–8)

In the Old Testament, all Africans were generally referred to as "Ethiopian" or "black-skinned," and sub-Saharan Africa was called "Ethiopia." "Ethiopian" was subsequently applied then to Africans in the diaspora as well (Sundquist 554).[3] It is this later application, resonating in historical overtones, that nineteenth-century speakers invoked.

The prophecy of Ethiopia stretching out her hands became the standard trope of salvation in sermons preached from black pulpits during the nineteenth century. In the words of theologian Gayraud Wilmore, it "became a forecast of the ultimate fulfillment of the people's spiritual yearning." He notes that such renowned preachers as Richard Allen, Henry Highland Garnet, Alexander Crummell, and Bishop Turner "made it the cornerstone of missionary emigrationism both in the United States and in Africa" (121). Albert Raboteau writes that in the search for signs of God's will for black people, black speakers found "two texts that served as the *classical loci* for interpreting black history in the nineteenth century: the book of Exodus and Psalms 68:31" (41). Speakers explored one of these two "places" when seeking to account for the various conditions and struggles of black people in America. The locale shifted from the Exodus story of delivery from bondage, when slavery was foremost, to Psalms, when post-slavery oppression continued.

Ironically, when the term "Ethiopia" was used by white writers to describe or refer to black people, it frequently suggested the condescension implicit in the adoration of the noble savage rather than the triumph conveyed in the celebration of survival and victory over oppressors. One striking example comes from an article on Sojourner Truth, "Sojourner Truth, the Libyan Sibyl," by Harriet Beecher Stowe. Writing in 1863, Stowe recalled that during an interview Truth sang several verses of a hymn: "Sojourner, singing this hymn, seemed to impersonate the fervor of Ethiopia, wild, savage, hunted of all nations, but burning after God in her tropic heart, and stretching her scarred hands towards the glory to be revealed" (477). In her critique of Stowe's essay, Peterson writes that "[wh]at is especially significant about these metaphoric and symbolic representations of Truth is the degree to which they privilege geography—first the geography of continent, then that of the body—over history, ultimately tending toward a dehistoricization of Truth herself" (38). But, as Peterson also points out, Truth was probably well aware of her various symbolic representations, the uses to which they were put, and the uses to which she could put them.[4]

Antebellum Black Society

With the gradual abolition of slavery in Northern states, many blacks migrated to the coastal cities of Boston and New York. Between 1790 and 1810, the free black population of New York City increased over 600 percent (Horton and Horton 83). By 1830, there were 1,875 blacks living in Boston, constituting 3.1 percent of the city's total population (Cromwell 156). These migrants faced attempts by threatened white citizens to exact other means of social control in the absence of slavery. These attempts took the form of restrictions of movement, proposals for colonization, emigration, and, in some states, deportation. After the elimination of slavery in Massachusetts in 1783—the first federal census in 1790 listed no blacks in Massachusetts as slaves—the state legislature passed laws designed to bar interracial marriages and expel all blacks who were not citizens. Boston reacted in 1800 by ordering 240 blacks deported, an action no doubt influenced by Gabriel Prosser's unsuccessful but portentous Virginia slave revolt earlier that year. In 1821, a legislative committee investigated the possibility of prohibiting blacks from migrating to Massachusetts on the grounds that they would create disorder and swell the welfare rolls. By the late 1830s, blacks in Boston were disproportionately incarcerated (Horton and Horton 102, 108).

At the federal level, Congress in 1790 restricted naturalization to white immigrants. In 1792, the newly organized militia limited enrollment to white males, although blacks were not barred from other branches of the armed forces. In 1810, Congress excluded blacks from carrying U.S. mail. In 1820, it gave white officials in Washington, D.C., authority to adopt governing regulations for its black residents (Litwack 31). But perhaps the most systematic and seductive form of white resistance to a free black presence in antebellum America was the colonization movement.

The American Colonization Society (ACS), formed in 1816, promoted the establishment of a colony in West Africa or elsewhere for free blacks. The society, whose charter members included the prominent leaders Frances Scott Key, Henry Clay, Daniel Webster, and Supreme Court Justice Bushrod Washington, actually supported disfranchisement and other racial restrictions for fear that equality would merely give blacks false hopes and encourage them to remain in what they saw as a hopeless situation. In its publication the *African Respository*, the ACS argued that colonization was the best solution. But most blacks strongly opposed the project. For example, shortly after the ACS was organized, approximately three thousand blacks crowded into Richard Allen's Bethel African Methodist Episcopal (AME) Church in Philadelphia, to protest (Litwack 24).

Throughout the late eighteenth and into the nineteenth centuries, blacks formed associations to address these and other threats to their survival in America. The black free masonry was one such association. Under the leadership of Prince Hall, in 1787, the African Masonic Lodge, with a British charter, was established in Boston. Later followed a host of other groups, to include the African Society of Boston in 1796; the African Benevolent Society of Newport and the African Society for Mutual Relief of New York City in 1808; and the Afric-American Female Intelligence Society of Boston in 1831, which Maria Stewart addressed. Black congregations also broke away from mainstream denominations to establish their own churches. In Philadelphia, the Free African Society, led by Richard Allen and Absalom Jones, was organized in 1797, and later, the Bethel AME Church was established under Allen's leadership. In Boston in 1805, the African Baptist Church, where Stewart would later be married, was established by Thomas Paul, and in 1811, with John Gloucester at its head, the African Presbyterian Church of Philadelphia opened its doors.[5] That the word "African" or "Afric" appears in the name of these organizations should not be overlooked. These early activists, even as they were fighting for equality as Americans, remained keenly aware of their African origins, an awareness articulated in their public discourse as well, as they invoked prophecies of Ethiopian ascendance.

Ethiopian Ascendance as Rhetorical Strategy

It is impossible to determine the first public use of this prophecy by an African American, but it generally supported a "jeremiadic theme," alluding to Jeremiah, the Old Testament prophet, who predicted that the southern kingdom of Judah would be destroyed. Wilson Moses defines the jeremiad, during this period, as "the constant warnings issued by blacks to whites, concerning the judgment that was to come from the sin of slavery" (*Messiahs* 30–31). Ingeniously adapting their rhetoric to this tradition as a dominant form of expression in revivalistic antebellum America, Moses adds, black speakers reinforced America's belief that it was a chosen nation, by admonishing that in the matter of slavery, it was not keeping the covenant. It has been pointed out that such charges against American society, by demonstrating a faith in the ultimate triumph of democracy, actually highlighted the inherent optimism of the jeremiad and the ways in which it conservatively supports the status quo (Howard-Pitney 483–90). But Stewart and other jeremiadic speakers pushed always toward an idealized notion of this society, raising the bar, so to speak, as each ideal approached reality.

This discursive strategy can also be cast as one variation of what Barbour calls the "deconversion" story common in early autobiographies by people of color, wherein the narrator makes a distinction between true Christianity and the "white man's religion" used to justify white superiority (Barbour 85). Promoting this deconversion from the belief that Christianity and white superiority were synonymous, black speakers argued that the practice of slavery and oppression prevented white America from assuming its rightful place as a chosen nation. Two early examples of this adaptation occurred at the close of the eighteenth century. In 1794, Richard Allen and Absalom Jones, founders of the AME Church, published *A Narrative of the Proceedings of the Black People During the Late Awful Calamity in Philadelphia, in the year 1793: and a Refutation of Some Censures, thrown upon them in some Late Publications*, which included an "Address to those who keep Slaves, and approve the Practice." In the address, they compared American slavery with Egypt's enslavement of the Jews and reminded their readers of the retribution that came to those who oppressed the Israelites:

We do not wish to make you angry, but excite your attention to consider, how hateful slavery is in the sight of that God, who hath destroyed kings and princes, for their oppression of the poor slaves; Pharaoh and his princes with the posterity of king Saul, were destroyed by the protector and avenger of slaves. Would you not suppose the Israelites to be utterly unfit for freedom, and that it was impossible for them to attain to any degree of excellence? (24)

The Ethiopianism of Allen and Jones would redeem Africa solely through the agency of Christianity.

Prince Hall, Revolutionary War soldier, abolitionist, preacher, and grand mason of the first African Masonic Lodge in America, delivered a sermon to the lodge in West Cambridge, Massachusetts, condemning the abusive treatment of people of color in Boston and enslaved people of color everywhere. In his 1797 speech, "Pray God Give Us the Strength to Bear Up Under All Our Troubles,"[6] he exhorts:

My brethren, let us remember what a dark day it was with our African brethren, six years ago, in the French West Indies. Nothing but the snap of the whip was heard, from morning to evening. Hanging, breaking on the wheel, burning, and all manner of tortures were inflicted upon those unhappy people. But, bless be God, the scene is changed. They now confess that God hath no respect of persons and, therefore, receive them as their friends and treat them as brothers. Thus does Ethiopia stretch forth her hand from slavery, to freedom and equality. (15)

Hall was aware of the anxiety created in America by the revolt in the West Indies. Moses speculates that Hall only mentions in passing the violence and bloodshed leading to the establishment of the Republic of Haiti, which is the real message of the address. Instead, he "leavened" his message, closing with the "rhetoric of racial reconciliation" exemplified in the passage above (*Messiahs* 34).

Of course, Prince Hall, as chief founder of the African Masonic Lodge, was aware of this organization's African origins. The Masons historically acknowledged that their principles originated in Egyptian instructions to the Greeks and Romans, which provided the knowledge base of Greco-Roman civilization. While contemporaneous European Masons may have been able to ignore these origins, the black Masons in America no doubt found them strongly appealing.[7]

Hardly conciliatory is Robert Alexander Young's 1829 pamphlet titled *The Ethiopian Manifesto, Issued in Defence of the Blackman's Rights, in the Scale of Universal Freedom*. Young addressed the pamphlet to "the whole of the Ethiopian people," and to their oppressors, whom he warns of a day of accounting. He invokes the passage from Psalms, but paraphrases it considerably to suit his purpose of proclaiming retribution: "[T]he decree hath already passed the judgment seat of an undeviating God, wherein he hath said, 'surely hath the cries of the black, a most persecuted people, ascended to my throne and craved my mercy; now behold! I will stretch forth mine hand and gather them to the palm, that they become unto me a people, and I unto them their God' " (92).

Maria Miller Stewart

The kind of rhetorical dissembling Prince Hall had engaged in can be observed in the discourse of Maria Miller Stewart, speaking thirty-five years later. In her first speech to a mixed group, Stewart claimed in 1832 at Franklin Hall that "were it not that the King eternal has declared that Ethiopia shall stretch forth her hand unto God, I should indeed despair" ("Franklin Hall" 47).[8]

Although black and white women were generally accepted as evangelists, preachers, and missionaries in most church denominations by the early nineteenth century, they were not expected to speak publicly on political matters.[9] Little is known about Stewart or what motivated her to come forward in this manner. Mary Helen Washington, in her foreword to Ida B. Wells's Memphis diary writes that "we have almost no . . . record of how well-known Black women lived their daily lives, and, because Black women writing are so constrained by the pressures of race and gender uplift, we have . . . very little sense of the daily events that have gone into the making of their lives" (Foreword xv). These pressures of race and gender uplift constrained Stewart. Moving to Boston after supporting herself for most of her early life, then Maria Miller married

James W. Stewart in 1826, at the age of twenty-three. James Stewart died three years later, leaving Maria Stewart, after a two-year legal battle, without the inheritance to which she was entitled. In the context that Boston, at the time, was heavily involved in abolitionism, Stewart experienced a religious conversion leading her to write and speak out against injustices. Stewart's religious conversion and emotionalism no doubt had roots in the series of Great Awakenings of the eighteenth and early nineteenth centuries. Piersen writes that the fire and emotion of the First Great Awakening of the 1730s and 1740s appealed to the black worshiper because it "more closely approximated the religious patterns to which Afro-Americans were pre-disposed," this predisposition originating in African religious practices (67). The Awakening also nurtured the kind of religious evangelical activity in which women like Zilpha Elaw, Jarena Lee, and Stewart, traditionally restricted by gender improprieties, could begin to participate.

For Stewart the promise of godly retribution for these injustices was a source of personal comfort and also a call to political action. Alluding again to this verse in her "Address Delivered at the African Masonic Hall" in 1833, Stewart predicted that

> many powerful sons and daughters of Africa will shortly arise, who will put down vice and immorality amongst us, and declare by Him that sitteth upon the throne, that they will have their rights; and if refused, I am afraid they will spread horror and devastation around. I believe that the oppression of injured Africa has come up before the majesty of Heaven; and when our cries shall have reached the ears of the Most High, it will be a tremendous day for the people of this land; for strong is the arm of the Lord God Almighty. (63)

Note that Stewart placed the "horror and devastation" in a subordinate clause, following the cautionary "I am afraid." The depicted rebellion of the sons and daughters of Africa is one sanctioned and supported by the strong arm of God. Richardson observes that for Stewart the biblical passage was "a rallying cry in joining the black past and present, religious and secular" (18). This rallying cry, heard repeatedly in Stewart's essays and speeches, can be understood as, what Perelman and Olbrechts-Tyteca label, a figure of communion. They describe the persuasive effect of allusion as such a figure:

> There is allusion when the interpretation of a passage would be incomplete if one neglected the deliberate reference of the author to something he evokes without actually

naming it; this thing may be an event of the past, a custom, or a cultural fact, knowledge of which is peculiar to the members of the group with whom the speaker is trying to establish communion. (177)

Maria Stewart established communion with her audience, moving them closer to social action, through reference to a common African origin and the redemption it promised.

In her 1831 pamphlet titled *Religion and the Pure Principles of Morality, the Sure Foundation on Which We Must Build*, published in 1831, she employed this figure in a familial way in addressing the "daughters of Africa," reminding them of their origins and of the promise that "Ethiopia might stretch forth her hand unto God." At the same time, however, Stewart advocated self help and communal action—"but we have a great work to do" (30). Stewart stressed the condition of this prophecy that God would help them only if they helped themselves, thereby marking her version of Ethiopianism activist. In a prayer inserted into this essay, Stewart requested rather than predicted divine intervention in support of this work: "[D]o thou grant that Ethiopia may soon stretch forth her hands unto thee. And now, Lord, be pleased to grant that Satan's kingdom may be destroyed" (34). "Satan's kingdom" was surely antebellum America.

When placed in the larger context of early feminist rhetoric, Stewart's use of the Bible was typical. Other early women speakers quoted and paraphrased scriptures extensively, adapting them to support their claims. For example, Lucretia Coffin Mott, in her 1849 "Discourse on Woman," refuted the use of the Bible to justify prohibitions against women's speaking by offering her own exegesis of certain biblical texts. She reminded her Philadelphia audience that "the first announcement, on the day of Pentecost, was the fulfillment of ancient prophesy, that God's spirit should be poured out upon *daughters* as well as sons, and they should prophesy." She continued: "It is important that we be familiar with these facts, because woman has been so long circumscribed in her influence by the perverted application of the text, rendering it improper for her to speak in the assemblies of the people, 'to edification, to exhortation, and to comfort'" (78). Sojourner Truth's now legendary biblical validation of women also matches Stewart's use of scripture. Almost an exact contemporary of Stewart, Truth, by most accounts, was born in 1797; Stewart, in 1803. Truth died in 1883, four years after Stewart. In her 1851 speech at the Woman's Rights Convention in Akron, Ohio, Truth countered the argument put forth by a minister earlier during the gathering, opposing woman's rights because Christ was a man, with her response: "Then that little man in black there, he says women can't have as much rights as man, 'cause Christ wasn't a woman. Where did your Christ come from? Where did your Christ come from? From God and a woman. Man had nothing to do with him" (26–27). The Old Testament also supplied Stewart with examples of competent women. Defending a woman's right to engage in public life in her "Farewell Address," she cites the leadership of Deborah, Esther, Mary Magdalene, and the woman of Samaria.

But, of course, Stewart evoked scripture to support her claim to the ascendance of African people as well. In the spring of 1832, Stewart addressed her sisters in the Afric-American Female Intelligence Society of Boston and spoke of God's promised ascendance of Ethiopia's sons and daughters, reminding them, as she did in the earlier pamphlet, that they had a role to play in this revolution. The society was formed in 1831, just a few months prior to this occasion. It appears to have been the first organized literary society, male or female, in Boston (Porter 569). The members, "women of color of the Commonwealth of Massachusetts," organized to share information and suppress "vice and immorality" (*The Liberator* 7 January 1832, qtd. in Richardson 127n73). Stewart, declaring assurance of God's sustaining presence, begins what was perhaps her first speech to any group. Clearly anxious about this bold move of public "exertion," Stewart, opens with *insinuatio*, a rhetorical move wherein the speaker claims her inadequacy or lack of qualifications for the task and asks the audience's indulgence. A way of ingratiating oneself with the audience, *insinuatio* allows the speaker to acquire the auditors' initial goodwill and support. It was clearly an essential move for a black woman speaking publicly in 1832. Stewart justified her presence as a mandate from the Almighty. She stated that while she has been called by God, others were more qualified than she for this work and that she came "purely to promote the cause of Christ, and the good of souls, in the hope that others more experienced, more able and talented than myself, might go forward and do likewise" (50). Throughout the speech, Stewart, communicating "dying mortal to dying mortal," locates her arguments in a day of retribution, a day when all the wrongs will be corrected, all the sinners punished.

After what probably amounted to twenty minutes of biblical recitation and justification, Stewart proposed to make "a few remarks upon moral subjects," promising afterward to "sink into oblivion." She expressed amazement at the way "the descendants of fallen Africa" treated each other not only because such treatment was harmful but also because of the bad impression it left on white observers. This preoccupation with cultivating the good opinions of the dominant culture pervades the exhortations of socially conscious nineteenth-century black women, perhaps more concerned for reputation and respectability than their white counterparts, since they were working against negative stereotypes. Stewart also recognized that any change of opinion must result from self-improvement and the help of providence. She invoked the passage from Psalms, at the same time reminding the women that they needed to get up and do for themselves as other oppressed people had—the Greeks, the French, the Haitians, the Poles, and Native Americans. Peterson points out that in calling for self-help through political action Stewart deviated from the standard solutionless jeremiad, seeking instead "to fill in that unnamed space in the jeremiad that lies between sin and redemption, promise and fulfillment, to specify the possibilities of secular history and human agency" (70). Stewart recognized that the women needed to assert themselves. Finally, Stewart appeals to the society women to assert their good influence as Christian wives and mothers in a continuing quest for respectability.

Approximately six months later, September 21, 1832, Stewart delivered her first speech to an audience of men and women, "Lecture Delivered at the Franklin Hall." For Stewart, now addressing a "promiscuous" audience, *insinuatio* becomes critical. Stewart again justified her appearance as response to a "spiritual interrogation": "Who shall go forward, and take off the reproach that is cast upon the people of color? Shall it be a woman? And my heart made this reply—'If it is thy will, be even so, Lord Jesus.'" In the opening section, again she alludes to her lack of qualifications for the task: "O, had I received the advantages of an early education, my ideas would, ere now, have expanded far and wide; but, alas! I possess nothing but moral capability—no teaching but the teachings of the Holy Spirit" (45). She had also used the same kind of ingratiation in her pamphlet titled *Religion and the Pure Principles of Morality, the Sure Foundation on Which We Must Build*, stating, "I hope my friends will not scrutinize these pages with too severe an eye, as I have not calculated to display either elegance or taste in their composition, but have merely written the meditations of my heart as far as my imagination led" (28). However, it is clear that Stewart has learned more than the "teachings of the Holy Spirit," particularly as demonstrated in her speech to the Afric-American Female Intelligence Society, where she enumerated past rebellions, and in her "Farewell Address," in which she summarized portions of a work identified by Richardson as *Woman, Sketches of the History, Genius, Disposition, Accomplishments, Employments, Customs and Importance of the Fair Sex in All Parts of the World Interspersed with Many Singular and Entertaining Anecdotes by a Friend of the Sex*, published in 1890, by a John Adams (Richardson 24). In the "Franklin Hall" address, Stewart followed this profession of inadequacy with a description of the discriminatory employment practices in Boston, where black women could find work only as domestics. Without denigrating the domestic work that she herself had performed, Stewart pointed out that many black women were called to other professions and should not be denied the opportunity to pursue their interests.

To develop communion in this lecture, Stewart made several explicit audience shifts, charging various categories of auditors to respond in different ways to her arguments. These shifts raise questions about the composition of Stewart's immediate audience and about who read her lectures in the *Liberator*. All of Stewart's extant Boston speeches, delivered between April 1832 and September 1833, were published in Garrison's *Liberator*, which had just been launched in January 1831. As for its readership, Garrison himself announced in a late 1834 issue that three-quarters of the newspaper's 2,300 subscribers were black (Jacobs 15). Lintin surmises that although Stewart's "Franklin Hall" lecture was advertised as one that might be of interest to whites, very few attended because of prevailing attitudes toward blacks (40–41). The opening inquiry of the "Franklin Hall" speech, "Why sit ye here and die?" (45), was clearly directed toward the black citizens of Boston as a rejection of proposed colonization. But in a later section of this lecture, Stewart addressed white women, urging them to recognize their privileged positions: "O, ye fairer sisters, whose hands are never soiled, whose nerves and muscles are never strained, go learn by experience! Had we had the opportunity that you have had to improve our moral and mental faculties, what would have hindered our intellects from being as bright, and our manners from being as dignified as yours?" (48). While directly addressing any "fairer sisters" who might have been in the audience, Stewart was probably also engaging the emotional figure apostrophe, crying out to those not present, drawing them in, and making them hearers. Perelman and Olbrechts-Tyteca classify apostrophe, along with allusion, as another figure of communion, wherein the speaker can increase identification by inviting the audience "to take part in the deliberation which he appears to carry on in front of them" (178). In this instance, Stewart cultivated communion with her black Boston audience by reminding them of their common indignation toward those addressed. Stewart's shift to the first person plural pronoun in this section— "[h]ad *we* the opportunity," "*our* moral and mental faculties," "*our* intellects," "*our* manners"—also strengthened communion through enallage of person, where, by changing the number of persons, Stewart identifies herself with her audience rather than with the women being figuratively addressed (Perelman and Olbrechts-Tyteca 178).

Stewart reserved her final comments in this lecture for black men in the immediate audience, exhorting them to "make some mighty effort to raise your sons and daughters from the horrible state of servitude and degradation in which they are placed. It is upon you that woman depends; she can do but little besides using her influence" (48). The idea that woman's power resided chiefly in her ability to influence decision makers was a common topos of nineteenth-century women's discourse.[10]

The prediction of a day of retribution in this speech comes at the midpoint and resonates doubly, as a hopeful promise to her black Boston audience and as an ominous threat to her white overhearers:

It is true, that the free people of color throughout these United States are neither bought nor sold, nor under the lash of the cruel driver; many obtain a comfortable support; but few, if any, have an opportunity of becoming rich and independent; and the enjoyments we most pursue are as unprofitable to us as the spider's web or the floating bubbles that vanish into air. As servants, we are respected; but let us presume to aspire higher, our employer regards us no longer. And were it not that the King eternal has declared that Ethiopia shall stretch forth her hands unto God, I should indeed despair. (47)

As Raboteau reminds us, "Princes shall come out of Egypt and Ethiopia shall soon stretch forth her hands unto God" was not so much a prophecy as it was a prayer (56).

In the 1833 "Address Delivered at the African Masonic Hall," Stewart explicitly targeted black men, challenging them to be productive as their ancestors had been. Calling them "sons of Afric," she reminded them of their African origins: "History informs us that we sprung from one of the most learned nations of the whole earth; from the seat, if not the parent, of science. Yes, poor despised Africa was once the resort of sages and legislators of other nations, was esteemed the school for learning, and the most illustrious men in Greece flocked thither for instruction" (58).

Stewart, like other nineteenth-century speakers, needed to reclaim an honorable African past that would place her black auditors in a superior rather than inferior relationship with Anglo-Americans. Stewart proclaimed that punishment for gross sins "provoked the Almighty to frown thus heavily upon us, and give our glory unto others" (58). The reference here to "our glory" parallels the belief that God had chosen African people ultimately to be the source of Christian redemption for all. The danger was that in proclaiming a Christianizing role for African Americans, speakers came close to using the same justification that Europeans offered for enslaving Africans in the first place—to evangelize and civilize them. Raboteau points out that black clergy avoided absolution by claiming that "God wills good; he only permits evil, and from it draws good" (45). According to this thinking, God permitted but did not will slavery. This perspective also had roots in a religious version of romantic racialism, a concept, as defined by George Fredrickson, based on a belief in essential differences in temperament among races of people. According to this belief, Africans have a natural aptitude for Christianity, being "believing," "affectionate," and "altruistic," with such characteristics as meekness, patience, and humility. Whites, on the other hand, are less suited for Christian benevolence, being "too cerebral, self-seeking, and aggressive to meet the standards of the Sermon on the Mount" (62). But, Stewart called on them to remember that God has promised that "Ethiopia shall again stretch forth her hands unto God" if only they would "strive to regain that which we have lost" (58). The "sons of Africa" could accomplish this recovery, Stewart pressed, through hard work and careful attention to "mental and moral improvement." For Stewart the return to Africa was symbolic.

Moses suggests that Stewart, Allen, Hall, and other jeremiadic speakers were fully aware of their wider audiences: "It is thus likely that much of the black messianic oratory and most of the pamphlets that spoke of divine retribution were produced for the benefit of whites, although ostensibly directed towards black audiences" (*Messiahs* 37). Of course some jeremiads were explicitly directed toward whites, as in the case of Allen and Jones's 1794 "Address to those who keep Slaves, and approve the Practice" (mentioned previously). But even those that were not directed toward whites clearly demonstrate an awareness of multiple audiences. Predicting divine retribution rather than a human rebellion was a way of warning the oppressors of doom on the horizon without naming names. The apologetic phrase "We do not wish to make you angry," which begins the ominous paragraph from Allen and Jones's speech quoted above, can be understood as having just that purpose. Their auditors were potentially faced with the dilemma of putting down a revolt led by God.

Black nationalists also used the call to Ethiopian retribution more specifically to forecast a literal national homeland, separate from the land they currently occupied. However, neither Stewart nor David Walker, whom Stewart knew well, could be labeled nationalists in this sense. Instead, both invoked an African past for strength and inspiration. Stewart admired Walker, a prominent abolitionist in the black Boston community, who in 1829 published a pamphlet titled *An Appeal in Four Articles, Together with a Preamble to the Colored Citizens of the World, but in Particular and Very Expressly to Those of the United States of America.* In the introduction to the third edition, he exhorted:

It is expected that all coloured men, women and children, of every nation, language and tongue under heaven, will try to procure a copy of this Appeal and read it, or get some one to read it to them, for it is designed more particularly for them. Let them remember, that though our cruel oppressors and murderers, may (if possible) treat us more cruel, as Pharaoh did the children of Israel, yet the God of the Etheopeans, has been pleased to hear our moans in consequence of oppression; and the day of our redemption from abject wretchedness draweth near, when we shall be enabled, in the most extended sense of the word, to stretch forth our hands to the LORD Our God, but there must be a willingness on our part, for GOD to do these things for us, for we may be assured that he will not take us by the hairs of our head against our will and desire, and drag us from our very, mean, low and abject condition. (H. Aptheker, *Continual* 62)

The religious theme is strong in Walker's appeal, especially the view that in rebelling the slaves would carry out God's divine will, perhaps through the leadership of some earthly messiah, who would lead the rebellion. This passage is echoed in Stewart's address to the Afric-American Female Intelligence Society:

But God has said, that Ethiopia shall stretch forth her hands unto him. True, but God uses means to bring about his purposes; and unless the rising generation manifest a different temper and disposition towards each other from what we have manifested, the generation following will never be an enlightened people. We this day are considered as one of the most degraded races upon the face of the earth. It is useless for us any longer to sit with our hands folded, reproaching the whites; for that will never elevate us. (53)

Moses concedes that Stewart's speeches do convey a nationalist spirit "despite her lack of willingness to carry her nationalism to its ultimate logical expression of territorial separatism" (*Wings* 161). But Stewart's version of the jeremiad was the dominant one that posits—in the words of Howard-Pitney—"a chosen people *within* a chosen people" and that "addresses *two* American chosen peoples—black and white—whose millenial destinies, while distinct, are also inextricably entwined" (15; emphasis in original). To Stewart, and to Walker, however, such a separation would have been no more "logical" than the efforts of the colonization movement to expatriate free blacks to West Africa. The American Society for Colonizing the Free People of Colour of the United States was formed in Washington, D.C., in 1817, in part out of the unwillingness of Anglo-Americans to share equal liberty with the increasing number of free blacks.[11] By 1810, there were close to 185,000 free blacks in the United States, and by 1830, two years before Stewart delivered her first address, there were 319,000 (Franklin and Moss 137). Of these, however, according to one quite possibly unreliable census, only 1,875 lived in Boston, with a total population of 61,392 (Richardson 4).

As Stewart points out in her speeches, free blacks were despised by many whites, who denied them voting rights and discriminated against them in education, housing, employment, and the use of public facilities. Even the opening sentences of her first public address at Franklin Hall constituted a rejection of colonization. Incorporating phasing from the Old Testament, 2 Kings, she asks, "Why sit ye here and die? If we say we will go to a foreign land, the famine and the pestilence are there, and there we shall die. If we sit here, we shall die. Come let us plead our cause before the whites: if they save us alive, we shall live—and if they kill us, we shall but die" (45). Stewart argued in her speech at the African Masonic Hall that blacks had earned a right to America, a point she expressed eloquently in a series of antithetical clauses: "We have pursued the shadow, they have obtained the substance; we have performed the labor, they have received the profits; we have planted the vines, they have eaten the fruits of them" (59). Stewart ended this speech with what was perhaps her strongest anticolonization statement: "They would drive us to a strange land. But before I go, the bayonet shall pierce me through" (64).

Stewart's career as a public speaker ended with her Boston farewell address, delivered on September 21, 1833. After two years of writing and speaking about the proud past and redemptive future of African peoples, Stewart wrote and spoke in Boston no longer. It is not clear what happened to Stewart during that year of public speaking, but in this address Stewart seems reconciled to living out her life in relative obscurity as a result of the year's condemnation. Following in the tradition of the apologia, Stewart cites biblical and historical precedents for her public performance as a woman, concluding: "What if such women as are here described should rise among our sable race? And it is not impossible. For it is not the color of the skin that makes the man or the woman, but the principle formed in the soul" (Richardson 70). She moved to New York City, where she taught school and participated in women's organizations and in a black women's literary society. Stewart later moved to Baltimore and finally to Washington, D.C., where she died on December 17, 1879. In 1838, just five years after Stewart's departure from Boston, the First African Baptist Church, with which she sustained a close affiliation, changed its name to the First Independent Baptist Church of the People of Color, of Boston, with the justification that "the term African is ill applied to a church composed of American citizens" (Levesque 509). This shift was influenced to a large extent by the anticolonization sentiments. The ACS had promoted the link between American blacks and Africa, using it to support their pro-emigration arguments. As a counter, blacks increasingly emphasized their identity as Americans, reflected in the titles of publications, such as the *Colored American* weekly newspaper and the names of various colored conventions. They were affirming their entitlements as Americans rather than rejecting African origins.

This chapter has considered the ways in which Stewart employed African and Western discursive practices syncretically to create community with her Boston audiences. Emerging from a tradition of faith in the ability of language to bring about change, Maria Stewart answered a call to come forward and "take off the reproach that is cast upon the people of color" ("Franklin Hall" 44). Stewart's call to communalism alluded to biblically prophesied black retribution. Through apostrophe, she conversed with the white women of Boston and proposed one of the earliest cross-racial alliances of women. Through voice shifts she aligned herself solidly with other "daughters of Africa." These figures of communion enabled a liberatory rhetoric of social action.

3

"We Are All Bound Up Together"
Frances Harper's Converging Communities of Interest

> I hold that between the white people and the colored there is a community
> of interests, and the sooner they find it out, the better it will be for both
> parties. . . .
>
> —Frances Harper, Letter to William Still, 1872

Frances Ellen Watkins Harper emerges as perhaps the most prominent, active, and productive black woman speaker of the nineteenth century. By the age of thirty-four, she was listed among the outstanding figures of her day. For more than fifty years, she lectured and wrote poetry, essays, and fiction on slavery, woman's rights, civil rights, blacks and the war effort, mob violence, temperance, racial uplift, and self-help. She belonged to abolitionist societies and supported the Underground Railroad. She was one of only two women to speak at the National Convention of Colored Men in 1864. She was a lifelong member of the white Unitarian denomination. She was a founding member of the National Association of Colored Women. She was associated with three predominantly white women's organizations, the Women's Christian Temperance Union, the American Woman's Suffrage Association, and the National Council of Women. She served as vice president of the Universal Peace Union. She traveled throughout the post-Reconstruction South speaking at crowded churches, at parlor gatherings of women, and in state legislatures.

Harper's career calls into question the practice of assuming that nineteenth-century black women, like their white counterparts, were not allowed to participate in the male-dominated public arena, other than in traditional gender roles. Entering a range of complex rhetorical situations during the last half of the century, Harper operated to some extent within both the Habermasian public sphere[1] of a dominant white male culture and within a black counter-public described by Michael Dawson. According to Dawson, this counterpublic was sustained in part through the activities of the black women's club movement, where Harper had considerable influence. He also notes that the club women served as a "crucial link between the women's suffrage and Black rights movements" (200–205). Through her work in black and white women's associations, Harper provided just such a link. Further, negotiating these various rhetorical domains gave Harper numerous opportunities to engage in the associative and dissociative processes discussed later in this chapter.

In spite of an extensive speaking career, Harper rarely spoke of herself. Most of what she did say can be found in excerpted letters written to abolitionist William Still between 1853 and 1871. Still, in his book titled *The Underground Rail Road*, included these excerpts in a chapter on Harper's abolitionist and reconstruction activities. Through these communications, we acquire a sense of what motivated her to write, travel, and speak tirelessly for so long. In one letter, she wrote:

I hold that between the white people and the colored there is a community of interests, and the sooner they find it out, the better it will be for both parties; but that community of interests does not consist in increasing the privileges of one class and curtailing the rights of the other, but in getting every citizen interested in the welfare, progress and durability of the state. I do not in lecturing confine myself to the political side of the question. (Still 770)

This theme of community interests recurs in Harper's speeches during a lifetime of lecturing. Harper articulated points of convergence and divergence between the rights of the slaveholder and the enslaved, between women's rights and the rights of newly enfranchised black men; between white women and black women; between black men and black women; between middle-class blacks and the masses of poor and enslaved blacks concentrated in the South. She confronted the tensions growing out of differences among class, race, and gender as they developed throughout the nineteenth century. Harper emphasized convergence in her persuasive discourse in the context of the reality that many of her audiences were composed of men and women who did not share her cultural experiences. It was necessary to direct their attention to what they

and those she represented did share in common, at the same time that she reminded them of what they did not.

In this chapter I consider selected persuasive texts by Harper, most of them
delivered speeches, that argue for common interests between diverging communities as they attempt to reduce tension and promote collective action. Antislavery treatises comprise the first set. "The Colored People in America" is
thought to be the text of Harper's first public lecture (Foster, *Brighter* 95). In
an August 1854 letter to Still, she wrote: "My 'maiden lecture' was Monday
night in New Bedford [Massachusetts] on the Elevation and Education of our
People" (758). This antislavery text addressed to Northern sympathizers dealt
with tensions between the alleged rights of slaveholders and the rights of the
enslaved. The second speech, "Could We Trace the Record of Every Human
Heart," portions of which were reported in the *National Anti-Slavery Standard*,
was delivered on May 13, 1857, at the annual meeting of the New York City
Anti-Slavery Society. Alluding to the Fugitive Slave Law of 1850, which made
it possible for a slaveholder, by presenting an affidavit, to declare almost any
black person a fugitive, Harper, in "Could We Trace the Record of Every Human Heart," addressed tensions between property rights and human liberty
through a hierarchic ranking of values. "Our Greatest Want" is the title of an
1859 article Harper wrote for the *Anglo-African Magazine*, thought to be the
first black literary journal. Here the appeal to middle-class black readers is for
economic prudence, balancing the desire for financial gain against the pressing
need to support racial uplift.

Four speeches addressed to gatherings of white women's groups and centered on interconnections between woman's rights and civil rights comprise
the second group. In the postbellum speech titled "We Are All Bound Up Together," the tensions between women's rights and civil rights are exposed. Delivered to the Eleventh National Woman's Rights Convention in 1866, this
speech clearly delineates points of converging and diverging interests between the white women in the audience and the black women Harper represented. "Coloured Women of America," published in part in the January 1878
Englishwoman's Review, was a speech delivered to the Women's Congress. In
this speech, Harper identified for her English audience independent and capable black women who defied the perception that black women were weak
and disempowered. "Duty to Dependent Races," an 1891 speech to the National
Council of Women, contradicts the perception that blacks were needy and de-

pendent upon the white race for survival, by arguing instead for rights and entitlements. The final text considered, "Woman's Political Future," was delivered in 1893 at the World's Congress of Representative Women in Chicago. Here again Harper parted company with many of the women in the audience who supported unrestricted universal suffrage, arguing instead for the power of woman's influence.

I discuss the rhetorical strategies Harper employed in these texts to resolve conflicting concerns arising out of race, class, and gender differences, in order to argue for a higher "community of interests." Using Karlyn Campbell's outline for descriptive analysis, I consider the purpose, audience, persona, tone, structure, supporting materials, and strategies for resolving this kind of rhetorical problem (*The Rhetorical Act* 28–33). Perelman and Olbrechts-Tyteca's *The New Rhetoric* also provides an instructive framework for considering the ways in which competing value hierarchies are ordered and reordered according to the principles employed for ranking them (81–83). Recognizing the incompatibilities of converging values, Harper often engaged in hierarchic ranking of conflicts among communities of interest. For example, as the debate heated up around the Fifteenth Amendment, enfranchising the newly citizened black male, Harper found it necessary to part company with many of her suffragist contemporaries, arguing that when "it was a question of race we let the lesser question of sex go." Drawing again from *The New Rhetoric*, I consider the applicability of the authors' discussion of association and dissociation to Harper's speeches. They write:

By processes of association we understand schemes which bring separate elements together and allow us to establish a unity among them, which aims either at organizing them or at evaluating them, positively or negatively, by means of one another. By processes of *dissociation*, we mean techniques of separation which have the purpose of dissociating, separating, disuniting elements which are regarded as forming a whole or at least a unified group within some system of thought. (190)

Calling for unity in diversity, Harper aligned her interests with those of her auditors to "bring separate elements together" on some issues; yet on others, she engaged in dissociation, pointing out ways in which her experiences had been different from theirs. This chapter examines these strategic shifts from "apart of" to "apart from" as they allow her first to build community, then to point out weaknesses in its construction.

Frances Ellen Watkins Harper, described by journalist Grace Greenwood as "the bronze muse" (H. Brown 102), lectured throughout the United States from 1854 until her death in 1911. Born free in Baltimore, Maryland, in 1825, Harper was orphaned by the age of three. She was reared by her aunt and uncle, Henrietta and William Watkins. William Watkins, a minister, directed the Watkins' Academy for Negro Youth, which he establish in 1820. Harper attended the academy, studying the Bible, classical literature, elocution, grammar, mathematics, music, philosophy, reading, and writing. According to a former student, William Watkins was a taskmaster who demanded "exact inflection of a pupil's voice" and was "so signally precise that every example in etymology, syntax and prosody had to be given as correctly as a sound upon a keyboard" (Johnson 11). Along with this rigorous training, Harper attended abolitionist meetings with her cousins, who were already well known for their oratorical skills. William Watkins frequently contributed articles to Garrison's *Liberator*.

At twenty-six, Harper left Baltimore to teach, first in Ohio and later in Pennsylvania. In 1853, a free black man, upon entering Harper's home state of Maryland, was sold into slavery and subsequently died trying to escape. In one of her letters to Still, she recorded her reaction to this incident: "Upon that grave I pledge myself to the Anti-Slavery cause" (Still 758). Largely because of this injustice, then, Harper gave up teaching to lecture for the abolitionist cause. A year later, Harper was employed by the Maine Anti-Slavery Society as a traveling lecturer. Her lectures carried her to a number of states, where her reputation as an abolitionist speaker grew. After marrying Fenton Harper in 1860, she moved to Grove City, Ohio, where their only child, Mary, was born. In 1864 when Fenton Harper died, Frances Harper returned to lecturing. With slavery no longer the issue, she turned her attention to Reconstruction, temperance, education, moral reform, and women's rights. Harper spoke both North and South, addressing on one occasion the South Carolina legislature, where, at the time, blacks were seated. In 1871, she established a permanent home in Philadelphia but continued to travel and speak. She involved herself with the Women's Christian Temperance Union, the American Woman's Suffrage Association, the Universal Peace Union, the National Association of Colored Women, and the AME Church. Harper died in 1911, having modeled the black feminist version of the Ciceronian citizen-orator.

The process of dissociation began for Harper when she mounted the platform. Recorded impressions suggest that a woman of Frances Harper's ability was not what most audiences were expecting. Greenwood found it difficult to conceive that Harper might have been "sold on the auction block" and, after hearing a series of Harper's lectures in Philadelphia, described her as follows: "She . . . speaks without notes, with gestures few and fitting. Her manner is marked by dignity and composure. She is never assuming, never theatrical" (Still 779). Greenwood's remarks echoed those of numerous other white auditors whose shock at her performance exposed their own limited expectations. The *Portland Daily Press* described Harper as having "splendid articulation," using "chaste, pure language," having "a pleasant voice," and allowing "no one to tire of hearing her" (Still 760). Peterson argues that such reviews of Harper's delivery represent an "attempt to eliminate the public presence of the black female body perceived as sexualized or grotesque and to promote the voice as pure melody, insubstantial sound, a negation of presence" (124). These reactions to Harper's style and delivery attempted to erase what for her auditors was an incongruity between the articulations of an intelligent mind and the body that housed it. In an effort to deny her blackness, some went so far as to declare, "She is not colored, she is painted" (Still 772). Curiously, such freighted commentaries on Harper's delivery were not restricted to nineteenth-century observers. One literary scholar writes in 1989 the following description: "She was anything but an unsightly female, no titaness in size, with a fair figure, long, lustrous hair, and facial features pleasant to behold" (Jackson 267). The emphasis here is on those characteristics that serve to make Harper appear more like her white auditors—for example, "long, lustrous hair"—and, therefore, more acceptable because less incongruous. These nonlinguistic assessments of Frances Harper suggest the range of preconceptions she carried to the platform with her and indicate why a strategy of dissociation was critical to her message. She had to distance herself from those preconceptions in order to be heard.

Harper's black female contemporaries responded to her differently, paying more attention to delivery. In 1858, Mary Ann Shadd Cary, a black abolitionist, journalist, and speaker in her own right, said of Harper's rhetorical skills: "She is the greatest female speaker as ever was here [Detroit]" (Sterling 174). Harper never lost this oratorical forcefulness. An article in the September 1894 issue of *Woman's Era*, reporting on a lecture she delivered at the weekly meeting of the National League, remarked that "[w]omen who, like Mrs. Harper, have spent their time in cultivating their heads and hearts for unselfish usefulness, are not old at sixty-seven [*sic* sixty-nine]. Fortunate for us is it that Mrs. Harper is still in the prime of her intellectual vigor, and her finished oratory is as persuasive as ever" ("Monthly Review" 7). These evaluations confirm Harper's lifelong command of the lectern.

It is unfortunate that the speeches Harper delivered in less formal settings before ordinary people were not recorded; the rhetorical context for these performances was characterized in 1871, by a correspondent of the *Christian Recorder*, the organ of the AME Church. Stressing the importance of black lecturers, he said that "[w]hile we need some to diffuse literature in the form of journals and periodicals, we also need those who instruct the masses orally, especially those who cannot read, nor will not subscribe for a paper to be read to them" (qtd. in Foner 6). After the Civil War, Harper traveled extensively throughout the South, speaking to Sunday schools and small gatherings of women, to both black and white people. She wrote to Still:

Last Saturday I spoke in Sumter [South Carolina]; a number of white persons were present, and I had been invited to speak there by the Mayor and editor of the paper. There had been some violence in the district, and some of my friends did not wish me to go, but I had promised, and, of course, I went. . . . I am in Darlington, and spoke yesterday, but my congregation was so large, that I stood near the door of the church, so that I might be heard both inside and out, for a large portion, perhaps nearly half of my congregation were on the outside. (Still 768)

Standing at the door in this way, Harper literally brings together a "divided" community in much the same way that, rhetorically, she united "divided" audiences. After the passage of the Thirteenth, Fourteenth, and Fifteenth Amendments, many naively assumed that advocacy was no longer needed, but new forms of oppression emerged, causing Douglass in 1870 to exhort, "Press, platform, pulpit should continue to direct their energies to the removal of the hardships and wrongs which continue to be the lot of the colored people of this country . . . " (qtd. in Foner 6). Harper was in the forefront of those who chose the platform as the medium through which she addressed these "hardships and wrongs." Still, other than accounts in Harper's letters to Still, few reports of these rhetorical occasions remain.

Antislavery Texts

Harper based her antislavery speeches on the widely accepted assumption that the existence of slavery anywhere endangered freedom everywhere. Harper's appeal to this assumption reinforced the theme of community interests. Further, two other prevailing assumptions supported Harper's antislavery rhetoric. The first was that the human family was all one, an assumption Harper glossed as the great American family tied up in one "bundle of humanity" in her 1866 speech to the Eleventh National Woman's Rights Convention. The home was the site for this humanitarian principle. The second was that slavery was a sin, with the church providing the moral ground for its abolition (O'Connor 177–82). These three assumptions—the pervasive effects of slavery, its immorality, and the interconnectedness of humanity—undergird the arguments in the three antislavery texts considered here.

"The Colored People in America"

Possibly her earliest antislavery speech was delivered in New Bedford, Massachusetts, at a meeting on the subject of the education and elevation of black people. The essay titled "The Colored People in America," thought to be the text of this speech, was appended to her 1854 collection, *Poems on Miscellaneous Subjects*, a book reprinted over twenty times. In the preface to the 1854 edition, what Robert Stepto calls the "authenticating document"[2] for Harper's book, William Lloyd Garrison felt the need to remind readers that hers was the writing of "one young in years, and identified in complexion and destiny with a depressed and outcaste race" and that "though Miss Watkins has never been a slave, she has always resided in a slave State," referring specifically to this essay and two others as "a specimen of her prose writings" (Garrison 4). Garrison's remarks place limitations on Harper's work because of her association with slavery. His misperception that readers would need to be alerted to her association with slavery, and, therefore, with its indignities, is one of many for which this essay served as corrective. In the second sentence Harper immediately identifies herself with her people, claiming "whatever concerns them, as a race, concerns me" (Harper, "Colored" 38). Harper showed through this identification that she knew she would be and had been treated the same as those enslaved, thereby building on the theme of connected humanity. Embedded in a sustained series of periodic sentences, the phrases in the first section describe this treatment and the depraved conditions of black people, ending with blunt pronouncements of their consequences.

Harper chastises those blacks who were beginning to advance economically for the tendency to "censure and upbraid" those who were not (38), appealing indirectly for racial unity. In the next section, Harper stressed that what she calls the "darkest faults" of the race could be found among any people who had experienced the same depraved conditions. Harper isolated the responses from the people who exhibited them, claiming that anyone placed in similar circumstances would react similarly:

Place any nation in the same condition which has been our hapless lot, fetter their limbs and degrade their souls, debase their sons and corrupt their daughters, and when the restless yearnings for liberty shall burn through hearts and brain—when, tortured by wrong and goaded by oppression, the hearts that would madden with misery, or break in despair, resolve to break their thrall, and escape from bondage, then let the bay of the bloodhound and the scent of the human tiger be upon their track;—let them feel that, from the ceaseless murmur of the Atlantic to the sullen roar of the Pacific, from the thunders of the rainbow-crowned Niagara to the swollen waters of the Mexican gulf, they have not shelter for their bleeding feet, or resting-place for their defenceless heads;—let them, when nominally free, feel that they have only exchanged the iron yoke of oppression for the galling fetters of a vitiated public opinion;—let prejudice assign them the lowest place and the humblest positions, and make them "hewers of wood and drawers of water;"—let their income be so small that they must from necessity bequeath to their children an inheritance of poverty and a limited education; and tell me, reviler of our race! censurer of our people! if there is a nation in whose veins runs the purest Caucasian blood, upon whom the same cause would not produce the same effects; whose social condition, intellectual and moral character, would present a more favorable aspect than ours? (38–39)

In this 254-word periodic sentence, Harper dissociated attributes considered by many to constitute a racial essence from the people to whom these attributes were ascribed. She argued instead that similar experiences would "produce the same effects" among any race. Harper's use of the term "race" here and in her other writings signified a group of people who were the product of certain social conditions. She addressed the ways in which those conditions shaped the group consciousness of those people, resulting in "hearts that would madden with misery, or break in despair." Harper herself identified with this "race" of specific people because they and she shared and had been shaped by a specific history rather than because of innate and immutable characteristics.[3]

Harper ended the third and final section on what would become her characteristically optimistic note. She highlighted the accomplishments of this "down-trodden and despised race" in the face of dire circumstances. She cited accomplishments in education, finance, and religion as indicators of the great promise of black people, who, if given the same opportunity as others, would become "a people to whom knowledge has given power, and righteousness exaltation" (40). If indeed this is the text of the "maiden lecture" she mentioned to Still, then it suggests the extent to which even residents of "the hot-bed of fugitives," New Bedford, needed, like Garrison, to have their misconceptions corrected.

The tensions in this essay reside in the differences between the lived experiences of most blacks in mid-nineteenth-century America and those of most of Harper's Northern white auditors. Harper determined to have those auditors understand the causal connection between the "inheritance of misery" to which blacks were born and the debased spirit and dwarfed intellect that resulted from it. Speaking to those who held stereotypical views of black people, she resolved to account for these views by describing the conditions emerging from slavery that engendered them.

"Could We Trace the Record"

The opening sentence of Harper's 1857 address to the gathering of the New York City Anti-Slavery Society makes an appeal to a common and natural desire for freedom: "Could we trace the record of every human heart, the aspirations of every immortal soul, perhaps we would find no man so imbruted and degraded that we could not trace the word liberty either written in living characters upon the soul or hidden away in some nook or corner of the heart."[4] Everyone, she pointed out, wants to be free to live, even those who have never experienced freedom. Other speakers on the convention program that day included Ernestine Rose, a native of Poland, who helped lay the foundation for the woman's rights movement, Wendell Phillips, activist for abolition and woman's rights, and William Lloyd Garrison. As on numerous other abolitionist platforms, Harper was the only black speaker. This speech, delivered during a period of sectional controversy, is a direct attack against Northern support of the Fugitive Slave Law of 1850. Harper talked tough on this occasion, referring in particular to the plight of a fugitive slave remanded into slavery. One such incident involved Anthony Burns. In 1854, Burns, having escaped from slavery, was recaptured in the city of Boston, jailed, and transported to Virginia and finally to North Carolina as a slave. The Fugitive Slave Law of 1850 had legitimized this chain of events. Eventually purchased out of slavery, he returned to Boston. Only in America, Harper stressed, could such a scenario have unfolded. She described this scenario again in general terms, the second time portraying the impact of the Fugitive Slave Law upon women: "Slavery is mean, because it tramples on the feeble and weak. A man comes with his affidavits from the South and hurries me before a commissioner; upon that evidence *ex parte* and alone he hitches me to the car of slavery and trails my womanhood in the dust." Harper holds up the treatment of fugitives in the Northern states of America against their treatment internationally in a shameful contrast. According to the report in the *National Anti-Slavery Standard*, these unfavorable comparisons elicited applause if not embarrassment. Applause also followed her apostrophic call to Southern slave hunters: "Ye bloodhounds, go back to your kennels! When you fail to catch the flying fugitive, when his stealthy tread is heard in the place where the bones of the revolutionary sires repose, the ready North is base enough to do your shameful service." Possibly expecting a speech against slaveholding practices in the South, the audience is confronted instead with its own complicity. Harper, through association, brought together for the purpose of negative evaluation, Southern slavery and Northern disinterest.

After this scathing attack on those who supported the Fugitive Slave Law by failing to protest it, Harper realigns herself with them by recognizing their common Christianity, returning again to the appeal with which she closed most of her speeches. However, in this speech, the appeal comes through direct challenge that those gathered never rest until "the death knell of human bondage [is] sounded." The tensions reside between respect for human liberty, concern for international reputation, and common Christianity, on the one hand, and greed and the desire to appease Southern slaveholders, on the other. "Instead of listening to the cry of agony," Harper proclaims, "they listen to the ring of dollars and stoop down to pick up the coin." Harper was speaking just three years after she delivered her first address. Although she does remind her auditors of their common faith and their common respect for human freedom, gone is much of the conciliatory tenor of the 1854 text. Along with the optimism of the earlier speech, missing here also is an explicit attempt to identify common bounds of community. Rather, Harper emphasized slavery's immorality and its "shameful" pervasive effects.

"Our Greatest Want"

"Our Greatest Want," the third antislavery treatise considered here, is an article Frances Harper, then Watkins, published in the June 1859 issue of the *Anglo-African Magazine*. The magazine was published in New York City by Thomas Hamilton, from January of 1859 to at least March of 1860.[5] It carried articles by many other prominent black intellectuals including Martin R. Delany,

William C. Nell, Grace Mapps, Sarah M. Douglass, Edward Blyden, and Frederick Douglass. Harper also served on the editorial board. Periodicals like the *Anglo-African Magazine* helped to create community among antebellum blacks in the North. In the prospectus printed in the *Liberator*, Hamilton stated that one of the magazine's purposes was "to present a clear and concise statement of the condition, the past history, and the coming prospects of the colored population of the U.S. free and enslaved" (211). This purpose emphasized, as did Harper's essay, the interconnectedness of all black people in America, regardless of condition. Harper confronted the tensions between the free black readers of the publication and the masses of poor and enslaved blacks in the South, challenging those who were just beginning to acquire material wealth to remember those who were not free to work for themselves. Opening with a series of deductive claims regarding the influence of prevailing ideas, Harper moved quickly to the example of the quest for wealth, especially wealth acquired as profit from slavery: "The money getter, who virtually says let me make money, though I coin it from blood and extract it from tears . . . in a word all who barter principle for expediency, the true and right for the available and convenient, are worshipers at the shrine of success" ("Greatest" 160).

Black people, in particular, were challenged in this essay to develop spiritually to the point where they would assume leadership in the struggle against slavery. "The important lesson we should learn and be able to teach," she concluded, "is how to make every gift, whether gold or talent, fortune or genius, subserve the cause of crushed humanity and carry out the greatest idea of the present age, the glorious ideas of human brotherhood" (160). Harper's lectures and regular contributions to the Underground Railroad are evidence of her personal contribution of "gold" and "talent" to the cause.

Harper here wanted to dissociate black readers from the push to get and spend that preoccupied white society, forcing them to recognize the inequities that continued to prevail. The acquisition of wealth did not guarantee, she assured her readers, the acquisition of equality: "The respect bought by gold is not worth much" (160). She further urged withdrawal of support from a government that did not support abolition.

Woman's Rights and Human Rights

Harper delivered the speeches in this section from 1866, at the close of the Civil War, to 1893, when woman's rights and suffrage were at the forefront. The speeches were all addressed to gatherings of predominantly white women's organizations. Given Harper's views on woman's rights and the rights of black people, speeches addressing the first topic of necessity took into consideration the second. The rhetorical context for each speech, then, can be viewed as a physical representation of the diverging and frequently competing terrains of race and gender that Harper—a black woman speaking to white women—negotiated. Perelman and Olbrechts-Tyteca describe the ways in which argument relies on hierarchies as well as basic values, especially in rhetorical situations like these. They suggest that when confronted with two or more competing values, rhetors construct a heterogeneous hierarchy that will give the advantage to the preferred value: "Most values," they write, "are indeed shared by a great number of audiences, and a particular audience is characterized less by which values it accepts than by the way it grades them. Values may be admitted by many different audiences, but the degree of their acceptance will vary from one audience to another" (81). This ranking is easier, they note, with homogeneous hierarchies established in order to rank similar values. In such situations, the values differ only in degree, resulting in a quantitative rather than a qualitative hierarchy. It is generally not difficult to argue for a course of action that will lead to the most good and/or avoid the most harm. The challenge is to argue for one good over another competing and incompatible good. Harper's general ranking of the needs of black people over those of black and white women reflects this hierarchical principle of competing values. Giving the vote to black men, she claimed, took precedence over insisting that women be included as well, since the first would benefit those with the greatest immediate need. Her paraphrased remarks at the 1869 meeting of the American Equal Rights Association that "[w]hen it was a question of race, she let the lesser question of sex go" presumes agreement among her auditors on an established hierarchy that places race above gender, "the lesser question" (Stanton, Anthony, and Gage 391).

Harper must have viewed the vote in much the same way as the black Richmond women about whom Elsa Barkley Brown writes. According to Brown, these women went to the polls with their husbands, although they could not vote, to gain "collective protection" and to affirm the sense of a "collective enfranchisement"; in their view, it was everyone's vote that the men were casting (127). Anna Julia Cooper, in an 1892 essay on Southern black women, also described the tendency among many wives to leave their husbands because they had "voted away" their family's privileges ("Status of Woman in America"

139). Yet Brown cautions against coming to the conclusion that the women did not desire the vote for themselves. She points out that for them "the question was not an abstract notion of individual gender equality but rather one of community" (129n34). It is important to remember, as well, that although Harper supported the Fifteenth Amendment, after it was ratified, she actively campaigned for the woman's vote.

"We Are All Bound Up Together"

In her speech titled "We Are All Bound Up Together," the developing theme of a community of interests becomes more apparent. This, the first of her post-war messages to be considered, was delivered at the Eleventh National Woman's Rights Convention on May 16, 1866. The convention, held in New York City at the Church of the Puritans, was presided over by Elizabeth Cady Stanton. The first women's rights convention held after the Civil War, this gathering unanimously adopted a resolution to form the American Equal Rights Association (AERA), charged with the task of "burying the black man and the woman in the citizen" (qtd. in DuBois 64) by fighting for universal suffrage. Susan B. Anthony presented the Equal Rights Amendment (ERA) resolution following Harper's speech, which Harper had closed with a reference to the abusive treatment experienced by Harriet Tubman on the Camden and Amboy Railroad. As Foster points out, the speech "marked the beginning of Harper's prominence in national feminist organizations" (*Brighter* 216).

Having already established her reputation as an abolitionist poet and orator, Harper, then forty-one, identified Harriet Tubman with the Old Testament Moses, requiring the white Protestant delegates "to absorb African American symbology into their frames of reference" (Foster, *Written* 140). Harper's participation at the conference represented, however, only a limited prominence for black women in the national women's movement. DuBois points out that during the three-year history of the AERA, only five black women—Hattie Purvis, Sarah Remond, Sojourner Truth, former slave Mattie Griffith, and Harper—participated actively (69). These women had all been active in the abolitionist movement.

In the opening section of this speech, Harper cites a personal experience as a recent widow. She had been married only four years when, in 1864, her husband's death resulted in the confiscation of her property to pay his debts. This happened, she explained to the conventioners, because she was a woman and a widow, not solely because she was black. Harper was speaking in the state of New York, which only six years earlier had passed an expanded Married Women's Property Law—among other provisions, allowing a woman to manage financial assets if her husband was absent or deceased. Some of the women listening to Harper must have found themselves recalling that piece of legislation. Her narrative of this experience ends with the proclamation, "I say, then, that justice is not fulfilled so long as woman is unequal before the law," drawing upon the notion that the fate of all humanity is "bound up together" ("Bound Up" 45). In this first paragraph, then, she located herself within the community of interests of these women, drawing, perhaps for the first time, from the intimacy of her own experiences rather than restricting herself to more distant historical examples.

Having established this common ground with her auditors, Harper proceeded to step away from it, analogizing the treatment of women and the treatment of blacks in the South: "We are all bound up together in one great bundle of humanity, and society cannot trample on the weakest and feeblest of its members without receiving the curse in its own soul. You tried that in the case of the negro" (46). Similarly, in the letter to Still proclaiming a "community of interests," she countered her own words, writing, "but that community of interests does not consist in increasing the privileges of one class and curtailing the rights of the other, but in getting every citizen interested in the welfare, progress and durability of the state" (Still 770). In her 1866 address, Harper moved toward the concept of *diverging* interests with the claim "You tried that in the case of the negro." The abrupt pronoun shift here from the "we" of community to the accusatory "you" signals this divergence as well. She claimed that in an effort to suppress black people, the entire country was torn asunder, and others, even poor whites, were neglected. Having united with and then separated from the women in the audience, she proceeded to outline other points of diversion, particularly with respect to suffrage:

I do not believe that giving the woman the ballot is immediately going to cure all the ills of life. I do not believe that white women are dewdrops just exhaled from the skies. I think that like men they may be divided into three classes, the good, the bad, and the indifferent. The good would vote according to their convictions and principles; the bad, as dictated by prejudice or malice; and the indifferent will vote on the strongest side of the question, with the winning party. ("Bound Up" 46)

She restrained her support of universal suffrage in favor of improved conditions for blacks. Recalling her own mistreatment on streetcars, even in the nation's capital, she asked the critical question, "Have women nothing to do with this?" (47). Harper, then, after identifying a common community of interests inhabited by all women, relocated herself in that half of a diverging community inhabited by black people. Harper was not sure that she could trust white women's organizations to protect the interests of black women, as the rhetorical questions, "Have women nothing to do with this?" and "Are there not wrongs to be righted?" (47) both indicate. Once Harper's arguments against unrestricted support of suffrage have been presented, these interspersed interrogations drive the point home.

In the closing section, Harper strongly criticized the women for their failure to support more actively the rights of black people and expressed the hope that perhaps the ballot might give them the courage they seemed to lack:

Talk of giving women the ballot-box? Go on. It is a normal school, and the white women of this country need it. While there exists this brutal element in society which tramples upon the feeble and treads down the weak, I tell you that if there is any class of people who need to be lifted out of their airy nothings and selfishness, it is the white women of America. ("Bound Up" 48)

When the AERA split three years later over the Fifteenth Amendment, some of the women who insisted that it be replaced by an amendment enfranchising women and black men voiced their opinions in racist language. Elizabeth Cady Stanton proposed that middle-class white women should be given the vote to offset the votes of poor people, black people, and immigrants. Frederick Douglass criticized Stanton and other woman's rights leaders for making negative comparisons between "the daughters of Jefferson and Washington, and the daughters of bootblacks and gardeners," charging further that they were "advancing the cause of women's rights on the backs of defenseless slave women" (qtd. in Giddings 67–68). Harper's recognition that white feminists could not always be counted on to support blacks led her to support the Fifteenth Amendment, which, of course, barred racial but not gender discrimination in voting. This historically significant debate becomes rhetorically significant to the extent that it enables an understanding of the continuous shifts and adjustments Frances Harper was compelled to make in this speech and the three others considered here. Harper was far from certain that it was wise to sacrifice all to woman's suffrage when she did not trust the white women who stood to benefit most from it. She easily met the challenge of establishing common ties but did not hesitate to sever those ties when personal principles demanded.

"Coloured Women of America"

An excerpt from Harper's speech to the English Women's Conference, "Coloured Women of America," was reprinted in the January 15, 1878, *Englishwoman's Review*. In it Harper returned to the economic constraints addressed in her earlier essay in the *Anglo-African*, "Our Greatest Want." The excerpt is prefaced by these remarks from the journal editors:

During the recent Women's Congress an interesting paper was read by Mrs. Harper, of Philadelphia, describing the present condition of some of the coloured women in the Southern States, and the speedy advance which they have made in civilization since independence. Their condition is so little known in England that we transcribe a portion of the essay for our readers. ("Coloured" 10)

These headnotes with their reference to black women's progress "in civilization since independence" point to the need for a speech that was essentially informative and corrective. Harper must have recognized this need since the excerpt seems heavily epideictic in its praise of black women generally, holding up several in particular. It anticipates Victoria Matthews's 1895 speech, "Value of Race Literature," in which she presented an extensive list of "race accomplishments" for the women gathered in Boston. Harper's purpose here was to cut across class boundaries in order to show how black women at all levels of education had achieved:

The women as a class are quite equal to the men in energy and executive ability. In fact I find by close observations, that the mothers are the levers which move in education. The men talk about it, especially about election time, if they want an office for self or their candidate, but the women work most for it. They labour in many ways to support the family, while the children attend school. (10)

Jacqueline Jones suggests that texts like this one and, for example, Fannie Barrier Williams's "The Intellectual Progress of the Colored Women of the United States since the Emancipation Proclamation," highlighting the domestic and economic achievements of black women, "marked the emergence of the 'black matriarchy thesis,' for they suggested that the main problem in Afro-American family life was an 'irresponsible' father who took advantage of his 'faithful, hardworking womenfolks' " (104). The message was that these women had to be strong and financially independent because their husbands, fathers, and brothers could not or would not provide the needed support.[6] It was, no doubt, hard to praise the accomplishments of Reconstruction black women without running the risk of denigrating black men at the same time. Further, this dissociation may not always have been desired. Consider, for example, this reported quote from an 1871 lecture Harper delivered in Mobile, Alabama. Reprinted in Still's *Underground Rail Road*, the report was included in a letter from Harper, where she described how she gave the Alabama rebel audience "more gospel truth than perhaps some of them have heard for some time" (Still 775).

I have actually heard since I have been South that sometimes colored husbands positively beat their wives! I do not mean to insinuate for a moment that such things can possibly happen in Mobile. The very appearance of this congregation forbids it; but I did hear of one terrible husband defending himself for the unmanly practice with 'Well, I have got to whip her or leave her' " (Still 776).

It is noteworthy that the reporter chose to relate this portion of her speech—possibly because it cast a negative light on black men—and omitted, in the reporter's words, those "parts of the discourse that grated a little on a white Southern ear" (776).

The opening statement in "Coloured Women of America," that "women as a class are quite equal to men in energy and executive ability," established the comparative strain running through the speech. Harper stressed to her audience of English women that black women were not only advancing economically but were doing so better than and independent from men. She claimed that black women took more initiative in educational and financial pursuits. Harper cited examples of women who managed large plots of farm land, performing "a man's share in the field, and a woman's part at home," some with the assistance of men, but most without (11). But this speech does not seem to push the contrast between the accomplishments of black men and black women as much as it stresses the perseverance and ingenuity of the women. Harper was more concerned here with correcting an image of black women as helpless and inadequate. One way to accomplish this was to associate the women's abilities with those of men.

Harper's detached recitation of ingenuity and perseverance could lead one to forget that she had a similar life experience herself. A widow after only a few years of marriage, with few resources and a daughter to rear, she supported them both for the rest of her life by selling her publications and lecturing. She could very well have included herself among those women who had managed "to keep the wolf from the door" (11). In the last section, she mentioned a woman who "has written several stories, poems, and sketches, which have appeared in different periodicals" (14), quite possibly a self-reference. She also listed in this section, women who had become teachers, lawyers, doctors, writers, social workers, journalists, and artists, naming names, in some instances, and only alluding to the careers of others.

The portion of Harper's speech excerpted here could have been the "evidence" for a larger claim made in unprinted portions. As it is reprinted, one has the sense that the examples have been separated from the thesis. At least in this excerpt, Harper does not invite her auditors to participate in the construction of an argument. They are only overhearers of a litany of accomplishments that could have taken place without them. The evidence, of course, makes its own point.

Peterson observed that Harper failed to address ways to expand the productive economies of women to move away from the traditional agrarian and domestic forms of wage-earning (232). Indeed, the chief activities described are farming, laundering, cooking, milking, and raising poultry and hogs. Perhaps, because she was addressing an audience of uninformed white Englishwomen, she chose to give an epideictic address praising the current state of affairs rather than a deliberative address proposing change.

"Duty to Dependent Races"

"Duty to Dependent Races" was delivered in 1891 at the first triennial meeting of the National Council of Women, held in Washington, D.C. It was presented along with five other speeches under the general subject "Charities and Philanthropies." Other topics under this heading were "State Control of Dependent Classes," "The Care of Dependent Children," "The Need of Women in Public Institutions," and "Women as Police Matrons." This entire speech unfolds in a process of dissociation. On this occasion, Harper needed to correct a number of misunderstandings about the conditions of black people in America at the time—their causes, effects, and remedy. Her immediate challenge was to counter the essentialized characterization of a "dependent race" put forth by Alice C. Fletcher, the previous speaker, but no doubt commonly accepted. Harper also took on the "New South" view articulated by Georgian Henry Grady, portraying Southern blacks as "ignorant and easily deluded." Finally, she attacks general resistance to granting citizenship to "an alien race among a people impatient of a rival."

Both Harper and Fletcher, fellow of the Museum of the Scientific School of Harvard, spoke under the subtopic "Our Duty to Dependent Races." Fletcher constructed two "dependent races," the "American Indian" and the "Negro," and described for her audience what she considered to be their duty to these two races, "each distinct from the other, and from our own race, physiologically and linguistically" (Avery 81). She went on to address the question, "What shall we from our abundance give to those dependent upon us?" (82). Harper opened her speech with the following sentence of refutation:

While Miss Fletcher has advocated the cause of the Indian and negro under the caption of Dependent Races, I deem it a privilege to present the negro, not as a mere dependent asking for Northern sympathy or Southern compassion, but as a member of the body politic who has a claim upon the nation for justice, simple justice, which is the right of every race, upon the government for protection, which is the rightful claim of every citizen, and upon our common Christianity for the best influences which can be exerted for peace on earth and good-will to man. ("Duty" 86)

With this opening sentence, she both rejected Fletcher's basic premise of dependence, arguing that black people are simply claiming what is rightfully theirs, and established a framework for an alternative view. Thus the title often attributed to this text is misleading, since it suggests that Harper spoke here on the duty of others to provide for the *dependent* Negro race, when, in fact, she argued not for duties but for rights, and not for a dependent race, but for a race entitled to the same rights and privileges as others. These opening remarks set the speech's refutational tone. Her claims were that black people have certain rights by virtue of membership in the human race, rights as citizens of the United States, and, finally, that the granting of such rights is the natural response of a Christian nation. It should be noted again that Harper and Fletcher used the term "race" in different ways. Harper employed it here and in her other writings to signify a group of people who were the product of certain social conditions that shaped a group consciousness and created certain disadvantages. Fletcher's use implies essentialized racial characteristics of a people differing "physiologically and linguistically" from the "white race [which] has led the march of human progress" (Avery 82). Harper challenged these assumptions by dissociating the fiction of Fletcher's construction of race from the reality of her own construction. She replaced the image of the Negro race as dependent, needy, inferior, and linguistically challenged, with one of a people entitled to certain rights by virtue of membership in the human race and as United States citizens.

Harper reasserted her claim of black equality and entitlements through inclusive and exclusive voice shifts. Her opening sentence suggests that she was speaking on behalf of the race as a third party: *I* deem it a privilege to present *the Negro*" (86) and "*I* claim for *the Negro* . . . " (87). Shifting voice, she later identified with the race stating, "*Our* first claim upon the nation and government is the claim for protection . . . " (86). Further into the opening section of the speech, speaking inclusively of the entire nation, she reconnected herself with the audience: "That claim should lie at the basis of *our* civilization, not simply in theory but in fact." With these voice shifts, Harper placed herself in various converging and diverging communities of interest. Harper here also bestows civilization upon African American citizens during the Darwinist 1890s, when civilization had come to be an attribute of whites only. In this view, whites were at a higher stage of evolution than other peoples, who were still in some lower pre-civilized state of savagery or barbarism (Bederman 410–11). Thus Harper's claim to civilization and citizenship was significant.

Condit and Lucaites write about the role of public rhetoric during the Colonial period in establishing a "legitimizing rationale" for the inability of Euro-Americans to acknowledge the equality of free blacks (2). Having accepted the theory of natural rights as justification for the declaration of independence from Great Britain, the colonists found it difficult to absorb the theory's implications for the treatment of free black men and women, especially as their numbers grew. They instead developed their own dissociative discourse clearly intended to exclude blacks, one which proposed colonization in another country as one way to correct the incompatibility that there was "no place for the freed Africans in America" (10), since they could not accept their citizenship status.

The following comment from an 1832 New England publication indicates the standard European-American interpretation of "we the people": "We do not admit with the writer, that America is as much the country of the blacks, bond or free, as it is ours" (Condit and Lucaites 12). It should be remembered that a year later, such proposals would lead Maria Stewart, in her "Address Delivered at the African Masonic Hall," to respond, "They drive us to a strange land. But before I go, the bayonet shall pierce me through" (64). The 1857 Dred Scott decision, which Harper had explicitly condemned in her 1866 speech at the Woman's Rights Convention, merely made official the colonist's interpretation by decreeing that "they [blacks] are not included, and were not intended to be included, under the word 'citizens' in the Constitution" (qtd. in Condit and Lucaites 12).

Now Harper engaged here in linguistic reclaiming of this denied equality through her careful pronoun shifts. With the Civil War over, emancipation proclaimed, and the colonization movement stilled, it continued to be necessary to insert a collective "we" that acknowledged difference into the public discourse.

Developing again the theme of a "community of interests," she emphasized the concept of a nation as bound up together, charging, "The strongest nation on earth cannot afford to deal unjustly towards its weakest and feeblest members" (87). She proceeded predictably to discuss in separate sections each of these justifications for her claims. Her first claim, for protection, is made in the context of the numerous lynchings that were taking place in the post-Reconstruction South.

She challenged the racist assumptions expressed by Henry Grady, who had been an editor of the *Atlanta Constitution* at the time of his death, two years earlier.[7] She quoted him as expressing the fear "that this vast swarm, ignorant, purchasable, will be impacted and controlled by desperate and unscrupulous white men and made to hold the balance of power when white men are divided" ("Duty" 88). Harper responded that blacks were being punished before having committed a crime and that if they were indeed ignorant, it is a consequence of a system which made it a crime to educate them. So again, the law had backfired against those who established it; the community of interests ignored produced a Southern majority of illiterates and the fear of "Negro domination." Following this argument is the same cataloguing of the accomplishments of the race which can be found in "We Are All Bound Up Together." She exhorts her audience to provide assistance in racial uplift not as a duty but as a privilege and because by so doing, these women would be investing in their own well-being and in the well-being of the country as a whole.

Harper's recognition of the need for value ranking is apparent in the next section, where, in order to defend her claims, she argues for a higher value than those her audience would use as standards for the granting of certain privileges: "But there are some rights *more precious* than the rights of property or the claims of superior intelligence: they are the rights of life and liberty, and to these the poorest and humblest man has just as much right as the richest and most influential man in the country" (88).

In order to counter the perception of blacks as constituting an "alien race," Harper ends this speech with her standard appeal to their "common Christianity." Appeal to this highest ranking community of interests she reserved for last in most of her speeches and essays. Here she operates in the realm of what Perelman and Olbrechts-Tyteca label an abstract hierarchy, in this instance, one that recognizes the superiority of the just over the useful and appeals to the absolute superiority of Christian principles (80). Belief in the supremacy of Christian principle is the value Harper assumes is commonly shared by her nineteenth-century audiences. She took her final answer to the question of duty to weaker or dependent races from the New Testament: "I hold that Jesus Christ answered that question nearly two thousand years since. 'Whatsoever ye would that men should do to you, do you even so to them' " (91). Harper produced a document worthy of rhetorical study because she effectively connects the community of interests of her people to the larger problems faced by all.

"Woman's Political Future"

"Woman's Political Future" was delivered at the World's Congress of Representative Women of all Lands during the 1893 Chicago World's Columbian Exposition. Harper spoke during the "Civil and Political Status of Women" session, along with eight other women.

Turning the tables in this speech, Harper adapted the tactics Henry Grady used to argue against the black vote to voice her own reservations about woman's suffrage. His apparent concern was for "a mass of ignorance voting." In "Woman's Political Future," Harper expressed concern that women could potentially become the ignorant mass voting. She problematized the call for

qualified voters by pointing to an even wider range of disqualifications, not one
of which was skin color:

I do not believe in unrestricted and universal suffrage for either men or women. I believe
in moral and educational tests. I do not believe that the most ignorant and brutal man
is better prepared to add value to the strength and durability of the government than
the most cultured, upright, and intelligent woman. I do not think that willful ignorance should swamp earnest intelligence at the ballot-box, nor that educated wickedness, violence, and fraud should cancel the votes of honest men. The unsteady hands of
a drunkard can not cast the ballot of a freeman. The hands of lynchers are too red with
blood to determine the political character of the government for even four short years.
The ballot in the hands of woman means power added to influence. How well she will
use that power I can not foretell. (435–36)

By proposing such tests for women as well as other potential voters,
Harper broadens the argument used to oppose an unmonitored black vote.
Voter screening had, of course, been proposed by others, but usually as a means
of screening out certain black voters, never women and never to test morality.
For example, during an interview staged to respond to Ida Wells's suggestion
that she had done little to oppose mob violence in America, Frances Willard,
president of the Woman's Christian Temperance Union, also articulated her
version of the "voter test" proposal: "It is not fair that they ["alien illiterates"]
should vote, nor is it fair that a plantation Negro who can neither read nor
write, whose ideas are bounded by the fence of his own field and the price of
his own mule should be entrusted with the ballot. We ought to have put an
educational test upon that ballot from the first" (Wells, *Crusade* 207). Harper,
then, turns the mainstream antiblack suffrage discourse on its side. She pro-
poses a way to screen a myriad of undesirable people out of the voting process,
thereby dissociating lack of qualification from race.

She next listed some of the evils that would need to be corrected with
"woman coming into her kingdom," targeting mob violence in particular.
Harper was speaking during a period when lynching and murders had reached
staggering heights. Earlier that same year, in a speech to the Boston Monday Lectureship, Ida Wells reported fifty-two lynchings in 1892 alone (Wells,
"Lynch Law" 93). Harper urged the use of influence rather than political enfranchisement to effect change in this area. She charged that woman "has not

done all she could by influence, tongue, and pen to keep men from making bonfires of the bodies of real or supposed criminals" (437). No explicit mention is made here of her power as a voter. Harper's was a form of social feminism that accepted traditional roles for women and argued that their "distinctive influence should be extended to areas outside the home" (Campbell, *Man* 121). This form of feminism attracted conservative women because it allowed them to move beyond the domestic sphere without tainting the cult of true womanhood.

Harper charged the women to "create a healthy public sentiment; to demand justice, simple justice, as the right of every race; to brand with everlasting infamy the lawless and brutal cowardice that lynches, burns, and tortures your own countrymen" (437). Harper wanted the women gathered here to speak out more forcefully against lynching. Her advocacy for woman's suffrage was subsumed under a larger concern for woman's activism in its many forms.

Margaret Windeyer, the Australian representative, who responded, clearly was not pleased with Harper's privileging of woman's influence over suffrage. The whole of her brief remarks refuted almost everything Harper had just said:

> I would like to point out that women have no political present when they do not exercise the franchise. . . . I can not conceive that the underhanded, secret influence which women try to have upon politicians is politics. It is not politics in the best sense; and it is an influence which we ought to do all in our power to remove. It is not politics for a clever woman to be able to get from men who are engaged in politics that which a woman who is not tactful, who has not a pleasant appearance, can not get. (Sewall 438)

Windeyer understood influence to mean a form of suggestive discursive power deriving from a close relationship or from physical attractiveness. Harper meant much more. Her use of influence would seem to refer more exclusively to the collective enfranchisement that many black women felt entitled them to a voice in the voting decisions of black men. They and Harper understood this influence as a precursor to their own enfranchisement, not as a substitute for it.

Harper predictably returned to religious appeal in the closing portion, promising that with women's collective action "Eden would spring up in our path, and Paradise be around our way" (46). Invited to speak at a gathering of women on their political future, Harper described this future in terms of responsible political activism for the purpose of "uplifting the human race" (437).

In the persuasive texts examined here, Frances Harper consistently posited an imperfect nation, one needing the joint corrective action of men and women whose destinies were "bound up together." She described this imperfection in terms of the devastation it created. Harper emphasized causes rather than effects, surrounding conditions rather than genetic flaws. The racist tendency to assign inferiority to a group of people because of apparent linguistic or physiological differences proved to be her most pervasive and persistent dissociative challenge. As Raymond Hedin writes, "The notion of black inferiority has become the 'countertext' of black writing" (36). He points out that in developing this countertext, however, black authors, addressing predominantly white audiences, have most often adopted a form of rational argument that works against those racist assumptions without addressing them directly; this strategy, he suggests, "has the additional advantage of making an 'argument' for their race's rationality indirectly and implicitly rather than overtly through content or comment" (37). It was another way to demonstrate the human civility of black people. This interpretation may well explain why many of the speakers considered here articulate a kind of controlled rage toward emotionally charge matters like lynching, rape, and denial of rights. Harper encountered this challenge in abolitionist discourse, even among those of purported good will. Harper had to remind Northern abolitionist audiences of their complicity in the criminal slavery system. She met this challenge during interactions with woman's rights activists, who, when a choice had to be made, were on numerous occasions unwilling to privilege race over gender and, in the process, often resorted to a language filled with racist innuendo. Harper, in contrast, found it difficult to give priority to women's issues when, in her opinion, the needs of a disadvantaged black community were more pressing. Her value hierarchy subjugated all else to the needs of her people.

4

"Out of Their Own Mouths"
Ida Wells and the Presence of Lynching

> The purpose of the pages which follow shall be to give the record which
> has been made, not by colored men, but that which is the result of compi-
> lations made by white men, of reports sent over the civilized world by
> white men in the South. Out of their own mouths shall the murderers be
> condemned.
>
> —Ida B. Wells, "A Red Record"

For almost forty years, beginning with her 1892 editorial in the Memphis *Free Speech* and continuing until her death in 1931, Ida B. Wells argued against racism and the practice of lynching. These arguments were conducted in a climate of national racial hostility, validated in 1883, when the Supreme Court struck down the Civil Rights Act of 1875, leaving blacks with little legal defense against a vengeful South and spawning an epidemic of Jim Crow laws. Lynching and murder reached staggering heights.[1] Between 1890 and 1920, more persons were lynched than were legally executed. One source estimates that the number of persons—most Southern blacks—lynched in the United States between 1882 and 1891 totaled 1,544 (R. Logan 76). The prevailing assumption that lynching was a crime perpetrated against black men suspected of raping or attempting to rape white women is false. Less than 25 percent of those reported lynched between 1882 and 1946 had been so accused. Further, many of those lynched were women. From 1884 to 1903, some forty black women, charged with such crimes as murder, "well poisoning," "race prejudice," arson, and theft, were lynched (Cutler 172). Moreover, the invisible victims of rape, particularly during Reconstruction, were black, not white, women. Testimony before a House of Representatives committee investigating the Memphis riot of 1865, as well as testimony in 1871 into activities of the Ku Klux Klan, document sustained violence against black women.[2] It was during the period labeled by Rayford Logan "the nadir" that Wells produced a discourse effectively deconstructing the lynching for rape scenario and awakening others to be more outspoken.

Rhetorical critics most frequently comment on the strong rational quality of Wells's style, generally considered to be masculine. As early as 1893, just a year after Wells's speaking and writing brought her international attention, T. Thomas Fortune, editor of the *New York Age*, wrote:

Her style is one of great strength and directness. She is so much in earnest that there is almost an entire absence of the witty and humorous in what she writes. She handles her subjects more as a man than as a woman; indeed, she has so long had the management of a large home and business interests that the sharpness of wit and self-possession which characterize men of affairs are hers in a large measure. (qtd. in Scruggs 39).

Fortune's sexist assumptions about what it means to "handle" material as would a man were widely held and account in part for the lasting impressions her rhetoric made on her surprised contemporaries (Penn 408). Rhetorical critic Karlyn Campbell also comments on the absence in the "Southern Horrors" speech of "stylistic markers that would have indicated attempts by a female to appear 'womanly' in what is perceived as a male role—that of rhetor" (*Man* 147). Thus Wells created an assertive and traditionally masculine persona that enabled her to speak candidly about lynching and rape.

But often overlooked in assessments of Wells's persuasive effectiveness is her use of descriptive detail. She engaged description as a primary means of support in every antilynching piece she wrote or delivered. Wells's reliance on description came out of this same determination to appear objective. In "Southern Horrors," an 1892 testimonial address, in "Lynch Law in All Its Phases," the 1893 speech delivered to the Boston Monday Lectureship at Tremont Temple, and in a series of other speeches and essays, Wells brought the issue of lynching to the attention of her Northern and British audiences chiefly by evoking its strong presence.

To support an argumentative claim, advise Perelman and Olbrechts-Tyteca in *The New Rhetoric*, the rhetor should select and narrate details with care. They write:

By the very fact of selecting certain elements and presenting them to the audience, their importance and pertinency to the discussion are implied. Indeed such a choice endows these elements with a *presence* which is an essential factor in argumentation and one that is far too much neglected in rationalistic conceptions of reasoning. (116; emphasis in original)

In making these choices, the rhetor interprets as well as constructs the available means of persuasion. Presence, then, they emphasize, is created and should not be confused with reality. From the storehouse of details, the arguer selects those most likely to move the audience closer to adherence. This shift of opinion is more likely to occur when the attributed meaning of these details is unambiguous, as in the case of Wells's descriptions of mob violence. No hearer or reader could misinterpret the implications of those carefully selected narrations.

The authors add that the choices a rhetor makes are also influenced by time and space constraints. The arguer must decide how to distribute details according to the impression she wants to leave in the minds of the audience, increasing the presence of some details by dwelling on them longer (143–44). Classical rhetoricians also point to the persuasive advantage of description. *De Inventione* defines this elaboration of details as especially useful in the first stages of argument, when "an exposition of events that have occurred or are supposed to have occurred" are narrated (Cicero I.xix.27). Following the *exordium* or opening section, designed to bring the audience into a receptive frame of mind, the narrative provides the audience with sufficient background to understand the argument to follow. *Enargeia* or the inclusion of vivid descriptions of past events, according to Quintilian, "make us seem not so much to narrate as to exhibit the actual scene, while our emotions will be no less actively stirred than if we were present at the actual occurrence" (*Institutio Oratoria*, VI.ii.32). In the *Ad Herennium*, this practice is labeled "ocular demonstration," wherein "an event is so described in words that the business seems to be enacted and the subject to pass vividly before our eyes" (Cicero IX.lv.1–4).

Depending upon the nature of the argument, a well-crafted narrative section alone will often make a speaker's point more effectively than any specific appeal for action. Certainly this may be said of much of Wells's early discourse against lynching in which she devotes more time to evidence than to specific argument. It was also the case in the opening "story" of antislavery speeches that abolitionists, especially if they were former slaves, had the opportunity to remind their auditors of or to rehearse for them in vivid detail the particulars of slavery. "Tell your story, Fred" was the instruction Garrison frequently whispered to Douglass on his way to the podium during Douglass's early abolitionist days. Douglass also employed this tactic in his *Narrative*—for example, in his description of Captain Anthony's sustained and bloody beating of his aunt (*Narrative*, ch. 1). As Douglass matured as a speaker, he began to want to do more than describe his experience; he wanted to present reasoned arguments against the institution of slavery, to move away from the specific to its compelling implications. This urge led to his eventual split with the Garrisonian camp. But during those initial performances, anecdotal evidence suggests that such descriptions were quite effective in creating the *presence* of slavery. Sojourner Truth, considered "the word made flesh," represented dramatic enactment of the lived experience of the female who was once enslaved. With enactment, personal testimony becomes a major source of appeal. Her physical "presence," at 5 feet 11 inches (Painter, *Sojourner Truth* 3), added further proof of the difficulties she argued to alleviate.

Some antislavery speakers, in their resolve to support abolitionist claims, went so far as to select concrete objects for presentation under the assumption that the "real thing [would] induce an adherence that its mere description would be unable to secure" (Perelman and Olbrechts-Tyteca 117). The theatrics of Henry Ward Beecher, a Congregational minister, provide an extreme but apparently effective example. On several occasions, Beecher brought someone to represent a slave in chains with him into the pulpit and preached a highly emotional sermon in which the slave would be auctioned off to freedom (Yellin 131).

Additionally, presence is created through repetition and amplification of those details the arguer wants to invoke. These amplified details may be described specifically, giving such information as time, place, and names, except in cases when more abstract language increases the possibility for agreement. Along with amplification, the authors note other figures that effectively make the object of discourse present to the mind. *Onomatopoeia*, the creation of a word or unusual use of an existing one to evoke an actual noise, has the effect of replicating actual events. *Synonymy*, the repetition of a single idea by means of different words, conveys presence by using a form that suggests progressive correction, for example, "Go, run, fly, and avenge us." The figure *interpretatio* also conveys presence: explaining one expression by another, not so much for clarification as to increase the feeling of presence, for example, "It is the republic you have completely destroyed; the state you have completely upset." *Enallage* of tense, the syntactical substitution of one tense for another, can produce a very strong impression of presence. For example, "If you speak, you are dead" suggests an immediate consequence of disobeying the injunction. The simplest figures for increasing the feeling of presence are those depending on repetition. These figures often have a more complex argumentative effect, giving a feeling of presence but also creating distinctions; with each restatement, the concept increases in significance. Anaphora, or repetition of beginnings, is one type of such repetition. Imaginary direct speech increases the feeling of presence by the fictitious attribution of words to a person (sermocinatio) or to a group of persons talking to one another (dialogism).

With subjects like lynching, invoking presence was especially important since that which is suppressed becomes very easy to ignore, dehumanize, and rationalize. Presence prevents such suppression because it is not an abstract philosophical construction. Perelman and Olbrechts-Tyteca further write that "it is not enough indeed that a thing should exist for a person to feel its presence. Accordingly one of the preoccupations of a speaker is to make present, by verbal magic alone, what is actually absent but what he considers important to his argument" (117).

Louise Karon summarizes five salient features of presence as outlined in *The New Rhetoric*:

First it is a felt quality in the auditor's consciousness. This quality, created by the rhetor's "verbal magic," enables him to impress upon the consciousness of his audience whatever he deems important. Second, presence fixes the audience's attention while altering its perceptions and perspectives. Third, its strongest agent is the imagination. Fourth, its purpose is to initiate action or to dispose the audience toward an action or judgment. Fifth, it is created chiefly through techniques traditionally studied under the headings of style, delivery, and disposition. (97)[3]

Ida Wells works "verbal magic" with her antilynching discourse—heightening consciousness, changing perceptions, stimulating the imagination, and initiating action through tactics of delivery, arrangement, and style. Applying some of the principles of presence identified in *The New Rhetoric* and summarized above, as well as other rhetorical probes, I consider in this chapter ways in which Wells employs selective description to persuade audiences geographically and emotionally removed from the circumstances to which they were asked to respond. Wells's discourse not only invokes the presence of the act of lynching but also heightens awareness of the perpetrators and the carnivalesque atmosphere among the spectators. Although the focus here is on "Southern Horrors" and "Lynch Law in All Its Phases," I also draw supporting evidence from other speeches and articles emerging from her verbal campaign in the United States and Great Britain. Since the extant texts all bear titles relating to this topic, the date and occasion are also used to distinguish among them. One of the later texts, a pamphlet titled *Lynch Law in Georgia*, was distributed by Wells out of Chicago in 1899 and described the lynchings of Samuel Hose and Elijah Strickland in Newnan, Georgia. This publication makes salient the presence of lynch mentality in the local press and among the "better" community citizens as well as the presence of lynch mobs.

Over the course of her life, Wells delivered numerous similar speeches on the horrors of mob violence, with apparent ease. In a Providence, Rhode Island, conversation with Frederick Douglass, while both were waiting backstage to speak, she explained the contrast between his nervousness and her composure: "That is because you are an orator, Mr. Douglass, and naturally you are concerned as to the presentation of your address. With me it is different. I am only a mouthpiece through which to tell the story of lynching and I have told it so often that I know it by heart. I do not have to embellish; it makes its own way" (*Crusade* 231). But, of course, there was art as well as nature in Wells's discourse against mob violence.

Wells delivered the Lyric Hall speech at a testimonial organized by a committee of 250 black women from New York and Brooklyn. The women held the event to honor Wells and to support her campaign against lynching. The affair was considered by many "to be the greatest demonstration ever attempted by race women for one of their number" (78). It was the first time Wells had delivered an address, speaking before she had developed the confidence expressed in her conversation with Douglass: "Although every detail of that horrible lynching affair was imprinted in my memory, I had to commit it all to paper. . . . [It was] the beginning of public speaking for me" (*Crusade* 78–81).

The "horrible lynching affair" to which she referred was the killing of three black Memphis entrepreneurs, her friends, who had opened a grocery store. This establishment was in competition with a white-owned store, which had had a monopoly on the trade of the black population. The friends were arrested for defending their store against white citizens who wanted to put them out of business. Before they had a chance to be tried in court, they were removed from their jail cells and murdered.

Wells spoke out against these and other acts of violence in an editorial in her paper, the *Free Speech*.[4] In response, outraged white Memphis citizens destroyed the offices of the *Free Speech*, and she was advised not to return to the city. Wells happened to be in Philadelphia when the editorial was published. Having been banished from Memphis, Wells went to New York and began writing a column for T. Thomas Fortune's *New York Age*. The June 25, 1892, edition described Wells's experience in a seven-column front page article and documented a number of other lynchings for alleged rape. Wells continued to write weekly columns in the *New York Age*, and in late October of 1892 published the pamphlet titled *Southern Horrors: Lynch Law in All Its Phases*.

The weekly articles in the *New York Age*, along with her moving performance at Lyric Hall, resulted in invitations to speak in a number of Eastern cities. It was not until 1893, however, during a visit to Boston, that she first addressed a predominantly white audience. This address, "Lynch Law in All Its Phases," was delivered at Tremont Temple in the Boston Monday Lectureship, February 13, 1893. According to Sterling, "[w]hen she spoke at Tremont Temple, where Ellen Craft had been cheered more than forty years earlier, the Boston *Transcript* published a detailed account of her speech" (*Foremothers* 85). Of paramount concern to Wells, as she traveled around the country and across the ocean, was that she project an image of objectivity. She assumed the persona of investigative reporter, one who merely presented the facts, the evidence, leaving it to the reader or auditor to draw the correct conclusions. She was particularly concerned about suppressing emotion, wanting the facts to speak for themselves. When delivering the Lyric Hall speech, she was annoyed that she began to cry, fearing that such an emotional display, or, as she called it, "an exhibition of weakness," would dilute the impact of her message. O'Connor, in *Pioneer Women Orators*, discusses the emphasis early nineteenth-century women speakers placed on allaying rather than arousing the emotions of their listeners, especially since the subjects they addressed were emotion laden. Their concern was to establish a dignified ethos for themselves, as women who were "out of their sphere," daring to speak publicly (159). Of course, this perception of impropriety must have been dimmer for a woman speaking in the last decade of the nineteenth century; yet for Wells, it was still a burning issue: "Whatever my feelings, I am not given to public demonstrations. And only once before in all my life had I given way to woman's weakness in public" (*Crusade* 80). Ironically, this unexpected but very natural emotional display of what Wells considered "woman's weakness" probably strengthened rather than weakened the impact.

In her autobiography, Wells revealed the qualities she appreciated in a good speech, admiring most its attention to concrete details. Of a speech delivered by W. T. Stead, editor of the British publication *Review of Reviews*, she commented that it was "eloquent with plain facts and deductions from those facts as applied to our race" (*Crusade* 123). Again, reporting on Frederick Douglass's speech delivered on "Negro Day" at the 1893 Chicago Columbian Exposition, an event that Wells had strongly opposed, she wrote, "Mr. Douglass's oration was a masterpiece of wit, humor, and actual statement of conditions under which the Negro race of this country labored" (*Crusade* 119). Both comments direct attention to the rhetorical appeal of presence.

Wells's purpose was "to deconstruct the myriad of Southern claims and pretenses to which otherwise progressive forces in the North acceded" (Carby 113). In all of her antilynching discourse, Wells wanted to make the point that lynching was used as a means of controlling or limiting the advancement of blacks under the guise of being in response to the rape of white women. In all cited instances, she pronounced, the accusations had turned out to be unfounded and prompted by opposition to some other behavior by the victim. She concentrated on proving that these were not rape cases, recognizing that any effective attack against lynching would have to be one that "disabused the Black man-as-rapist syndrome" (B. Aptheker 62). Wells harnessed her outrage within the reins of concrete and well-documented evidence. Proceeding under the assumption that her listeners were intelligent but uninformed persons who simply needed to be presented with the facts of the case, Wells, in "Southern Horrors," made present to her largely black and female audience the monstrous acts. She opened with a quote from her editorial in the May 21, 1892, edition of the *Free Speech* (the quote was also included in the 1893 Tremont Temple speech). In the original editorial, since Wells was addressing readers quite familiar and perhaps, in many instances, more familiar than she with the particular incidents, she spent little editorial space on descriptive details, instead boldly making the following controversial claim:

Nobody in this section of the country believes the old thread bare lie that Negro men rape white women. If Southern white men are not careful they will over-reach themselves, and public sentiment will have a reaction; and a conclusion will be reached which will be very damaging to the moral reputation of their women. (Wells, "Southern" 6)

With the audience of Memphis citizens, she could move directly to her conclusions. Lynching was a continuous presence; it was not necessary to call it forth. But to the New York women those incidents needed to be rehearsed in greater detail.

The 1892 speech titled "Southern Horrors," printed in pamphlet form by the New York Age Print is divided into six chapters. These divisions provide a loose unity for some sections but appear to be purely arbitrary for others. A summary of these chapters highlights this framework.

Chapter I, "The Offense," opens with a description of the response of white Memphis to the editorial that appeared in the *Free Speech*, May 21, 1892. Wells first quoted the controversial editorial, then the response, in the *Daily Commercial*, three days later; she followed this citation with a response from another Memphis paper, the *Evening Scimitar*. Then there is further narration of events to demonstrate that these acts of mob violence were being committed by more than the "lawless element." Next is personal commentary on what prompted the editorial in the *Free Speech*. She then declared her twofold purpose in delivering this speech: to tell the true story of what happened in Memphis and to defend black men who have become involved with white women, those "Afro-American Sampsons [*sic*] who suffer themselves to be betrayed by white Delilahs" ("Southern Horrors" 5). She considered the case of J. C. Duke, the editor of a newspaper in Alabama, who questioned these so-called rapes as "the growing appreciation of white Juliets for colored Romeos." She developed the point that white women are willingly forming liaisons with black men: "White men lynch the offending Afro-American, not because he is a despoiler of virtue, but because he succumbs to the smiles of white women" (6). In the Arno Press reprinting, Chapter I ends here.

However, chapter II, "The Black and White of It," is essentially an elaboration upon the point just made in the previous section. She cited the case of a woman in Ohio, who, after accusing a black man of rape, later confessed to her husband that the man was innocent. In this case, the accused was released, having served four years in jail. Wells then argued that this outcome was the exception and that in most cases, the accused rapists are lynched without benefit of due process. Drawing on stories from the Southern press, she cited several similar instances of complicity by white women, with many culminating in the delivery of black babies. These instances, she claimed, called for the full establishment of the guilt or innocence of Afro-Americans accused of rape. To support her claim that "it is not the crime but the class," she then cited several stories, in the white press, of black women who were assaulted by white men with little or no consequence to the offender. Parallel instances of black men, jailed and subsequently lynched after being accused only of "visiting" white women, were cited, supporting the claim that the issue was race, not rape. Judging from its title, one may conclude that the chapter's main purpose was to contrast the treatment of black and of white accused rapists and black and white women who claim to have been raped.

"The New Cry" is the title of Chapter III. This section contains much of the causal analysis described above. Having dispensed with the alleged cause, she examined a series of other justifications for lynching. First was the justification that lynching grows out of a desire to suppress the newly freed Afro-American lest he acquire too much power: "Honest white men practically conceded the necessity of intelligence murdering ignorance to correct the mistake of the general government. . . . " (*Southern Horrors* 13). As Wells reiterated in *A Red Record*, her 1894 antilynching treatise, once the effectiveness of this response became apparent, it was necessary to invent another justification. From this need developed the "new cry" that these acts were being perpetuated in defense of Southern womanhood—the new cry was rape. This justification turned out to be the most effective, the one against which few would raise objections, even many blacks who believed that education and good manners would finally make them acceptable.

In Chapter IV, "The Malicious and Untruthful White Press," Wells quoted long passages from two Memphis newspapers calling for more lynching to curb the "brute passion of the Negro" and lamenting the loss of the enslaved Negro's "learned politeness from association with White people." It is also in this chapter that she related in detail the specific events leading to her own exile from Memphis. After the three businessmen were lynched, she, through her newspaper, encouraged blacks to leave Memphis. The inflammatory editorials appearing in her paper gave the local citizens another excuse to react violently. This chapter does live up to its title in that it focused on the ways in which mob violence in Memphis and throughout the South were misrepresented in the white press.

Chapter V, "The South's Position," chronicles the Southern white response to the accusations of mob violence. This frequently articulated response was that the North should let the South handle its own affairs. She did acknowledge that some organizations, like the Methodist Episcopal Church and the Republican party, some major newspapers, the president, governors, judges, and concerned citizens across the South had expressed disapproval of the practice of lynching. These responses brought a "short halt" to the practice, but the lynching soon resumed. She accused those who were silent of being accomplices in this outrage and called for stronger action from those who raise only mild objections.

The concluding chapter, "Self Help," was a direct appeal to blacks to act in their own behalf and was both a literal and figurative call to arms. She outlined a specific three-pronged proposal: economic boycotts of white-owned businesses, including the railroads, a proposal reinforced with one for self-protection ("a Winchester rifle should have a place of honor in every black home, and it should be used for that protection which the law refuses to give"), emigration, or mass exodus from those areas where such crimes are perpetuated to the new Oklahoma territory, and journalistic investigations, documenting claims of mob violence, conducted by and published in black-owned newspapers.

Disregarding these chapter divisions, one may recognize an organization that is essentially logical rather than topical or chronological. Wells examined causal relationships among the various responses to lynch law and proposed specific solutions to her empirical audience of black women and men.

Wells used examples as her primary means of support; in fact the first three chapters are essentially a collection of examples linked with interpretive commentary. These examples are backed up with statistics compiled by the *Chicago Tribune*. In Chapter III, "The New Cry," she cited 728 instances of blacks lynched during the previous eight years. In *A Red Record*, she drew from this same source to chronicle victims of lynch law during 1883. Wells was always conscious of the importance of authenticity and credibility, especially in addressing a topic surrounded with such controversy.

Wells developed a close analogy between slavery and lynching. In the 1893

Tremont Temple speech, "Lynch Law in All Its Phases," she develops this equation by suggesting that Northern response to lynching is similar to the past Northern apathy toward slavery:

In a former generation the ancestors of these same people refused to believe that slavery was the "league with death and the covenant with hell," Wm. Lloyd Garrison declared it to be, until he was thrown into a dungeon in Baltimore, until the signal lights of Nat Turner lit the dull skies of Northampton County, and until sturdy old John Brown made his attack on Harper's Ferry. . . . The lawlessness which has been here described is like unto that which prevailed under slavery. *The very same forces are at work now as then.* ("Lynch Law" 344; emphasis in original)

She also developed a compelling argument around the analogy in "Southern Horrors" between the treatment of men accused of the rape of white women and those accused of the rape of black women. This analogy makes the point mentioned earlier that at issue was class, not crime. Wells drew still another contrast between the rejection faced by white women bearing illegitimate black babies and that faced by women bearing illegitimate white babies. Through these analogies, she was able to compare issues falling on one or the other side of what W. E. B. Du Bois would later call the "color line" (54). This was, in fact, the tactic of analogy she developed in the 1893 "Lynch Law in All Its Phases" speech, where she compared response to the lynching of blacks, generally, with the 1891 lynching of Italians. After three Italian citizens, along with eight others, were lynched in New Orleans, Italy demanded redress. Even the federal government could not prevail over the state of Louisiana and eventually offered the Italian government $25,000 and an inconclusive verdict. The verdict was similar to those offered in most pseudo-investigations of black lynching, but the international response and outrage was markedly different, and at least some remuneration was offered. Ironically, it was this incident and not the violence perpetrated against black citizens that led to the first proposal for federal action to prevent lynching, a proposal that would have protected only foreign nationals in the United States.

Still another comparative tactic for Wells was an *a fortiori* argument, using it to build a strong case against the likelihood of black men raping white women: "The thinking public will not easily believe freedom and education more brutalizing than slavery, and the world knows that the crime of rape was unknown during four years of civil war, when the White women of the South were at the mercy of the race which is all at once charged with being a bestial one" (*Southern Horrors* 5).

The point would be made frequently in arguments against lynching. Why was it, Wells asked, that when these "brutes" had been left alone on the plantations with only women and children, there was no concern that they might be overcome with a desire to rape? One explanation posited that once the black men were no longer enslaved, they lost the civilizing effect resulting from association with white people, and their more brutish native instincts reemerged.

Unlike many of her predecessors and contemporaries,[5] her use of biblical allusion is limited to the Samson-Delilah reference in the opening section of *Southern Horrors:* "They [the facts] will serve at the same time as a defense for the Afro-American Sampsons who suffer themselves to be betrayed by White Delilahs" (5). In the 1893 "Lynch Law in All Its Phases" speech, rather than appeal to biblical authority, Wells appealed to the Constitution, particularly the freedoms outlined in the Bill of Rights. Lambasting mob violence, Wells pointed out that it threatens the "foundation of government, law and order" and appeals not to sentiment, "not even so much from a standpoint of justice to a weak race, as from a desire to preserve our institutions" (333). Perhaps in her determination to avoid woman's weakness, Wells steered clear of Christian biblical reference, most often associated with women as guardians of morality.

Wells's use of irony to contrast perceptions with the reality she wanted her audience to face persists throughout *Southern Horrors*. She variously described the perpetrators of mob violence as "the guardians of the honor of Southern White women," as "the leading citizens" (8) of the community, or as "these civilized whites" (12). In describing the fruits of her investigations into the liaisons between white women and black men, she claimed to have proven that in most instances, "[t]he woman was a willing partner in the victim's guilt, and being of the 'superior' race must naturally have been more guilty" (10). She located this violence in "the land of liberty." Describing a murder in Vicksburg by a gang of burglars, Wells commented that "[o]f course it must have been done by Negroes" (24). This trope was especially effective in the context of her speech because it was clear just where she stood in relation to the issues under discussion.

Her argument also achieved presence through the synonymous terms used to characterize the practice of lynching. At various times, she referred to it as "the deviltry of the South," "inhuman and fiendish" behavior, the actions of "cruel and blood-thirsty mobs," "butcheries of Black men," "this great outrage," "frequent and revolting crimes," "this awful hurling of men into eternity on supposition," "the most heinous crimes that ever stained the history of a country," and as "the Black shadow of lawlessness . . . spreading its wings over the whole country." Clearly this constant amplification by synonym, pointed out in *The New Rhetoric*, enhances presence, in the instance of Wells's speech, by reinforcing the perception of mob violence she wanted to convey.

A consideration of what Campbell calls "the rhetorical problem" or "the discourse in relation to its context" aids in understanding the challenge Wells faced (*The Rhetorical Act* 149). The problems associated with *Southern Horrors* arise from the nature and cultural history of the subject itself, the resistance of the audience to respond, and Wells's own forceful personality.

The subject of rape itself demanded reeducation on several issues. Aptheker has aptly categorized the most salient of these issues:

In defending the racial integrity of Black manhood, Wells simultaneously affirmed the virtue of Black womanhood, and the independence of white womanhood. For the dialectics of the lynch mentality required the dehumanization of Black men (as rapists), Black women (as prostitutes), and White women (as property whose honor was to be avenged by the men who possessed them). (B. Aptheker 62)

Many of those who heard her were reluctant to respond, for they were being asked not only to question the motives of their fellow citizens in the South, with whom they were attempting to mend the broken fences of the Civil War, but also to question the virtue of the Southern woman and to give up some of their own stereotypes about Black men, leaving open the possibility that such a violent crime would go unpunished. In her autobiography, *Crusade for Justice*, Wells offers her own assessment of the audience she needed to reach: "Only in one city—Boston—had I been given even a meager hearing, and the press was dumb. I refer, of course, to the White press, since it was the medium through which I hoped to reach the White people of the country, who alone could mold public opinion" (86).

As her subsequent travels suggest, Wells soon came to realize that a more effective campaign could be made abroad, where public opinion and economic sanctions could both have an impact. She was invited to England and Scotland by Catherine Impy and Isabelle Mayo, both prestigious international crusaders against oppression, after an interview in Philadelphia with Impy (*Crusade* 82–85). In these countries she was favorably received, even as the Southern press in America lambasted her efforts. In fact, British interest in lynch law actually facilitated the campaign in America. This shift in attention to the British Isles parallels the transatlantic strategies of Frederick Douglass, Sara Parker Remond, and others in the abolitionist cause who found more receptive audiences abroad.

Another aspect of this rhetorical problem was Wells's reputation, her prior ethos. Wells had already established herself as an outspoken journalist. T. Thomas Fortune felt that Wells had "become famous as one of the few of our women who handle a goose quill with diamond point as easily as any man in newspaper work" (*Crusade* 33). Lucy Smith, a journalist and organizer of black Baptist women, said of Wells: "No writer, the male fraternity not excepted, has been more extensively quoted, none struck harder blows at the wrongs and weakness of the race. Her readers are equally divided between the sexes. She reaches the men by dealing with the political aspect of the race question, and the women she meets around the fireside" (qtd. in *Crusade* 33).

How then may we assess Wells's 1892 "Southern Horrors" speech? Campbell suggests that a rhetorical act may be evaluated on the basis of the responses it evokes, its truthfulness or the accuracy of the evidence used in support of its claims, the skill with which the rhetor overcomes the rhetorical constraints—which she calls the artistic or aesthetic criterion—and, finally, its ethical value (*The Rhetorical Act* 152–56).

In the light of the many rhetorical obstacles, what responses did Wells's speech and her entire lynching campaign evoke? As Wells outlines in *Crusade for Justice* (80–82), the 1892 speech titled "Southern Horrors" had several long-range effects. It was, of course, the beginning of her own public speaking career, a career that would continue until her death in 1931. She also saw it as the beginning of organized black women's clubs. Following her speech, the women of New York, Brooklyn, and Boston formed the Women's Loyal Union and the Women's Era Club, under the leadership of Josephine St. Pierre Ruffin and others. These and other "clubs" formed by black women during this time were united in 1896 as the National Association of Colored Women (NACW), with

Mary Church Terrell as its first president. According to Giddings, Wells's antilynching campaign "had not only helped to launch the modern civil rights movement, but it had brought black women into the forefront of the struggle for Black and women's rights" (94).

Another long-range effect was that the speech launched a worldwide campaign against lynching. It was, in fact, Wells's tour of England that seemed to have given the issue national and international attention. As mentioned earlier, Wells herself recognized the need for this kind of international attention. Before she left England, the British Anti-Lynching Committee was formed, and in Aberdeen, Scotland, the Society for the Recognition of the Brotherhood of Man was formed. English reaction also caused many Americans to break their silence, and many influential American leaders supported the campaign. Giddings describes the impact of this international campaign, launched by the "Southern Horrors" speech:

The number of lynchings decreased in 1893—and continued to do so thereafter. The decline in the murders may be directly attributed to the efforts of Ida B. Wells. The effect of Wells's campaign was aptly demonstrated in her home city. Memphis exported more cotton than any other city in the world, and Wells's assertions had been especially damaging to its image. So, as a direct result of her efforts, the city fathers were pressed to take an official stand against lynching—and for the next twenty years there was not another incident of vigilante violence there. (92)

Mossell quotes Wells regarding response to her oratorical campaign: "The Afro-American has the ear of the civilized world for the first time since emancipation" (1894, 1988, 45).

Following Campbell's outline, we may now consider the truth criterion. According to Campbell, this criterion "is a measure of similarity between the 'reality' presented in a speech or essay and 'reality' as presented in other sources" (*The Rhetorical Act* 153). The validity of the facts Wells presented could hardly have been questioned by her audience, as these facts were drawn from the Southern press itself. We also have the evidence presented in such texts as Cutler's *Lynch-Law: An Investigation into the History of Lynching in the United States*, published in 1905. His research covered 140 years, beginning with the lynching in 1763 of Indians in Lancaster, Pennsylvania, and ending in 1903 with a total of 1,997 between 1882 and 1903. The aspects of her speech that could be called into question are those associated with motives and with guilt or innocence. Because these are the social truths associated with an argument, they may never be validated with certainty.

Again according to Campbell, "the aesthetic criterion is a measure of *how well* an act achieves its purpose, of how creatively a rhetor responds to the obstacles faced, of how inventively a rhetor fulfills the requirements of a form" (154). Given the rhetorical obstacles with which she was faced, one may conclude that Wells handled the rhetorical situation skillfully, focusing not on her personal experience but on the facts of the cases and carrying her auditors through an elimination process that would allow them to draw their own conclusions about motive. She minimized pathetic appeal most often associated with female rhetors and, again, allowed the evidence to make the case. Despite the immediate or long-range effects, one may argue that the speech as a rhetorical act has withstood the test of time.

The final criterion, the ethical, seems to us today overwhelmingly met. Ethical assessment "evaluates the social consequences of rhetorical action" (Campbell, *The Rhetorical Act* 54). If anything, one could question what appears to be a restrained ethical appeal in Wells's antilynching discourse. In almost all cited examples, the question of whether lynching should ever occur was not raised. The thrust is toward providing evidence that the crime did not occur. Perhaps for Wells it was more important to prove that in most instances the crime itself never occurred. By focusing on the appropriateness of the punishment, the argument would have moved away from the real motives for lynching that Wells wanted to unveil. Arguing about whether lynching was justifiable or suitable punishment for rape would only have distracted her auditors from the more important issue of whether indeed rapes were being committed.

W. G. Sumner in 1905 advanced the ethical argument against this method of punishment in his foreword to Cutler's *Lynch Law*: "The badness of the victim is not an element in the case at all. Torture and burning are forbidden, not because the victim is not bad enough, but because we are too good. It is on account of what we owe to ourselves that these methods are shameful to us, if we descend to them" (v).

In her arguments, Ida Wells adopted the position that the absence of a general outcry was due to ignorance if not disinterest. A passage from a December 30, 1891, *New York Times* editorial suggests the level of tolerance for mob violence. Describing the pursuit of an alleged culprit, the editorial concluded,

"If they catch him they will lynch him, but this incident will not be likely to add to the prevailing excitement" of the more "serious moonshining problem" (qtd. in Bederman 407). The illegal production of liquor was considered a more serious problem than lynching. Thus, the opening sentences of "Lynch Law in All Its Phases" announce her intention to invoke the *presence* of mob violence, confronting her Northern audience with the specific details:

I am before the American people to-day through no inclination of my own, but because of a deep-seated conviction that the country at large does not know the extent to which lynch law prevails in parts of the Republic, nor the conditions which force into exile those who speak the truth. I cannot believe that the apathy and indifference which so largely obtains regarding mob rule is other than the result of ignorance of the true situation." (333).

Speaking here to the Boston Monday Lectureship on February 13, 1893, almost a year after her three friends were lynched in Memphis and she herself was forced into exile, Wells described in even greater detail the particulars surrounding those events. The Boston Monday Lectureship, formed in 1875 and composed of white clergymen and lay men and women, was a spin-off of the popular Monday noon prayer meetings at Tremont Temple. Under the influence of its founder, Presbyterian orator Falvius Josephus Cook, the lectureship became a center of Boston intellectual life for over twenty years. In this speech, as in "Southern Horrors," she drew extensively from accounts in Southern white newspapers, believing that their own language would convict them. Like most nineteenth-century Bostonians, the members no doubt relied heavily on the press for accurate information on national and world events. In addition, Wells pitted the North against the South, evoking Civil War Yankee versus Rebel sentiments. She implied further that the South had defamed the Constitution by destroying its civil rights provisions.

This address chronicles Wells's own evolving understanding of the race problem in America at the turn of the century. She began with the assertion quoted above that those who had done little to reduce mob violence in the South failed to act out of ignorance rather than apathy. She identified with their lack of knowledge, comparing it with her own misunderstanding about the possibility for black progress. Wells had believed, along with many of the so-called "better class of Afro-Americans," that by practicing self-help, education, and good manners, the race problem would be solved and black people would finally

be welcomed as acceptable and equal members into mainstream American society. "But there was a rude awakening," Wells declared, resulting from the 1892
Memphis lynchings of her friends. This awakening led her to probe the naive
assumptions of black Memphis that if they simply cooperated, the law would
protect them. It propelled her into a lifelong rhetorical campaign against mob
violence and reduced her certainty in self-improvement as a means of survival.
Instead, self-help took the form of a Winchester rifle, economic boycotts, and
emigration to other areas, tactics delineated in *Southern Horrors.*

To evoke the presence of this 1892 lynching affair, fully half of the 1893
speech is given over to relating its details. In the 1892 "Southern Horrors" address, she tells of this event for the first time but then included fewer specific
details. For those women gathered in Lyric Hall, she chose instead to present
evidence from less publicized cases occurring in places like Anniston, Alabama;
Chestertown, Maryland; Carrolton, Mississippi; and Waycross, Georgia. The
second speech, "Lynch Law in All Its Phases," addressed to an audience of
Northern white women less aware of the horrors, incorporated more specific,
focused details—dates, times, numbers of people involved, smells, sounds, type
of clothing worn by the attackers, and direct quotations from spectators. For
this audience Wells created presence.

In the midst of retelling, Wells claimed, "I have no power to describe the
feeling of horror that possessed every member of the race in Memphis when
the truth dawned upon us that the protection of the law which we had so long
enjoyed was no longer ours" (337). Having declared "the feeling of horror" beyond description, Wells devoted her attention to recreating for her audiences
the horrors that provoked those feelings. This re-creation relied heavily on
lengthy quotations from the Southern press, giving truth to her claim that "out
of their own mouths shall the murderers be condemned," since Wells herself
was not present at these events. These reports were written by those who were.
Of course in many instances, the details were gleaned from cooperative spectators rather than the reporters themselves. Although the thought of a "reporter"
standing on the sidelines witnessing and "objectively" recording such horrid
acts is disturbing, the difficulty of calming a mob bent on violence cannot be
exaggerated, especially when the observer was black. In *A Red Record,* Wells tells
of a minister who had witnessed the Paris, Texas, lynching and who barely escaped the town alive when he tried to stop it (30). Often these reports of mob

violence were published in full, along with the names of the victims and the accused offenders, but as Wells pointed out, only on rare occasions were those accused ever questioned or charged. After relating a detailed account of the Arkansas murders of Hamp Briscoe, his wife, and son, Wells remarked:

Perhaps the civilized world will think, that with all these facts laid before the public, by a writer who signs his name to his communication, in a land . . . where judges and juries are sworn to administer the law, . . . that this matter was duly investigated, the criminals apprehended and the punishment meted out to the murderers. But this is a mistake; nothing of this kind was done or attempted. (*Red Record* 24)

Following a similar description of the Memphis horror, in the 1893 "Lynch Law in All Its Phases" speech, Wells argued for its typicality, contrasting, at the same time, the sharp difference between the government's response to mob violence committed against visitors to the United States and the response to ten years of over a thousand black lynchings.

Wells employs presence most compellingly in her recounting of two contemporary examples of the "lynching mania." She prefaced these descriptions with a request for patience from her audience while she directed their attention again to atrocities in America against American citizens.

The first example was of Ed Coy, from Texarkana, Texas, charged with assault on a white woman:

A mob pronounced him guilty, strapped him to a tree, chipped the flesh from his body, poured coal oil over him and the woman in the case set fire to him. The country looked on and in many cases applauded, because it was published that this man had violated the honor of the white woman, although he protested his innocence to the last. Judge Tourgee in the Chicago *Inter-Ocean* of recent date says investigation has shown that Ed Coy had supported this woman, (who was known to be of bad character,) and her drunken husband for over a year previous to the burning. ("Lynch Law" 342)

Second, she described the Paris, Texas, burning of Henry Smith, which had taken place just two weeks earlier. Smith had been accused of assaulting a four-year-old girl, the daughter of a white man with whom he had had a disagreement. Wells creates presence through the following "verbal magic":

The man was drawn through the streets on a float, as the Roman generals used to parade their trophies of war, while the scaffold ten feet high, was being built, and irons were heated in the fire. He was bound on it, and red-hot irons began at his feet and slowly branded his body, while the mob howled with delight at his shrieks. Red hot irons were run down his throat and cooked his tongue; his eyes were burned out, and when he was at last unconscious, cotton seed hulls were placed under him, coal oil poured all over him, and a torch applied to the mass. When the flames burned away the ropes which bound Smith and scorched his flesh, he was brought back to sensibility and burned and maimed and sightless as he was, he rolled off the platform and away from the fire. His half-cooked body was seized and trampled and thrown back into the flames while a mob of twenty thousand persons who came from all over the country howled with delight, and gathered up some buttons and ashes after all was over to preserve for relics. ("Lynch Law" 342–43)

Detailed description evokes presence in these passages. In the second passage, Wells pairs the gruesome details of the lynching syncretically with the carnivalesque delight of the twenty thousand people from "all over the country" gathering relics of "buttons and ashes" and "howling with delight at his shrieks." In the remaining sections of the speech, Wells moved from graphic description of these incidents to a general cataloguing of statistics to demonstrate their typicality. These statistics documented the lynching of men and women for such crimes as being "drunk and saucy to white folks." Only after an extended critique of several other incidents did Wells propose corrective action. Thus, in a twenty-page speech, Wells, choosing to let her well-crafted facts speak for themselves, devoted only three explicitly to proposing a specific course of action. She began this brief section with the question, "Do you ask the remedy?" and appealed for strong public sentiment against such crimes to provoke change. Ending with lines from a patriotic anthem, the speech returned to its opening call for national pride.

In *A Red Record*, Wells included an extended account of the Paris, Texas, incident, as reported in the New York *Sun* by an eyewitness. This account was probably the one from which Wells abstracted her version, quoted above. In the *Sun* version, the observer narrates from the perspective of one who believed the inflicted atrocities justified. Describing the accused variously as "negro ravisher," "brute," "fiend," "most inhumane monster," and "slayer," this narrator revealed much more than the actual events. By quoting from this account verbatim, Wells effectively exposed much of the twisted logic of mob mentality, without direct comment or interpretation. In "Lynch Law in All Its Phases," faced with the time constraints of public performance, Wells summarized the affair's salient features. "A Red Record" carried not only the full newspaper account but also the contrasting account from the minister who tried to stop the torture. Wells created the presence of the 1893 Paris, Texas, lynching in both instances by selecting a version appropriate to the rhetorical situation, one that neither audience could misinterpret.

In the opening section of the pamphlet titled *Lynch Law in Georgia*, Wells announced her intention to "let the [Atlanta] *Constitution* tell the story of his torture and death," referring here to the lynching of Samuel Wilkes, alias Hose, on April 23, 1899, in Newnan, Georgia (9). Of course in telling the story of Hose, the *Constitution* also reveals a great deal about itself. The omniscient narrator seems to have been on hand at all stages of the affair, "objectively" reporting while lynch law did its work. The presence of bias and complicity in the Southern press is the real story these accounts tell. In declaring, "Out of their own mouths shall the murderers be condemned," Wells conflated messenger and message. The mouths of the murderers were the mouths of the press, a press that all too often dropped its feigned reportorial stance and engaged in the "inflammatory work" of suggesting or predicting appropriate punishment for the accused. The *Constitution*, narrating the events leading to the murder of Hose, persisted in predicting that he would be burned as soon as caught and offered a reward for his arrest. Such statements made it clear that the impulse to burn the captive originated in "the leading citizens of Georgia," as did the following: "The spot selected was an ideal one for such an affair and the stake was in full view," and "[I]t required only a few minutes to arrange to make Sam Hose pay the penalty of his crime" (*Lynch Law in Georgia*, 8, 9). The *Constitution* further implicates the community in collusive behavior through descriptions of the sign posted on the body of Elijah Strickland, lynched on the same day as Hose for his alleged involvement: "We must protect our Ladies," written on one side, and "Beware all darkies. You will be treated the same way," written on the other. The Chicago detective, Louis P. Le Vin, sent to investigate these murders commented on the casual way in which the citizens spoke about Sam Hose's lynching: "I found no difficulty in securing interviews from white people. There was no disposition on their part to conceal any part that they took in the lynchings. They discussed the details of the burning of Sam Hose with the freedom which one would talk about an afternoon's divertisement in which he had very pleasantly participated" (13). This investigator confirmed Wells's claim that the leading citizens, like Clark Howell of the Atlanta *Constitution*, "contributed more to the burning than any other men and all other forces in Georgia" (15).

Simone Davis points out that by quoting such revealing passages from the Southern press and weaving in her own commentary, Wells was also giving lessons in rhetorical criticism: "Collaging a great patch work of quotations from both the white and the African-American press, she allows the dialogic dynamics of the resulting text to teach the reader how context can modify meaning" (77). Davis argues that the heavy use of quotations not only authenticates Wells's evidence but also allows her to "sensitize her audience to idealogically loaded language" and to "train the discriminating reader to internalize" a mode of inquiry (79). In *Lynch Law in Georgia*'s prefatory remarks to the reader, for example, Wells announced that reports from Southern papers would be followed by the "true facts as to the cause of lynchings," as uncovered by the Chicago detective. Through careful placement of metadiscourse, Wells proceeded to expose what Davis refers to as the "causal convergence between racist language and racist violence" (79). The presence created in Wells's speeches, then, was intensified in her pamphlets, where she was able to direct the reader's ability to perceive how reality can be constructed through language.

"Lynch Law in America," an article appearing in the January 1900 *Arena, A Monthly Review of Social Advance*, carried essentially the same message Wells had been delivering by that time for eight years, presented more abstractly than in her earlier antilynching discourse. In this article, she traced the practice of lynching from the vigilante days of the West, when no other system of justice was in place, to the current practice of lynching black men and women in disregard of the judicial system. Wells here did not detail any particular act of violence specifically, comparing instead some contemporary characteristics of lynching practices with those of earlier times, as in the following passage: "The nineteenth century lynching mob cuts off ears, toes, and fingers, strips off flesh, and distributes portions of the body as souvenirs among the crowd. If the leaders of the mob are so minded, coal-oil is poured over the body and the victim is then roasted to death" ("America" 19). Two years before writing this article, in April of 1898, Wells had presented a petition of protest from the citizens of Chicago to President William McKinley at the White House. The petition protested the lynching of a black postmaster in Lake City, South

Carolina. Marshaling the same kind of concrete but generalized evidence, in her statement to the president she said:

Nowhere in the civilized world save the United States of America do men, possessing all civil and political power, go out in bands of 50 to 5,000 to hunt down, shoot, hang or burn to death a single individual, unarmed and absolutely powerless. Statistics show that nearly 10,000 American citizens have been lynched in the past 20 years. (H. Aptheker, *Documentary* 798)

The hope, in this instance, was that since the postmaster was a federal officer, the government could intercede without facing a charge of legal impropriety; however, no action was ever taken against those involved.

In the essay, the title, with its emphasis on America, highlights the international implications of mob violence committed against people generally, not just against blacks. Her arguments emphasized the damage to America's reputation abroad. She offered four consequences of this continued practice. First, she noted the country's inconsistency in protecting the rights of oppressed peoples in other countries—Russian Jews, Siberian exiles, Armenian Christians—while failing to protect many of its own citizens. Blacks had made the mistake of assuming that "a government that was good enough to create a citizenship was strong enough to protect it" (16). Second, Wells noted the cost of mob violence. When mobs had murdered foreigners, the federal government paid to the home countries nearly half a million dollars in indemnities. The third consequence was that such acts called into question America's claim to be a civilized nation. Civilized nations do not handle alleged injustices by resorting to "such brutal, inhuman, and degrading exhibitions as characterize 'lynching bees' " (23).[6] The final consequence Wells identified as loss of respect abroad, a significant consequence for those who wanted to feel pride in America when they traveled. Wells chastised Americans who protested the French military court's rulings against Alfred Dreyfus, Jewish officer in the French army convicted of treason, while in this country "one thousand men, women, and children . . . were put to death without trial before any tribunal on earth" (24).

At the time Wells wrote this piece from Chicago, she was married to Ferdinand E. Barnett and was the mother of two children. After her marriage in 1895, she continued her antilynching activities from her home, not working again outside the home until 1912, when her youngest child was eight. But Wells never lost her zeal for the cause. Even the date of her wedding had to be changed three times to accommodate her speaking schedule, a schedule which had Wells deliver an address in Kansas only a week before the marriage took place.

In September of 1900, Wells published the pamphlet titled *Mob Rule in New Orleans*. In this final piece of antilynching discourse to be considered here, Wells again employed accounts from local newspapers to state her case. The newspapers, the New Orleans *Times-Democrat* and the New Orleans *Picayune*, graphically chronicled the events surrounding the murders of Robert Charles and a number of other "suspicious-looking Negro[es]." The murders occurred during the mob violence that took place in New Orleans in July 1900. The violence was sparked by the "unprovoked assault" of three New Orleans policemen upon Charles and another man. Charles shot one of the officers in self-defense and fled. In pursuit of Charles, the mob wreaked havoc on the black community at large, killing men and women, merely to satiate its desire for vengeance.

Wells here followed her usual strategy, claiming that as publisher she "simply presents the facts in a plain, unvarnished, connected way, so that he who runs may read" (*Mob Rule* 3). Although she denied any attempt to "moralize over the deplorable condition of affairs shown in this publication," she was clearly aware that through presentation, such conditions carried their own message, and, in fact, Wells does seem to have engaged in more editorializing here than in her other pamphlets. As in other writings, Wells taught her audience how to read these accounts critically. Her commentary, sprinkled throughout, compared discrepancies in the two versions and pointed to certain telling discourse features, as in this passage:

> It is interesting to note how the two leading papers of New Orleans, the *Picayune* and the *Times-Democrat*, exert themselves to justify the policemen in the absolutely unprovoked attack upon the two colored men. As these two papers did all in their power to give an excuse for the action of the policemen, it is interesting to note their versions. (*Mob Rule* 6)

Wells followed this critique with conflicting newspaper accounts of several events surrounding the incident, then interjected further analysis: "Both of the two accounts cannot be true, and the unquestioned fact is that neither of them sets out the facts as they occurred" (7). It seems that as Wells continued to pursue her antilynching campaign, she grew less satisfied with merely letting the facts speak for themselves, just as Douglass had during his abolitionist days. While direct accounts from newspapers, letters attesting to the fine character of Robert Charles, narrative summaries of lynching over the past ten years, and statistics compiled by the *Chicago Tribune* comprise fully four-fifths of this pamphlet, Wells's own direct commentary also increases.

Moving in the final section of *Mob Rule in New Orleans* from evidence to argument, Wells mounted a direct appeal to her readers that every person charged with a crime be given a fair trial. Wells closed with the standard *a fortiori* argument that since black men had not attacked white women during the absence of their "protectors" during the Civil War, they were even less likely to do so now that the women were "surrounded by their husbands, brothers, lovers and friends" (48). Since Robert Charles had not been accused of "assaulting a white woman," Wells's deployment of this argument seems somewhat incongruous. But given the larger truth that most of the victims of mob violence had been charged with this crime, Wells may have chosen to end with this strong rebuttal in any case.

Further evidence of Wells's effectiveness as a speaker as well as of the general level of resistance to antilynching discourse was that in 1894, having established herself as an accomplished orator, she was offered a lucrative contract by the head of a Chicago lyceum bureau to deliver four addresses a week, as long as she agreed to "leave out any talks on lynching," since the American people would not pay to hear them (*Crusade* 226). It seems that many nineteenth-century Americans admired her oratory but were uncomfortable with its content. They had been paying more attention to the style than the substance. The creation of presence may have been effective for Wells only when done for the benefit of neutral or sympathetic audiences for whom the events being described were not within the realm of their experience. The hope was that such audiences would be shocked into action.

This analysis of Ida B. Wells's antilynching discourse comments as well on her ability to invoke the presence of mob violence. In many respects, her descriptive choices were shaped by the experiences of her own life, a life providing a model for resistance, beginning as it did in 1862, several months before the Emancipation Proclamation freed all slaves in the states in rebellion. After yellow fever took the lives of her parents, she found herself the sole support of her sisters and brothers. She met this challenge by taking a teaching job in her home in Holly Springs, Mississippi, and later in Memphis. Her resistance was demonstrated in her refusal to move to the smoking car of a train and her subsequent law suit against the offending railroad. Her resistance was evident in her decision to publish an article in the *Free Speech*, criticizing conditions in the black Memphis schools, which resulted in the loss of her teaching job. But her best-known act of resistance was the barrage of editorial appeals in the *Free Speech*, following the murders of her three friends. Revealing the true motives for lynching, these editorials urged the people to leave Memphis and ultimately prevented her from returning to the city for many years.

Given such a history of defiance, it should surprise few that her rhetorical strategies also evinced determined resistance. To some extent, the subject itself, mob violence, dictated a confrontational stance. As Stepto points out, Booker T. Washington in *Up from Slavery*, written nearly ten years after Well's first antilynching speech, "cautiously inveighs against 'the evil habit of lynching' " (39). But few could speak of such action with restraint, and certainly not Wells. The use of statistics, the suppression of emotion, the marshaling of example after example, the admonitions about a course of action, the clear statement of true motivation for lynching, all converge to produce a text that was direct and confrontational, yet factually irrefutable.

It should be clear that Wells was one of many black women who campaigned against mob violence in the 1890s. The 250 women who participated in the 1892 testimonial for Wells were collectively demonstrating against lynch law. An article in the May 1, 1894, *Woman's Era*, "How to Stop Lynching," and a response to it debate the effective ways to punish perpetrators of mob violence (8–9). At the December 1895 Atlanta Congress of Colored Women of the United States, the delegates drafted antilynching resolutions. Following the meeting, Victoria Matthews toured the South, partially at the request of the National Federation of Afro-American Women, investigating, among other atrocities, the practice of lynching. In the years following, the NACW formed local and national antilynching committees. Individually, black women incorporated protest again lynching into their public addresses. In her 1891 address to the National Council of Women, Frances Harper referred to the government's failure to protect and defend all citizens from mob violence, as she had in earlier addresses.[7] At the start of the twentieth century, Nannie Helen Burroughs protested against lynching at the 1900 meeting of the Women's Auxiliary to the National Baptist Convention. Mary Church Terrell refuted the standard lynching-for-rape connection, associating it instead with slavery, race hatred, and lawlessness in her 1904 article "Lynching from a Negro's Point of View." In 1922, Mary B. Talbert, then president of the NACW, helped organize the "Anti-Lynching Crusaders" to rally women's support for various antilynching initiatives, including Missouri Congressman Leonidas Dyer's Anti-Lynching Bill. The legislation passed in the House but never came to a vote in the Senate, failing as had a 1901 attempt by black post-Reconstruction Congressman George White to make lynching a federal crime. In 1930, under the leadership of Jessie Daniel Ames, who apparently knew nothing of Wells's pioneering work, white women finally organized against mob violence, forming the Association of Southern Women for the Prevention of Lynching. Still, all these antilynching activities pale in comparison to the unflagging and persistent efforts of Ida B. Wells.

An obituary in the *Chicago Defender* described Wells as "somewhat intolerant and impulsive" (qtd. in Townes 286). Perhaps a more fitting description is that, true to her impulses, Ida Wells spoke out forcefully against conditions that others were willing to tolerate. Comparing her to the Old Testament Queen Esther, an article in the October 5, 1894, issue of the *National Baptist World* paid tribute to her antilynching oratory, characterizing it as

a voice . . . that God has seen fit to send forth in behalf of a down-trodden race, a voice that has sounded the alarm[;] the bugle is blown, which is to call the christian and liberty loving part of this nation to the defence of a weak and helpless people, that is being murdered daily by the brutal and merciless whites of the south. (H. Davis 1)

5

"Women of a Common Country, with Common Interests"
Fannie Barrier Williams, Anna Julia Cooper, Identification and Arrangement

> It is not the intelligent woman vs. the ignorant woman; nor the white woman vs. the black, the brown, and the red,—it is not even the cause of woman vs. man. Nay, 'tis woman's strongest vindication for speaking that *the world needs to hear her voice*. It would be subversive of every human interest that the cry of one-half the human family be stifled.
>
> —Anna Julia Cooper, "Woman Versus the Indian"

In her introduction to *Invented Lives*, Mary Helen Washington identifies the "distinguishing feature" of black women's writing as being about black women. She elaborates that such writing "takes the trouble to record the thoughts, words, feelings, and deeds of black women" (xxi). The extant essays and speeches of Fannie Barrier Williams and Anna Julia Cooper focus on black women perhaps more consistently than those of any other women discussed in this volume. Maria Stewart addressed her first recorded speech to a gathering of black women, but neither that speech nor her subsequent speeches were exclusively about black women. Frances Harper, with the exception of her speech titled "Coloured Women of America," concentrated more on the needs of black people generally. "Woman's Political Future" challenged the women in the audience to become more active in human uplift without specific reference to the needs and accomplishments of black women. Ida Wells, while acknowledging the impact of mob violence on black women as well as black men, devoted her rhetorical career primarily to exposing the driving forces behind this practice.

Victoria Matthews, like Harper, focused more on "race problems" generally, although we do have a wonderful tribute to black women in "The Awakening of the Afro-American Woman."

Both Williams and Cooper spoke at the 1893 World's Congress of Representative Women in Chicago. Williams, a major speaker, addressed the audience of predominantly white women on the progress of black women since emancipation from slavery. Cooper followed Williams's address with remarks on the same subject. A year earlier, Cooper had published her collection of essays and speeches titled *A Voice from the South, By a Black Woman of the South*. Highly educated women—Williams, from a middle-class New England family, and Cooper, a self-made woman born into slavery—they both faced the challenge of praising the accomplishments and rehearsing the needs of black women with whom, in many respects, they were no longer identified. They occupied a precarious position between many of the audiences they addressed and the women they represented. In order to gain the support they felt was needed from white women, they had to represent themselves as the models of "true womanhood" they claimed all black women had the potential to become. As Claudia Tate observes, turn-of-the-century blacks generally "regarded bourgeois decorum as an important emancipatory cultural discourse" (4). At the same time, they had to present a true account of these women's current circumstances, simultaneously emphasizing similarities and differences. To meet this challenge, both Williams and Cooper engaged in rhetorical strategies that placed black women in the same category, "woman," as the white women reading and listening to their texts. To bolster this linkage, Williams employed strategies best understood in the context of Burkean identification and division. Kenneth Burke writes that "[i]dentification is affirmed with earnestness precisely because there is division. Identification is compensatory to division. If men were not apart from one another, there would be no need for the rhetorician to proclaim their unity" (22). Williams proclaimed unity with her auditors by pointing out ways in which they all were, after all, the same. Burke points out that "we might well keep it in mind that a speaker persuades an audience by the use of stylistic identifications; his act of persuasion may be for the purpose of causing the audience to identify itself with the speaker's interests; and the speaker draws an identification of interests to establish rapport between himself and his audience" (46). Cooper placed black women into the universal category "woman" by first locating the arguments to her predominantly black male audiences within this larger realm and disposing subsequent arguments with increasing specificity. By analyzing two salient rhetorical features, identification and arrangement, respectively, I consider in this chapter how Williams and Cooper argued in defense of black women.

Fannie Barrier Williams was born in 1855 to a prominent Brockport, New York, family, the only black family in Brockport at the time. She attended the Collegiate Institute of Brockport, the New England Conservatory of Music, and the School of Fine Arts in Washington, D.C. In her essay titled "A Northern Negro's Autobiography," Williams documented her introduction to blatant racism, which took place in a Southern state where she had gone to teach and where she "began life as a colored person, in all that that term implies" (12). In 1887, she returned home to be married and found there again the prejudice-free environment of her youth. When she and her husband, S. Laing Williams, moved to Chicago, she again experienced what she called "very few evidences of race prejudice," but she made a significant discovery that would affect the course of her life:

[T]his kindness to me as an individual did not satisfy me or blind me to the many inequalities suffered by young colored women seeking employment and other advantages of metropolitan life. I soon discovered that it was much easier for progressive white women to be considerate and even companionable to one colored woman whom they chanced to know and like than to be just and generous to colored young women as a race who needed their sympathy and influence in securing employment and recognition according to their tastes and ability. To this end I began to use my influences and associations to further the cause of these helpless young colored women, in an effort to save them to themselves and society, by finding, for those who must work, suitable employment. ("Northern" 14–15)

Williams's recognition that the generosity the women showed to her, whom they viewed as a model of true womanhood, did not extend to black women generally led her to focus her energy on the uplift of young black women. In *Black Chicago*, Allan Spear writes that Williams "soon won a reputation as an able speaker, writer, and organizer," even eventually overshadowing her husband, a prominent attorney and protégé of Booker T. Washington (69). She helped raise funds to establish the Provident Hospital and School of Nursing, to train black women for health care. She was a member of the Illinois Woman's Alliance. Williams was the Chicago reporter for the *Woman's Era*. She was the first black member of the Chicago Woman's Club and the first black woman to serve on the Chicago Library Board. She was also the only black woman to give remarks at the eulogy for Susan B. Anthony at the 1907 meeting of the National American Woman's Suffrage Association. She certainly seemed a likely candidate for an invitation to speak at the World's Congress of Representative Women. Further comments from Mossell attest to her generally favorable reception among black and white audiences:

> Her wide and favorable acquaintance with nearly all the leading Afro-American men and women of the country, and her peculiar faculty to reach and interest influential men and women of the dominant race in presenting the peculiar needs of her people, together with her active intelligence, are destined to make Mrs. Williams a woman of conspicuous usefulness. (112)

Although Williams's advocacy for black women began long before her appearance at the 1893 Woman's Congress, the speech delivered on that occasion will be considered as her first extant piece of persuasive discourse. Addressed to a gathering of international women at such a highly publicized affair, it demonstrates a range of rhetorical maneuvers. Williams, while Chicago editor for the *Woman's Era*, published "Women in Politics" in the November 1894 issue. In it she challenged black women, as they became more political, to bring their own refinement and individuality into the process rather than follow established practices blindly. "The Club Movement among Colored Women of America" is the last chapter in the 1900 collection of essays titled *A New Negro for a New Century*. Informative as well as persuasive, this essay argued for the significant influence of black women's clubs all over the United States. In a November 1904 *Voice of the Negro* article titled "The Woman's Part in a Man's Business," Williams proclaimed the important roles that black women had played in helping black men entrepreneurially. She linked the success of black businessmen to better protection for black women. "The Colored Girl," also published in the *Voice of the Negro*, six months later, called for greater respect for young black women, regardless of social status or occupation, and placed the chief responsibility for this change upon black men. Of these texts, only the 1893 Woman's Congress speech was targeted for an audience overwhelmingly nonblack, making identification a more salient concern.

In her 1893 speech to the World's Congress of Representative Woman, "The Intellectual Progress of the Colored Women of the United States since the Emancipation Proclamation," Fannie Barrier Williams stressed throughout the common womanhood shared by all the women in her audience. Given the difficult circumstances under which she spoke—the Board of Managers had not wanted any black women to speak—Williams wisely emphasized similarities rather than differences. "The Solidarity of Human Interests," title of the session and the first speech of the session, established this theme of common interests. The World's Congress of Representative Women was held from May 15 to May 22, 1893, in Chicago, as part of the Columbian Exposition. The Exposition's alleged purpose was to display the achievements of America to the rest of the world. The women's exhibit, housed in a building designed by a woman architect, was to illuminate the accomplishments of American women. That purpose, however, was riddled with flawed assumptions. The Columbian Exposition was racist from the start. Gail Bederman points out that the exhibit was divided into a "civilized section, known as the 'White City,'" developed around a half-mile long basin framed by seven white buildings, each representing advances in Western civilization: Manufactures, Mines, Agriculture, Art, Administrations, Machinery, and Electricity. The Woman's Building was located at the edge of this White City, at the point where one exited to the "uncurled Midway." There displayed were villages of Samoans, Egyptians, and other so-called exotic races (411–12). To have African American men and women representing aspects of the White City, then, worked against this split; consequently, as Ida Wells wrote in her autobiography, *Crusade for Justice*, the "United States government had refused her Negro citizens participation therein" (116).[1] Hallie Quinn Brown of Wilberforce, Ohio, requested of Bertha Palmer, the head of the Lady Board of Managers of this Congress, to let her join. She was told that membership was by organization rather than by individual and that Brown represented no organization. Prompted by this response, Brown went to Washington, D.C., to speak to a group of women at the Fifteenth Street Presbyterian Church, requesting that they select her to represent them on this board. While they did not grant her request, as a result of her talk, the women did organize themselves into the Colored Woman's League, and according to Elizabeth Davis, they "stepped across the threshold of the home into the wider arena of organized womanhood" (20).

   After a great deal of protest about the absence of black participation, Williams was appointed to a token supervisory position, chosen, no doubt, for her demeanor. A few black women were eventually invited to speak at the Congress: Williams and Cooper, Frances Jackson Coppin from Philadelphia, and Sarah Early and Hallie Quinn Brown, both from Wilberforce, Ohio. Frances Harper spoke during an earlier session, "The Civil and Political Status of Women." Frederick Douglass, who presided over the Congress's Haitian exhibit, was a platform guest during Williams's session. In the tradition of authentication prominent in nineteenth-century slave narrative introductions, Douglass was prevailed upon to speak after Frances Coppin's discussion of Williams's speech, as if to validate what the women had said. He was the only man allowed to make remarks after the opening session of the General Congress. Douglass, exhibiting his well-honed rhetorical charm, expressed excitement at hearing "refined, educated colored ladies addressing—and addressing successfully—one of the most intelligent white audiences that I ever looked upon." He went on to proclaim, rather prematurely, that "a new heaven is dawning upon us and a new earth is ours, in which all discriminations against men and women on account of color and sex is [*sic*] passing away, and will pass away" (qtd. in Sewall 717). Hazel Carby suggests that the participation of these black women was less a recognition of their right to be there than it was part of a "discourse of exoticism that pervaded the fair" (5). The board presented these women as anomalies to the received and accepted views of blacks at the time. Williams was indeed "selected as an interesting representative of the colored people" (E. Davis 266). The choice of Williams was to some extent also based on the persuasiveness of her earlier arguments to the board, described by Gertrude Mossell in her epideictic on the work of nineteenth-century black women:

Some months ago wide publicity was given to the brilliant sallies of wit and eloquence of a young Afro-American woman of Chicago in appealing to the Board of Control of the World's Columbian Exposition in behalf of the American Negro. The grave and matter-of-fact members of the Commission were at first inclined to treat lightly any proposition to recognize the Afro-American's claim to representation in the World's Fair management. They soon found, however, that puzzling cross-questions and evasions awakened in this young woman such resources of repartee, readiness of knowledge and nimbleness of logic that they were amazed into admiration and with eager unanimity embraced her arguments in a resolution of approval, and strongly recommended her appointment to some representative position. (109–10)

Whatever the convergence of motives, Fannie Barrier Williams was there, and she delivered her address to the World's Congress of Representative Women in grand style. In preparation for the speech, Williams wrote to Albion W. Tourgée for ideas: "If there be any literature upon this sex phase of the negro question that you can refer me to or any accessible data that tell unmistakably of the steady and sure development from a degraded peasantry toward noble womanhood, I would be duly obligated" (qtd. in McFeely 367). No doubt a valuable source, Tourgée, jurist and author, had lived in the South during Reconstruction. At the time of the fair, he was editor of a column for the Chicago *Inter-Ocean*, in which he wrote about the civil and political conditions of Southern blacks. Williams was also chosen to address the World's Parliament of Religions at the Exposition, delivering her speech titled "Religious Duty to the Negro" on September 23, 1893. Already a prominent Chicago figure, after the delivery of these two speeches, Williams "received invitations from all parts of the country" (E. Davis 266).

In the speech titled "The Intellectual Progress of the Colored Women," Williams spoke first of similarities, then of differences, in much the same way as Frances Harper, in her speech titled "We Are All Bound Up Together," delivered to a similar group almost thirty years earlier. Harper identified with the women through her experiences as a disinherited widow but then quickly moved to issues that divided them. Williams attempted to overcome the rhetorical problems arising from addressing women from whom she was divided and who had been, in fact, reluctant to allow any black women to speak. To establish identification, Williams stressed the points of agreement between these women and the black women she claimed to represent. Based on Williams's prior ethos, the women were probably expecting a nonthreatening speech filled with hopes for improved relations between black and white women, and the first half of the speech was just that.

Williams appealed to the widely held beliefs of her audience, particularly concerning womanhood and religion. She first commended them for their decision to recognize the progress of black women: "That the discussion of progressive womanhood in this great assemblage of the representative women of the world is considered incomplete without some account of the colored women's status is a most noteworthy evidence that we have not failed to impress ourselves on the higher side of American life" (696). She then made a series of claims about black women based on assumptions of pre-emancipation moral, intellectual, and spiritual depravity. Williams described them as having emerged from slavery with "inherited inaptitudes for the moralities." She created a picture of women struggling to "catch up" with their white sisters in all things and to develop morally and intellectually in order to achieve the "blessedness of intelligent womanhood." She pictured black women not as claiming a rightful equality as Harper had in her 1891 speech titled "Duty to Dependent Races" but as striving to earn that equality, speaking of the "native gentleness" that made them more susceptible to developing intelligence and righteousness. She dwelled upon what she called a "lack of morals" among the formerly enslaved and emphasized the need, after emancipation, for learning family values. Participating in nineteenth-century emancipatory discourse, Williams described again and again the ways in which black women had assimilated the conservative Victorian gender roles of their white sisters. Williams and other black women felt that racial advancement would follow on the heels of social respectability. Tate reminds us that "[t]his was the society that the rising black middle class became intent on imitating after the Civil War, not because of pretentious social desire but because appropriation of gentility meant approximating racial equality" (59). Williams concerned herself with moral rectitude no doubt because she recognized the extent to which negative stereotypes worked against social and employment opportunities for late nineteenth-century black women. Later in the speech she made the point that "the morality of our home life has been commented upon so disparagingly and meanly that we are placed in the unfortunate position of being defenders of our name." She added that such a discussion of morals was relevant to the occasion only to the extent that it centered on the ways in which once-enslaved women had freed themselves from the "demoralization of their enslavement" (703) Williams located the demoralization within the slavery system itself, not within the women themselves; they were suffering under "an enforced degradation" (703). It was the enslavement, not the enslaved, that was demoralized.

She proceeded to compliment "those saintly women of the white race" who went South as school teachers, without mentioning that she herself had done so (696–7). She then introduced the theme of common concerns among black and white women by pointing to the eagerness with which black women strived "to overtake and keep pace with women whose emancipation has been a slow and painful process for a thousand years" (697). She added that these rapidly developing black women would soon join white women in this continuing process. She commented that newly freed black women were attempting to join the struggles of all women to gain their rights and that the character of the black women was lacking in "[s]ullenness of disposition, hatefulness, and revenge against the master class," concluding that these attributes "are not in the nature of our women" (698).

In the next section, Williams further identified black women with white women through an appeal to common religious faith, specifically as members of a range of denominations: "In their religious life, . . . our women show a progressiveness parallel in every important particular to that of white women in all Christian churches." The women, she claimed, had insisted upon a "more godly and cultivated ministry" and that "[l]ike the nineteenth century woman generally, our women find congeniality in all the creeds, from the Catholic creed to the no-creed of Emerson" (699). Determined to show that black women were no different, Williams even argued similarity in their lack of faith, as further evidence of "growing intelligence" and a "sense of religious discrimination" (699).

In education, she outlined specific areas of progress, describing how black women had taught themselves and gone on to teach others, even to become "prize teachers in the mixed schools of nearly every Northern city" (699). This example "serves as further evidence," she said, "that our women have the same spirit and mettle that characterize the best of American women. Everywhere they are following in the tracks of those women who are swiftest in the race for higher knowledge" (700). She highlighted the fact that black women were working to improve the quality of higher education for all: "As American women generally are fighting against the nineteenth century narrowness that still keeps women out of the higher institutions of learning, so our women are eagerly demanding the best of education open to their race" (699–700). She summarized with the claim that "our women are ambitious to be contributors to all the great moral and intellectual forces that make for the greater weal of our common country" (700). She stated that these women thus ask for "the same opportunity for the acquisition of all kinds of knowledge that may be accorded to other women" (700). Almost every paragraph here constructs a comparison between the emerging accomplishments of black women and those privileges already acquired by white women.

The appeal for united action through participation in women's organizations becomes most apparent in the next section where she places this appeal within the context of the progress of women's groups generally. She first asked the question, "If it be a fact that this spirit of organization among women generally is the distinguishing mark of the nineteenth century woman, dare we ask if the colored women of the United States have made any progress in this respect?" Answering, she claimed that black women had taken a leading role in organizing to work "for a common destiny" (701) She followed this claim with the assertion that "[a]ll the associated interests of church, temperance, and social reform in which American women are winning distinction can be wonderfully advanced when our women shall be welcomed as co-workers" (702).

In the second half of the speech, Williams shifted to a more critical tone. Having established that black women were essentially the same as white women, Williams then argued that they should therefore, be treated the same. She broached the subject of "American slavery," almost apologetically, although the subject was surely implied in the speech's title if not in everything she had said up to that point. "It is unavoidable," she explained, "to charge to that system every moral imperfection that mars the character of the colored American" (703). Williams emphasized progress and change rather than the degradation itself. Calling for black women's protection, Williams, in the next paragraph, alluded to their sexual exploitation: "I do not wish to disturb the serenity of this conference by suggesting why this protection is needed and the kind of men against whom it is needed" (703). Williams's tone here contrasted sharply with the tone of Ida Wells's comments on the same subject in "Southern Horrors." In that speech, Wells skillfully dissected the motives behind lynching. But Williams's speech was not exclusively about lynching.

In the final section, she addressed the difficulty black women had finding jobs, women with "real ability, virtue, and special talents." It is here that she provided her first and only specific example, for, as she said, "[o]ne of countless instances will show how the best as well as the meanest of American society are responsible for the special injustice to our women" (705). It is the case of a young woman—being considered for a job as a stenographer at a Chicago bank—whose application was turned down when "the slight tinge of African blood that identified her as colored woman" was made known. Returning to the tactic of identification, she reminded the audience that these women who were being denied employment shared common bonds with them: "We are so essentially American in speech, in instincts, in sentiments and in destiny that the things that interest you equally interest us" (709). Her final claim to this group was that all of these forms of discrimination would hurt all women—they were "dangerously contagious" since "[c]olored women are becoming more and more a part of the social forces that must help to determine the questions that so concern women generally" (709–10). In her closing paragraphs, as throughout, her strongest appeal is to common interest, common needs, common consequences: "As women of a common country, with common interests, and a destiny that will certainly bring us closer to each other, we come to this altar with our contribution of hopefulness as well as with our complaints" (710).

Williams made a final appeal for unity across race and gender:

The colored women, as well as all women, will realize that the inalienable right to life, liberty, and the pursuit of happiness is a maxim that will become more blessed in its significance when the hand of woman shall take it from its sepulture in books and make it the gospel of every-day life and the unerring guide in the relations of all men, women, and children. (711)

Expressions such as "like other American women," "same experiences," "like nineteenth century women generally," "common interest," "common country," and "parallel accomplishments" appear in almost every paragraph. Williams, then, established not only through the logical appeal of her argument but also through her very presence her powerful ethos that surely if black and white women are the same, if they share a common destiny, they both deserve equal treatment from a just society. This was the only text addressed almost exclusively to white women, with identification as the main persuasive strategy. When Williams wrote and spoke to predominantly black audiences, she rarely employed it.

"Women in Politics" was the title of Williams's November 1894 Chicago column for the *Woman's Era*. Although the Woman's Era Club of Boston declared itself "not necessarily a colored woman's club, but a club started and led by colored women" ("News from the Clubs" 4), most of the readers of their publication were middle-class educated black club women from around the country. They were models of what Williams claimed other black women could become with opportunity. This article developed in the context of increasing political activism in Chicago, where women had been granted permission to vote for trustees of the state university. Williams challenged the black women to use the leverage of their vote to insist that white women candidates demonstrate their support of employment and civil privileges for black women. "We should never forget that the exclusion of colored women and girls from nearly all places of respectable employment is due mostly to the meanness of American women." Not restricting her criticism to white women only, she incorporated a strong critique of black men's voting patterns as well: "If, however, we burden our hearts and minds solely with the anxiety for the success of a party ticket for party reasons, we shall be guilty of the same folly and neglect of self-interest that have made colored men for the past twenty years vote persistently more for the special interests of white men than for the peculiar interests of the colored race" (13).

Williams had no need to establish identification with this audience. They were all part of the same community. The identification here is invoked, as through language Williams sustains and transforms their collective experiences. Expressions such as "our own women" signaled this common community, as did the explicit criticism of black men, usually not carried on before uninitiated groups. Williams had criticized black men's organizational failures earlier in a June 1894 letter to the *Woman's Era*, cautioning the women against rushing into convention: "We should be careful to avoid the examples of our colored men, whose innumerable Conventions, Councils, and Conferences during the last twenty-five years have all begun in talk and ended in talk" (Letter 5). In the essay, "Women in Politics," we have the same strong advocacy for black women found in the 1893 speech, with the added message to black women that they could do better politically than black men had done. The tactics of identification have been suppressed here because the point is not that she and the women share common experiences but that they should use those experiences to political advantage.

"The Club Movement among Colored Women of America," published at the turn of the century, continued Williams's advocacy for black women by chronicling spawning black women's clubs. Appearing in the aptly titled 1900 collection *A New Negro for a New Century*, the article informs as it persuades. Williams pointed out that the interests of black women are subsumed and rendered invisible under such categories as "alien race," "a problem," an "industrial factor," or "ex-slaves." The special needs of women performing conventional gender roles were ignored. The essay described how black club women were rectifying this oversight and distinguished black club women's activities as having the serious purpose of improving conditions for those less fortunate, in contrast to the white women's clubs' "onward movement of the already uplifted" (383). She located the origins of black uplift work in the church.

In this article, Williams discussed ways in which the National Association of Colored Women's Clubs had helped to create a "race public opinion," making it possible "to reach the whole people with questions and interests that concerned the whole race" (404). Carla Peterson described the central role that antebellum organizational initiatives played in establishing black group unity, especially critical among subordinate groups. She writes that such institutional efforts

create organized consent among their members by means of specific cultural, social, and intellectual activities; they work to promote the welfare of the population as a whole over that of specific individuals or groups; they encourage the careful planning of resistance strategies; they make public and thus more effective hitherto privately held sentiments. (11) ·

The essay lists the connections established between the club women and their less fortunate sisters, giving evidence that these women did not separate themselves from the masses even though they pointed out differences from them. The process of identification here is internal, as Williams argued for the club women's totally unselfish approach to race uplift. The closing paragraph of the second of two chapters on the club movement gives a good sense of its spirit:

The club movement is well purposed. There is in it a strong faith, an enthusiasm born of love and sympathy, and an ever-increasing intelligence in the ways and means of affecting noble results. It is not a fad. It is not an imitation. It is not a passing sentiment. It is not an expedient or an experiment. It is rather the force of a new intelligence against the old ignorance. The struggle of an enlightened conscience against the whole brood of social miseries born out of the stress and pain of a hated past. (428)

"The Woman's Part in a Man's Business" was published in the November 1904 issue of the *Voice of the Negro*. One of the leading black magazines at the turn of the century and the first black-edited Southern magazine, the *Voice of the Negro* was produced in Atlanta from 1904–1906 and in Chicago for three months before it ceased. The inaugural issue of January 1904 targeted dual readers, promising that it would become "a necessity in the cultured colored homes and a source of information on Negro inspirations and aspirations in the white homes" (2). Given this initial purpose for the publication, one would expect the writers to engage in various tactics of identification in their efforts to inform white readers. Williams, herself a frequent contributor, in this article appealed to the standards of ideal womanhood to which white but not black women were held:

> She is the only woman in America who is almost unknown; the only woman for whom nothing is done; the only woman without sufficient defenders when assailed; the only woman who is still outside of that world of chivalry that in all the ages has apotheosized woman kind. . . . Yet colored women must face an age in this part of the world, that insists that they shall not be included in this world of exalted and protected womanhood. (544–45)

She challenged black businessmen to engage in a modified form of racial uplift, doing all they could to "exalt Negro womanhood in America" (545). As they succeeded in business and demonstrated that they could manage as well as white businessmen, they would also have a chance to elevate their wives, "bringing them nearer that sphere of chivalry and protection" enjoyed by white women" (545). Williams's view of the possibilities for black women was still narrowly defined in terms of what white women had accomplished by that time. "The colored girl," she wrote, "like the white girl, is pushing her way into every school whose doors are not closed to her complexion" (545). She stressed that they were making headway in "hairwork" and bread making, often going into business for themselves in response to hiring discrimination. Williams shifted from merely describing the black woman's supportive roles in male-dominated businesses to her role as an independent entrepreneur. Echoing the comparisons of her 1893 speech, she claimed that black women, like white women, worked in a wide range of occupations. The women would not, she assured readers, abandon their traditional roles; they would perform double duty. Williams here struggled to maintain a value balance between women's traditional roles as wives, homemakers, and helpmeets and their new opportunities as entrepreneurs. Because, Williams continued, black men and women had been equally deprived, the women had a better chance of progressing at the same pace. This was a somewhat contradictory claim, since she had argued earlier that black women, doubly oppressed, were at a greater disadvantage than black men. In the closing section, Williams even characterized the black woman as the "one woman in America, who must find her enjoyment in contemplating a remote future and not by living in a joyous present" (547). Having imagined the "colored woman" engaging in an array of independent activities, Williams in the last sentences returned her to a supporting role: "With the interest of this kind of woman in a man's business, he cannot fail, and without her he has already failed" (547). Williams performed here another version of the balancing act staged linguistically by many of these women, especially after the Civil War and into the twentieth century. They wanted to argue black women into the cult of true womanhood and at the same time leave them enough independence to engage in personal and racial uplift.

The title of this piece belies its emphasis on this societal progress of black women. The supporting role for women, which Williams returned to at the end, was downplayed; and singular opportunities for personal advancement moved to center stage. Perhaps a better title would have been "The Future of Black Business Women."

"The Colored Girl" appeared in the June 1905 *Voice of the Negro*. In this article Williams lashed out at black men who failed to show proper respect for "the colored girl." Instead of comparing black women with white women, Williams advised black men to adopt a black standard of beauty. The strong call to accept black women on their own terms and on the strength of their character rather than their material possessions or occupation reminds us that her primary readers here were black. Williams paid special tribute to ordinary, hardworking women engaged in racial uplift work, not the prominent society women: "Would you know the real heroines of the colored race, do not look for them among the well dressed throngs that parade our streets and fill our churches, but look in obscure places" (402). For the first time, Williams questioned a standard of beauty based on the appearance of other women: "Too many colored men entertain very careless, if not contemptible, opinions of the colored girl. They are apt to look to other races for their types of beauty and character" (402). Williams seemed more openly critical of the disrespect shown black women in this piece.

Williams continued to write and speak in defense of black women. Her advocacy evolved from the 1893 effort to demonstrate all the ways in which black women were similar to white women to the 1905 article submitted to the *Voice of the Negro*, declaring that black women needed to be accepted as well for the ways in which they are unique. In the article on black women's clubs,

Williams emphasized that the black women's clubs were not imitating white women's but were charting their own course based on the unique needs of black people in America. Their clubs represented, wrote Williams, "the organized anxiety of women who have become intelligent enough to recognize their own low social condition and strong enough to initiate the forces of reform" (384).

Anna Julia Cooper

If one's introduction to Cooper's early persuasive discourse is the brief speech she delivered following Williams's address at the Woman's Congress, that introduction could be misleading, for it presents a feisty, no-nonsense Cooper, less willing, it seems, than Williams to accommodate to or identify with the white women to whom she spoke. The factual support, so typical of her previous scholarly work, is still there, but it is presented so as to suggest that it is "old news," broadcast, if not heeded, many times before. The text of Cooper's remarks in the conference proceedings is placed under the heading "Discussion of the Same Subject by Mrs. A. J. Cooper of Washington, D.C." (Sewall 711). She said to those assembled that it would be impossible for any group of women to advance very far only thirty years after enslavement. Black women, Cooper continued, had, nonetheless, showed amazing courage, struggling to "keep hallowed their own persons" (Cooper, "Discussion" 711). But unlike the white woman, who "could at least plead for her own emancipation," the black woman, "doubly enslaved, could but suffer and struggle and be silent." Cooper then boldly announced her intention to break the silence, an announcement she had made the previous year in the preface to her collection of essays: "I speak for the colored women of the South" ("Discussion" 712).

Unlike the sweeping world history lessons of earlier speeches, the lesson that opens this one is brief and to the point. Having said it would be hard to give evidence of progress in thirty short years, Cooper proceeded to do just that, listing the schools established, citing statistics on black pupils and teachers recruited, and naming specific women who had achieved. She concluded by offering to summarize not only her "sentiments" but also those of her constituency: "We want, then, as toilers for the universal triumph of justice and human rights, to go to our homes from this Congress, demanding an entrance not through a gateway for ourselves, our race, our sex, or our sect, but a grand highway for humanity" (714–15). Calling here for human solidarity, Cooper changed the ground of the discussion from a question of what can be done to help black women to what must be done to help "the cause of every man and of every woman who has writhed silently under a mighty wrong" (715). Fannie Jackson Coppin, taking her cue from Cooper, continued in this same vein, reminding the gathering that the plight of black women was "not simply a side issue in which you feel that out of consideration for a certain class of people you ask them to give the history of their life" (715). Both Cooper's and Coppin's remarks represented counter-texts to the official and more conciliatory address Williams delivered.

When Cooper made those remarks, she had already published *A Voice from the South*, her collection of essays. By then, she had helped to organize the Colored Woman's League of Washington, D.C. She had, by that time, also served as "Woman's Department" editor for the *Southland*, a publication founded in 1890 by the Reverend Joseph C. Price, president of Livingstone College in Salisbury, North Carolina. Three years earlier, she had delivered her speech titled "The Higher Education of Women" to the American Conference of Educators. By then, she had addressed the Fourth Annual Convocation of Colored Clergy of the Protestant Episcopalian Church in Washington, D.C., delivering her speech titled "Woman a Vital Element in the Regeneration and Progress of a Race." Six years before making these remarks, she had been awarded a master's degree in mathematics from Oberlin. Further, by the time of this speech, she had taught at Wilberforce College in Ohio and at St. Augustine's College in Raleigh, North Carolina, and was completing her sixth year as mathematics and science teacher at the Washington [D.C.] Colored High School. This position, Cooper wrote, she had "received, unsought, through the kindly office of my Alma Mater" (Cooper, *Life and Writings* 1: 8).

While Williams was probably chosen over Cooper to give the main address because of her greater prominence in Chicago women's organizations, Cooper had certainly been more intellectually active than most of the other black women on the podium. But, as Paul Cooke, a Cooper scholar, points out, Cooper was more scholar and educator than public figure (Washington, Introduction [*Voice*] xxvii). The August 1895 Conference Souvenir issue of the *Woman's Era's* "Social Notes" section, commenting on some of the "most conspicuous women of the convention," described Cooper as "calm, thoughtful, and analytical,—a woman to mould opinion, rather than a leader of men. Mrs. Cooper, the student" (19). Her fondness for the classroom is clear from the advice offered in her 1930 article titled "The Humor of Teaching." In that article, she encouraged black teachers to relax and give their acquired book knowledge time to "inwardly digest," thereby fostering more original thinking in their students. She admonished that "[a]n instructor who is himself keen about the enigma of the Universe, or even about the enigma of Mississippi and Texas, will find his flaming torch as 'catching' from a chair in Greek and Latin as he would with a stereotyped or borrowed syllabus in Civics or a book 'plan' on the Reconstruction period" (394).[2] Cooper continued her intellectual and scholarly work for fully two-thirds of the 105 years of her life. By the time she was awarded the degree of doctor of philosophy from the University of Paris at the age of sixty-six, she had served as principal of the M Street High School and as chief administrator of the Frelinghuysen Group of Schools for Employed Colored Persons, commonly known as Frelinghuysen University.

This scholarly analytical bent was the distinguishing feature of her persuasive discourse. It shaped her criticism of restrictive nineteenth-century gender conventions. Claudia Tate makes the point that Cooper refused to "direct her turn-of-the-century campaign for black women's access to academic education to white society; she directed it to the new black academic patriarchs" (58). With such a long life span, Cooper came to know most, if not all, of the prominent post-Reconstruction black male leaders, including Frederick Douglass, Booker T. Washington, W. E. B. Du Bois, Alexander Crummell, Francis J. Grimké, and Edward Blyden. Explicit references in Cooper's writing to the misunderstandings of black men regarding the proper place for black women give evidence that such prominent figures as these were the targeted audiences for much of her persuasive discourse. Consider, for example, this direct salvo from her essay titled "The Higher Education of Women": "It hardly seems a gracious thing to say, but it strikes me as true, that while our men seem thoroughly abreast of the times on almost every other subject, when they strike the woman question they drop back into sixteenth century logic" (75). Cooper was just as eager to correct their false assumptions of superiority as to correct those of white society. Further, it is not surprising that Cooper concentrated on woman's equality, having herself been, since the age of twenty-one, a self-supporting widow, also helping to support her mother and a deceased brother's children. It is hard to imagine, then, that such an independent woman would develop a discourse of submission to men.

Perhaps more typical of the rhetorical strategies Cooper employed to articulate her feminist views are those in two essays: "Womanhood a Vital Element in the Regeneration and Progress of a Race" and "The Higher Education of Women," from the first section of *A Voice from the South*, the section Cooper labels "Soprano Obligato," referring to woman's accompanying but distinctly independent role. These two essays—both also delivered speeches[3]—were addressed to audiences of mostly black male intellectuals—one to black Episcopalian clergy and the other to "some of the best-trained black educators of the day" (Hutchinson 92). So we are considering here two addresses from a black woman intellectual to gatherings predominated by black male intellectuals on the subject of black women. Cooper recognized that both rhetorical situations risked becoming "mere intellectual entertainment" ("Womanhood" 23). Both speeches are filled with classical, biblical, and historical allusions, characteristic of much nineteenth-century prose. Just two years out of college at the time she addressed the black clergy, Cooper could easily recall such illustrations. "Her self-confidence and earnestness now and then leave a youthful ring suggestive of a recent college graduate," writes Leona Gabel in her characterization of Cooper's early prose (73). With such an arsenal of material, the challenge for Cooper may have been not what to say but what to say first.

"Womanhood a Vital Element in the Regeneration and Progress of a Race" was delivered at a conference of black Episcopalian clergy. Alexander Crummell convened this conference on Wednesday, September 22, 1886, in the St. Luke's Episcopal Church. George Bragg, in his brief church history, described its particular focus:

> It was at the Conference of 1886 in St. Luke's Church Washington that it was determined to change the Conference from an exclusively Negro body to one composed of Church Workers among Colored People, so as to include in its membership white as well as colored persons. And in the same Conference, following the change above noted, were introduced the first white members of this body. . . . (Bragg 5)

The black clergy had organized in 1883 in response to a conference that same year attended solely by white Episcopalians "to deliberate concerning the Negro" (Bragg 40). In 1886 the clergy decided to make their gathering more inclusive with the hope of increasing black influence on policy in this overwhelmingly white denomination. While Bragg does not list Cooper among the participants—only the clergy are listed—it is possible that she was invited because of her work at St. Augustine's, an Episcopal school, and her church work among the people in the Raleigh, North Carolina, community.

A salient feature of this speech is its length, which could well have taxed the attention span of even this august and committed nineteenth-century group. In print, the speech contains about 7,850 words, 82 paragraphs of varying length, and covers approximately 25 double-spaced typed pages. If read in its entirety at a normal speaking rate, the speech must have taken nearly an hour and a half to deliver. Given its length and the points Cooper wanted to cover on what she referred to as the "subject assigned"—an indication that a topic had been suggested to her—one of her primary considerations must have been effective arrangement.

Using Perelman and Olbrechts-Tyteca's discussion as a framework can help to explain Cooper's method for selecting and disposing the arguments in this speech. The authors stress the persuasive effect of arrangement or order in arguments. Arrangement is important in persuasive discourse, they point out, because changes in the audience are contingent upon the order in which the elements in an argument are presented. The authors list three approaches to decisions about order: responding to the argumentative situation itself, paying attention to the conditioning of the audience, and focusing on the audience's reaction to its perception of the speech's order. They explain:

In all three cases it is a question of effects on the audience. What distinguishes the three viewpoints is that, under the first, attention is mainly focused on the premises the audience is progressively led to admit, while under the second . . . the speaker is principally concerned with successive impressions made on the audience; the third viewpoint . . . pays attention to order or arrangement as a matter for reflection. (492)

While speakers adapt their arguments to situations, they note, the order of argumentative components can change those situations. The strength of arguments derives entirely, then, from their position in the text. Additionally, speakers can call attention to the arrangement of elements if they are presented in some recognizable order, giving the audience the impression that the arrangement has not been manipulated. Particularly useful in identifying the logic to the way Cooper marshaled arguments in a speech the length of "Womanhood a Vital Element in the Regeneration and Progress of a Race" is a proportioned outline of its development:

I. Statement and support of the first claim that Christianity and Feudalism engendered the "ennobling ideal of woman" (paragraphs 1–23, 28 percent)

II. Statement and support of second claim that societies that recognize the influence of women progress (paragraphs 24–28, 6 percent)

III. Statement and support of third claim that if the black race is to survive and progress it must invest more in its women (paragraphs 29–54, 32 percent)

IV. Discussion of what the Episcopalian Church, specifically, needs to do to support black women (paragraphs 55–82, 34 percent)

One important decision Cooper had to make was how to begin. With no transcription of the actual performance, we can only speculate that Cooper began with appropriate gestures to the occasion and the distinguished audience assembled. No doubt, she edited out these various forms of ingratiation in preparing this piece for publication; the first sentence of the printed text represents the beginning of the speech proper. This opening is a direct statement of one of the speech's main points, that Christianity and feudalism together shaped the idea of an ennobled womanhood. This claim would have captured the attention of a group of late nineteenth-century Christian church workers without offending or shocking them. It also "takes possession of the ground," suggesting a potential direction to the speech and allowing the clergymen to follow its development (Perelman and Olbrechts-Tyteca 498).

As the outline reveals, the speech can be roughly separated into thirds, with the first third covering the origins and implications of elevated womanhood, the second covering the urgent need to elevate black womanhood, and the final section challenging the representatives of the Episcopal Church to respond to this need. Cooper's main strategy of arrangement was first of all to base her arguments on their common Christianity's historical reverence for women. Devoting 28 percent of the speech to developing this point, Cooper appeared to inform rather than remind the clergy of Christianity's vital role in promoting the uplift of woman. Yet, references to this concept can be found in contemporary documents. For example, T. Thomas Fortune opened his 1892 biographical sketch of Ida Wells with the claim that "[o]nly in Christian countries has woman secured a measure of equality with the forceful agents that make the world's history" (Scruggs 3). Rather than begin with her main message that the Episcopal Church needed to do much more to support the development of black women if it and the race expected to progress, Cooper chose to open with this originary claim. She demonstrated that the notion of honoring and uplifting women came from the very Christianity they professed.

Using this approach, Cooper developed premises that the clergy were progressively led to admit. She first characterized the oppression of the Eastern woman, an oppression that had "enervated and blighted her mental and moral life" (9).[4] Cooper, at paragraph five, moved to a consideration of the "European bud and the American flower of modern civilization," quickly cautioning, however, that America's flower had not yet bloomed. That it would bloom, Cooper predicted, could be attributed to "the influence of good women" in the homes. Then began Cooper's narration of the chivalry of the Middle Ages, tainted by elitism. Christianity, she continued, extended this respect to all women, at least in principle.

The shortest section of the speech develops the second claim "that the position of woman in a society determines the vital elements of its regeneration and progress" (21). Cooper sets aside only four paragraphs to remind the churchmen that "this is so on *a priori* grounds." She ended this section with an apostropic challenge to women to fulfill their awesome responsibility.

Then comes the transition to the "subject assigned," a paragraph of metadiscourse indicating Cooper's clear understanding of the rhetorical situation—the audience of highly educated churchmen, the constraints of time, and the urgency of the message:

Now the fact of woman's influence on society being granted, what are its practical bearings on the work which brought together this conference of colored clergy and laymen in Washington? "We come not here to talk." Life is too busy, too pregnant with meaning and far reaching consequences to allow you to come this far for mere intellectual entertainment. (23)

Thus, at paragraph twenty-nine, with one-third of the speech delivered, Cooper mentioned, for the first time, the black woman of the South and moved from "intellectual entertainment" to intellectual challenge, from epideictic to deliberative discourse.

Cooper respectfully acknowledged that Dr. Crummell, most certainly in the front row if not in the pulpit at the time, had already called attention to the needs of black women in his speech titled "The Black Woman of the South: Her Neglects and Her Needs," delivered before the Freedman's Aid Society in

1883. Drawing from contemporary masculine discourse, Crummell stressed the need to protect women: "I do not stand here today to plead for the black *man*. He is a man; and if he is weak he must go the wall. He is a man; he must fight his own ways, and if he is strong in mind and body, he can take care of himself. But for the mothers, sisters, and daughters of my race I have a right to speak" (167). To create a space for her own discourse, Cooper, "with the Doctor's permission," proposed to call attention specifically to the needs of "colored girls" rather than women, upon whom "rests the foundation stone of our future as a race" (25).

This portion of the speech directly attacked the privileged position of those assembled. Cooper reminded them that their personal accomplishments meant little in isolation, for they represented exceptions. "Not by pointing to sunbathed mountain tops do we prove that Phoebus warms the valleys" (30–31). Their advancement, she proclaimed, was not as significant as the progress of the black women who helped to mold them. Such statements must surely have reduced the comfort level of this elite body. Although they had convened this conference specifically to address discrimination at all church levels, their gaze was outward. Few probably expected to hear that they were implicated in societal neglect of black women.

Cooper wisely chose to place this more accusative section between the general claim of elevated womanhood's Christian origins and the final appeal to the Episcopal Church at large to take action. Placing the most directly antagonist portion of a speech in the middle could be viewed as a variation of the so-called "Nestorian" practice of assigning the middle position to the weakest arguments, with the stronger arguments at the beginning and end.[5] The difference here, of course, is that Cooper's placement is based on relative potential for alienating the audience. It would not have been wise to alienate the clergymen, especially before they had had a chance to hear her arguments nor to close with such a direct attack. She closed, instead, with a challenge to the denomination to redefine the clergy's role as church workers. This role, she acknowledged, was less clear because of the church's timidity. In this final section, comprising 34 percent of the speech, Cooper came close to recommending defection, as she points to the denomination's inability to attract more black members in spite of what Cooper calls their "deeply rooted religious instincts." She said that other denominations had been much more successful than the Protestant Episcopal Church, with less than two dozen black priests in the

South. The younger "Christian workers for the race" had gravitated to more progressive denominations.

Cooper then traced the problems between the Episcopal Church and black people back to the church's failure to include black people in its deliberations about them and to make the training of black women a priority. She explored these two oversights, concentrating first on the claim of exclusivity, and then, finally, with nearly 90 percent of the speech delivered, she announced her intention to develop her "proper theme," the charge against the church of neglect:

To return, however, it is not on this broader view of Church work, which I mentioned as a primary cause of its halting progress with the colored people, that I am to speak. My proper theme is the second oversight of which in my judgment our Christian propagandists have been guilty: or, the necessity of church training, protecting and uplifting our colored womanhood as indispensable to the evangelization of the race. (42)

The remaining ten paragraphs contrasted the church's failure to take action on any of Crummell's earlier proposals to meet the black woman's pressing needs to the exemplary work of the Congregationalists. She urged financial support of the women of the South. In these closing paragraphs, Cooper developed a value hierarchy in which she ranked the needs of the race over loyalty to the Episcopal Church because, she reminded them,

[o]ur life as a race is at stake. The dearest interests of our hearts are in the scales. We must either break away from dear old landmarks and plunge out in any line and every line that enables us to meet the pressing need of our people, or we must ask the Church to allow and help us, untrammelled by the prejudices and theories of individuals, to work aggressively under her direction as we alone can, with God's help, for the salvation of our people. (45–46)

Her consistent use of transitional metadiscourse points to the fact that Cooper wanted to communicate clearly to her auditors the relationships among her various points as she moved through her text. Expressions, such as "And here let me say parenthetically," "It is pleasing to turn," and "It may help us to recall," as well as the paragraph-long partitioning quoted above, allow Cooper to identify the points at issue, predict the parts of the argument to follow, and position herself in relation to those parts.

If we return to Perelman and Olbrechts-Tyteca's discussion of arrangement to consider Cooper's ordering, we can see that Cooper was most heavily influenced by the argumentative situation itself in disposing her arguments. Addressing an assembly of church workers, she grounded her appeal in the Christian origins of respect for womanhood, a respect based on woman as mother, homemaker, the first influence on personality. She charged the black clergymen, then, with various forms of neglect but launched her strongest attack against the Episcopal Church itself, a church that had failed to reach out to black people generally and to support black women in particular. Cooper exhorted black church workers to take charge of the survival of their people. She charged the church to provide the needed support and step back.

The second speech to be considered here for analysis of arrangement, "The Higher Education of Woman," is shorter by twenty paragraphs but exhibits a similar pattern of arrangement. It was delivered at the American Conference of Educators, held in Washington, D.C., from March 25–27, 1890. Cooper had been invited to speak at the conference by Howard University alumni. The governing board of the conference included only two women, Lucy Ellen Moten and Julia Waugh Mason, both Washington, D.C., educators. The April 1890 *Southland* carried a report on the conference and some of the speeches, but Cooper's speech was not mentioned. The text appeared a year later in the April 1891 issue of the *Southland*, in the "Woman's Department," which Cooper edited.

Evidence of the significance of this occasion is provided in a letter to West African statesman Edward W. Blyden from the Reverend Francis J. Grimké, pastor of the Fifteenth Street Presbyterian Church in Washington: "We are to have an Educational Convention in our City this week. Mrs. Cooper is to read a paper on 'the Higher Education of Women.' I wish you were here to hear it" (qtd. in Gabel x). Blyden was among those who met frequently at the Grimkés' and at Cooper's own home, "when on this side of the Atlantic," for cultural and intellectual stimulation (Cooper, *Life and Writings* 1: 8).

For discussion purposes, the speech can be proportioned as follows:

I. Eighteenth-century ideas regarding the higher education of women and the general contempt for weakness (paragraphs 1–16, 27 percent)

II. Unconscious feminine influence, for example, at Oberlin (paragraphs 17–27, 18 percent)

III. Refutation of anticipated objection that there have been highly educated women throughout history (paragraphs 28–34, 12 percent)

IV. Nineteenth-century turn to valuing higher education for women (paragraphs 35–39, 8 percent)

V. Education not a deterrent to marriage (paragraphs 40–49, 17 percent)

VI. Importance of higher education for black women (paragraphs 50–60, 18 percent)

Cooper did not begin this speech as far back as she began "Womanhood a Vital Element in the Regeneration and Progress of a Race," but Cooper the scholar was still drawn by the need to establish historical underpinnings. She incorporated the earlier stages of the discussion, those occurring outside of the speech situation, into the opening section. These prior arguments needed to be rehearsed. The fact that this opening section represents over one-quarter of the address is not without consequence, for as Perelman and Olbrechts-Tyteca point out, careful ordering ensures that adequate emphasis ("presence") is given to essential background information (493). Dwelling on the history of neglect helped to prepare her auditors to hear of needed changes. She began with a discussion of Sylvain Marechal's *Can Woman Learn the Alphabet*, as well as other manifestations of the fear of educated women. This first section takes up nearly one-third of the speech, as Cooper narrated examples from the collegiate dark ages of women's higher education.

But, she declares, woman's influence could not be downed, despite the efforts of many to suppress it. Often unconsciously, the feminine presence had an impact, as she demonstrated in the case of Oberlin, where young women "threading the streets of the village every evening unattended" caused crime "to slink away, like frost before the rising sun" (56). This section pays attention to the indirect influence that Cooper claimed for women, "an influence subtle and often involuntary, an influence so intimately interwoven in, so intricately interpenetrated by the masculine influence of the time that it is often difficult to extricate the delicate meshes and analyze and identify the closely clinging fibers" (56). With this placement Cooper juxtaposed a counter to the masculine meanspiritedness of the eighteenth century she had just described. In contrast, these attributes, comprising "the feminine side to truth," increase in appeal.

Nearly halfway through the speech, Cooper paused to anticipate an objection on the part of her audience that highly educated women—for example, Sappho, Aspasia, Renaissance women professors—existed prior to the nineteenth century. She reminded them that these women were the few exceptions to the general rule of exclusion and discouragement. Cooper carefully placed this anticipatory refutation at a critical point where the auditors were most likely to need it: "Now you will argue, perhaps, rightly, that higher education for women is not a modern idea, and that, if that is the means of setting free and invigorating the long desired feminine force in the world, it has already had a trial and should, in the past, have produced some of those glowing effects" (62). Perelman and Olbrechts-Tyteca stress the importance of disposing of objections at the appropriate point in order to make room for the speaker's own arguments. Engaging in prolepsis here, raising and refuting this anticipated objection to her own claim, Cooper cleared the ground for the rest of the speech, just at the point when this objection might have interfered. Cooper's placement in this instance plays an important part in audience conditioning.

At paragraph thirty-five, Cooper shifted her attention to the somewhat more progressive nineteenth-century attitudes supporting change. These attitudes were reflected in the solicitations of Ralph Emerson, the "magnanimous" remarks of Grant Allen, and the curious concern of Matthew Arnold that higher education for women "spoils their *chances*" (68; emphasis in original). She addressed Arnold's concern and no doubt the concern of many in this overwhelmingly male gathering, though they would have been reluctant to raise it—the effect of higher education on woman's marriageability. In response, Cooper, at the time a self-supporting widow for over ten years, problematized the value of marriage, arguing that "intellectual development . . . renders woman less dependent on the marriage relation for physical support (which, by the way, does not always accompany it)" (68). With educated women perceiving broader horizons, the challenge, she continued, was for men to raise themselves to women's level, concluding that "[i]f it makes them [men] work, all the better for them" (71). She also argued that the knowledge acquired by educated women can actually make them better mothers and homemakers. Cooper again engaged in refutation, anticipating the objection that education would make women less suitable for marriage, "the most serious argument ever used against the higher education" (68). Cooper knew that this male-dominated audience would have considered it so and devoted eleven paragraphs or nearly 20 percent of the speech to refutation.

With more than three-fourths of the speech completed—Cooper must have been speaking for at least forty-five minutes by then—she summarized what had been said and moved finally to a discussion of the higher education of black women. It is significant that while the two objectives of the conference were to address subjects relevant "only to the educational interest and needs of black people" and to call national attention to black achievements (Hutchinson 92), Cooper does not mention black people specifically prior to this point, speaking instead from "the higher ground of generalities." Although the title of Cooper's speech is unmarked, the audience was no doubt anticipating a focus on black women. Such a delay must surely have built suspense as members of this racially mixed audience waited confidently for the other shoe to fall. This is the tactic of arrangement Cooper followed in her 1886 speech titled "Womanhood a Vital Element in the Regeneration and Progress of a Race," as well. She transitioned in both with metadiscourse designed to shift attention to black women, expressing regrets that their needs still required special and separate consideration. Resisting the temptation to end with optimistic predictions surrounding the twin masculine and feminine forces, Cooper writes that "duty is nearer home. The high ground of generalities is alluring but my pen is devoted to a special cause: and with a view to further enlightenment on the achievements of the century for the Higher Education of Colored Women" (73; emphasis in original). She followed with the results of research into black women college graduates, indicating slow progress and chastising black men in the passage quoted above. In the remaining paragraphs, Cooper addressed this "special cause," narrating, apologetically, her own experience with classroom gender discrimination. Her ultimate challenge, as in "Womanhood a Vital Element in the Regeneration and Progress of a Race," was that black women seeking higher education be given encouragement and financial support, "not the boys less, but the girls more" (79).

Cooper employed the funnel approach in this speech, beginning with the larger argument, placing black women within the larger context of all women, emphasizing the universal as well as the local, and finally narrowing to her "special cause."

Both Williams and Cooper always brought their discussions round to black women's interests. They approached those interests from a range of directions, charting their courses according to the particular rhetorical situations. Williams, when addressing white women, argued that black women were like them in all essential qualities, with the hope that through identification, these more privileged auditors would be moved to support aggressively the advancement of their sisters. But when addressing this same topic to black men, as in her article titled "The Colored Girl," Williams pressed the need to apply a different standard for valuing the contributions of black women, elevating them—in the tradition of the cult of true womanhood—but on their own terms. In articles to the *Woman's Era*, read primarily by black women, Williams also pushed the distinction between black and white women, suggesting that where black women's interests were concerned, white women could not always be trusted. Through strategic arrangement of her arguments, Cooper, in two speeches delivered primarily to black intellectuals, arrived finally at the interests of black women after several historical detours. She was careful to place their concerns in the global context of neglect and respect for women, showing, by selecting this circuitous route, that the black woman, a member of this global community, was entitled to no less than other women.

6

3°

"To Embalm Her Memory
in Song and Story"
Victoria Earle Matthews and Situated Sisterhood

As consistent women, jealous of our good name, we should not hesitate
through mistaken ideas as to wise policy, etc., in sending broadcast our
burning contempt for any creature who can assail with viperous touch a
subject that involves the innate mystery of hidden life out of our reverence
for those who preceded us, made a place in history, song and story for us.
Our indignation should know no limit. We as women have been too un-
obtrusive, too little known; we have been hidden by our close adherence to
high endeavor. The dross has forced to the front too long.

—Victoria Matthews, *Woman's Era*, July 1895

Victoria Earle Matthews organized and spoke at numerous gatherings
of black women at the turn of the nineteenth century, serving as a prototype of the emerging black woman public intellectual. The definition of a public intellectual is not fixed, especially as it would apply to the
women of this era. I use it here to mean one who participates in public discourse that has as its purpose the application of ideas to the understanding and
possible modification of social and political phenomena. Over one hundred
years after Matthews delivered her speech titled "The Value of Race Literature"
at the 1895 Boston Conference of Colored Women, Michael Dyson provides a
definition of public intellectuals that, I would argue, can be applied retrospec-
tively to nineteenth-century women like Matthews. He writes that they "bring
their considerable critical resources to bear on problems of public life that demand complexity of vision, economy of expression, clarity of thought, and rigor
of analysis," adding that "the public intellectual must be just that: an *intellectual*

thinking out loud in various *publics*" (xvi–xvii; emphasis in original). In this chapter, I explore ways in which Matthews's persuasive discourse performed just this kind of cultural work.

In the epigraph above, Matthews urged her sisters to abandon the self-effacing restrictions associated with middle-class respectability and the cult of true womanhood that prevented them from defending their own name. When Matthews wrote the column from which the quote was taken, she had already been selected as one of three delegates to represent the Woman's Loyal Union of New York and Brooklyn at the National Conference of Colored Women, held later that same month in Boston. The Conference had been called in part to provide black women a forum in which to express their "burning contempt" publicly. But these expressions were not only counters to assaults on their moral character. They also addressed the mental, physical, and financial well-being of black people generally. Elsa Barkley Brown reminds us in her discussion of black women's political activity in Richmond from 1880–1920 that the emergence of black women's clubs in the 1890s cannot be tied solely to external factors such as a response to attacks on their morality or to the general proliferation of white women's clubs (111–45).[1] In fact black women's associations and attacks on black morality were both long-standing "traditions," predating the 1890s (Shaw 20).

Victoria Matthews was arguably the most active woman at the conference. She had been president of the Woman's Loyal Union since it was organized in 1892 and had arranged, along with Marichita Lyons and other club women, the testimonial for Ida B. Wells at Lyric Hall in New York.[2] During the Boston conference, Matthews, known in the literary world as Victoria Earle, made use of her executive ability to serve on the platform committee and developed a set of resolutions in response to John Jacks's letter disparaging Wells and all black women. She was one of the women appointed to draw up resolutions to be forwarded to Albion W. Tourgée, author and jurist who had represented Homer A. Plessy in his challenge to the Louisiana Separate Car Law. At the close of the conference, when it was proposed that a national organization be formed, Matthews, as a member of the organizing committee, drafted the resolution to frame a constitution. She was also a member of the committee charged to "gather up the loose ends of the convention" (*History* 10). During the closing session at the Charles Street AME Church, it was Matthews who officially moved the creation of the National Federation of Afro-American

Women (NFA-AW) and was later named chairman of the organization's executive board.

The speech titles listed on the conference program suggest that Matthews's address, delivered on the second day of the conference, was a curious response to Josephine St. Pierre Ruffin's call for proposals. But a closer consideration of the rhetorical context suggests otherwise. Paul Lauter, in an article advocating the inclusion of Frances Harper's writing in the curriculum, stresses context as a prerequisite for understanding certain literary productions. He argues that "any institutional arrangement which systematically separates the texts from the world in which they are embedded arrests our capacity to read them" (32). One clear advantage of studying the public discourse of a previous era is that these performances reunite texts and "the world in which they are embedded," capturing the nuances of the time and the tenor of the occasion, perhaps more precisely than any other historical artifact.

Rhetorical theorist Lloyd Bitzer's definition of the components of a rhetorical situation, as modified by Carolyn Miller, is particularly helpful in capturing nuance and tenor. Bitzer offers a *situational* perspective on the subject of rhetoric, defining a rhetorical situation as consisting of an *audience* or those capable of being influenced and in a position to respond; an *exigence*, or an undesirable element in a situation that needs to be addressed; and certain *constraints*, possibilities and limitations as to what the speaker may and may not say. According to Bitzer, each rhetorical situation gives rise to a "fitting response." This response may not necessarily produce the desired effect; it may not, in other words, be successful in achieving its goals but can nonetheless be characterized as fitting. One may lose an issue while still responding in a "fitting" way (Bitzer 1–14). Bitzer's deterministic language suggests an objective reality independent of human awareness, which if properly understood, should evoke one fitting response.[3] While Bitzer's definition gives us a critical language with which to talk about rhetorical contexts, Miller's modified definition of exigence, based on an understanding of the rhetorical situation as a "social construct" or "semiotic structure," provides a more meaningful way to understand Matthews's response on this occasion:

If rhetorical situation is not material and objective, but a social construct, or semiotic structure, how are we to understand exigence, which is at the core of situation? Exigence must be located in the social world, neither in a private perception nor in material circumstance. It cannot be broken into two components without destroying it as a rhetorical and social phenomenon. Exigence is a form of social knowledge—a mutual construing of objects, events, interests, and purposes that not only links them but also makes them what they are: an objectified social need. This is quite different from Bitzer's characterization of exigence as a "defect" or danger. Conversely, although exigence provides the rhetor with a sense of rhetorical purpose, it is clearly not the same as the rhetor's intention, for that can be ill-formed, dissembling, or at odds with what the situation conventionally supports. The exigence provides the rhetor with a socially recognizable way to make his or her intentions known. It provides an occasion, and thus a form, for making public our private versions of things. (157–58)

Miller's redefinition widens the range of possible "fitting responses," equipping us to ask how Matthews, constrained, to some extent, by the particularities of the situation, managed certain "indeterminate contexts" in order to make her intentions known (Consigny 176). What follows is an analysis of "The Value of Race Literature" as Matthews's response to the immediate rhetorical situation and as a response to prior texts with which it participates intertextually in ongoing public debates about racial progress. I consider, as well, how her two other extant speeches, "The Awakening of the Afro-American Woman," an 1897 address to the Society of Christian Endeavor, and "Some of the Dangers Confronting Southern Girls in the North," her 1898 address to the Hampton Negro Conference, also participated contrastively in these same public conversations.

Matthews spent most of her short life in public service, modeling the activism she solicited from her audiences. She was born Victoria Smith on May 27, 1861, in Fort Valley, Houston County—at the time among the top five cotton-producing counties in the slave state of Georgia. According to Matthews's marriage record, her parents were William Smith and Caroline. Fleeing to New York, Victoria's mother returned to Georgia after emancipation and obtained custody of four of her nine children, including Victoria, her youngest, and Victoria's sister Anna. She first moved them to Richmond, then Norfolk, Virginia, where they remained for four years before settling in New York City in 1873, when Victoria was twelve. In New York, Matthews attended Grammar School 48 until the illness of a family member made it necessary for her to end her formal education. Driven by a passion for learning, Matthews took advantage of every opportunity to educate herself.

On October 22, 1879, at the age of eighteen, Victoria Smith married

William E. Matthews, a coachman from Petersburg, Virginia. They had one son, Lamartine, who died at sixteen. Shortly after their marriage, Matthews began writing for various newspapers, first substituting for reporters of the large New York daily papers, including the *Times, Herald, Mail and Express, Sunday Mercury, Earth,* and *Phonographic World.* She was New York correspondent to the *National Leader, Detroit Plaindealer,* and *Southern Christian Recorder* and also wrote for other black publications, including the *Boston Advocate, Washington Bee, Richmond Planet, Catholic Tribune, Cleveland Gazette, New York Globe, New York Age, New York Enterprise, Ringwood's Journal of Fashion, AME Church Recorder,* and *Woman's Era.* Matthews was also a member of the Women's National Press Association. In 1891, I. Garland Penn declared her the most popular woman journalist among her peers, pointing out that contributions from Matthews were eagerly solicited by the best papers of the black and white press (375–6). After the founding of the NACW in 1896, Matthews maintained a prominent role in its activities, serving as NACW National Organizer from 1897–1899. Locally, her club work revolved around the Woman's Loyal Union of New York and Brooklyn.

Matthews often delivered speeches based on direct investigations of the kind Ida Wells called for in her Lyric Hall speech, "Southern Horrors: Lynch Law in All Its Phases," speeches that would "get [the] facts laid before the public" (Wells, *Red Record* 24). In December of 1895, Matthews attended the Congress of Colored Women of the United States in Atlanta, in conjunction with the Cotton States and International Exposition. Some club women, including Josephine Ruffin, complained that the contributions of black people to America would be displayed separately, but Matthews attended anyway as a representative of New York women. Following the meeting, Matthews toured the South, investigating, among other atrocities, methods by which Southern black women became victims of unethical employment practices, often leading to prostitution. In a speech delivered at the 1898 Hampton (Institute) Negro Conference in Hampton, Virginia, she reported her findings, challenging others to investigate as well. The speech, "Some of the Dangers Confronting Southern Girls in the North," charged that "no women here can shirk without sin the obligation to study into this matter, to the end that the evil may be completely exterminated, and protection guaranteed to the lives and reputations of the generations yet to come" ("Dangers" 64).[4] The "women" addressed here were, like Matthews, prominent in turn-of-the-century racial uplift work. She also observed during this trip South the effects of chain gang law, particularly on children, and reported those findings in an 1896 lecture to the NFA-AW, calling the system "a blot on the fair fame of the United States" (*History* 41). Her interest in the plight of young black women migrating to the North led her to found the White Rose Mission Industrial Association in New York City in 1897, which trained and cared for such women. This mission eventually became part of the National Urban League.

Her extant published works include *Black Belt Diamonds* (1898), a collection of excerpts from Booker T. Washington's speeches; three short stories, "Aunt Lindy: A Story Founded on Real Life" (1889), later published in a single volume, "Eugenia's Mistake: A Story" (1892), and "Zelika: A Story" (1892); and three speeches, "The Value of Race Literature" (1895/1986), "The Awakening of the Afro-American Woman" (1897/1995), and "Some of the Dangers Confronting Southern Girls in the North" (1898). Matthews died in 1907, at the age of forty-six, from complications of tuberculosis.

The Exigence

On June 1, 1895, Josephine St. Pierre Ruffin, activist in the women's movement and president of the Woman's Era Club of Boston, issued a call for black women to gather in defense of themselves. The 1895 call came in part as a response to an open letter from the president of the Missouri Press Association, John W. Jacks, denigrating black women, claiming that they were "wholly devoid of morality and that they were prostitutes, thieves and liars" (Wesley 28). In another section of the letter, he wrote, "Out of some 200 [Negroes] in this vicinity it is doubtful if there are a dozen virtuous women of that number who are not daily thieving from the white people" (Moses, *Golden* 115). The letter had been sent to Florence Balgarnie of the British Anti-Lynching Committee in an attempt to discredit Ida Wells and her accounts of lynching in the South. The committee had been organized to investigate claims of lynching and mob violence in the United States and to publicly condemn such activities. Balgarnie had forwarded Jacks's letter to the editors of the *Woman's Era*, the first periodical owned and published solely by black women. Instead of publishing it, the editors decided to include a summary of its contents.

In her call to black women, Ruffin admonishes: "Read this document carefully and use it discriminately and decide if it be not time for us to stand before

the world and declare ourselves and our principles. The time is short but everything is ripe and remember, earnest women can do anything" (*History* 4). In response to Ruffin's call, the First Congress of Colored Women convened July 29,
1895, in Boston, with 104 delegates, representing fifty-four clubs from fourteen
states and the District of Columbia, to develop plans for a national organization. It is important to remember that this conference was the culmination of
at least sixteen months of active networking, particularly though the *Woman's
Era*, to organize nationally. The paper's correspondents from various women's
clubs around the country helped to fuel interest in such a gathering. This interest is evident in the pages of the first edition of *Woman's Era*, on March 24,
1894. The editors pose the question: "A Congress of the colored women's
leagues and clubs of the country was suggested long ago—should we not be
moving in the matter now?" (*Woman's Era* 7) In the next edition of May 1, 1894,
can be found enthusiastic responses from various club women to the query, "Do
you favor a convention of the colored women's clubs?" Josephine Silone Yates
of Missouri wrote, "By all means let us have a congress of colored women at
some time in the near future to give solidity, unity of purpose, national character, and other requisites of success necessary to a movement so broad and far
reaching as a race organization should be"; R. E. Moore of Massachusetts responded that "great good would result from an interchange of ideas as to how
we could best accomplish the more lasting results of the work each league is
engaged in"; Maria Baldwin of Massachusetts wrote, "I know of nothing that
would prove more stimulating than a congress of their [colored women's]
clubs"; and Matthews herself replied, "By all means let us have a conference"
(*Woman's Era* 1 May 1894, 3–4). Fully a year before the conference, then, interest
was high in such a gathering. Jacks's 1895 letter merely provided the exigence
for specific action, the occasion for making the private public. Ruffin articulated
as much in her call: "The letter of Mr. Jacks which is also enclosed is only used
to show how pressing is the need of our banding together if only for our protection; this is only one of the many matters upon which we need to confer"
(*History* 4–5).

The speeches on the opening day of the 1895 conference included Ruffin's
"Address of the President," Helen Cook's "Woman and the Higher Education,"
and Anna J. Cooper's "Need of Organization," calling on the women to organize not merely to fight against the maligning of black women but to unite in
the common effort of racial uplift. Ruffin's speech set the tone by admonishing:

"This conference will not be what I expect if it does not show the wisdom, indeed the absolute necessity of a national organization of our women." Ruffin saw the meeting as an opportunity for women to gain inspiration and renewal from "the mingling of congenial souls, of those working for the same ends"; and of course the other precipitating concern, mentioned in her call as well, was that black women's reputations be restored: "It is 'mete, right, and our bounden duty' to stand forth and declare ourselves and principles, to teach an ignorant and suspicious world that our aims and interests are identical with those of all good aspiring women" (*History* 32–34).

The Response

Speaking on the evening of the second day, Matthews shared the podium with Margaret Murray Washington, whose address was titled "Individual Work for Moral Elevation," and William Lloyd Garrison, T. Thomas Fortune, and Henry B. Blackwell, all listed under the subject "Political Equality." Given the exigence and occasion just described, one might ask whether Matthews's speech was a fitting response. In his afterword to the first reprinting, Fred Miller Robinson comments on "its bite and its hopefulness" (186). The speech is hard hitting and optimistic at the same time. How did Matthews define this rhetorical situation? The exigence or opportunity that gave rise to Matthews's speech was expressed in Ruffin's call, "Let Us Confer Together," when she asked the women to come forward and speak out. Now Matthews, in keeping with Ruffin's caution, never mentioned Jacks's letter. She had already berated it in her July 1895 column, quoted from in the chapter epigraph. Further, it appears from the paper titles that none of the speakers addressed that occurrence specifically. Although Jacks's letter may have precipitated the conference, the women spent very little time discussing it once assembled.

Instead, Matthews opened with her definition of "race literature" as "all the writings emanating from a distinct class—not necessarily race matter; but a general collection of what has been written by the men and women of that Race: History, Biographies, Scientific Treatises, Sermons, Addresses, Novels, Poems, Books of Travel, miscellaneous essays and the contributions to magazines and newspapers" (126).[5] And she proclaimed that more was needed. So we have here in 1895 one of the earliest arguments in defense of a separate consideration of such work, a defense still being put forth in various forms today.

Matthews argued that black literature was and always had been different and deserving of special consideration because the "conditions which govern the people of African descent in the United States have been and still are, such as create a very marked difference in the limitations, characteristics, aspirations and ambitions of this class of people, in decidedly strong contrast with the more or less powerful races which dominate it" (127). In other words, out of this common experience of oppression had emerged a "race literature." As did Frances Harper in what may have been her first public speech—"The Colored People in America," forty-one years earlier—Matthews here posited a definition of race as a socially constructed entity, resulting, for those defined as "colored," "Negro," or "black," in commonly constrained and restricted historical experiences.[6] This definition runs counter to a characterization based on essentialist assumptions, according to Michael Omi and Howard Winant, that "race is a matter of innate characteristics, of which skin color and other physical attributes provide only the most obvious, and in some respects most superficial, indicators" (64). They posit an interpretation of "race" that while acknowledging its constructed nature also notes its material social consequences. Matthews knew from personal experience the shifting character of the color line. When investigating social conditions in the South, she was able to enter many establishments only because of racialized assumptions about her identity. As black people wrote about these common experiences of prejudice, a "race" literature emerged.

Matthews's response to Ruffin's challenge crossed traditional generic boundaries. As the title "The Value of Race Literature" suggests, the speech Matthews delivered was essentially epideictic, calling attention to both praiseworthy and condemnable literary acts. But in keeping with the contemporary discourse of self-help and racial uplift, it was also deliberative, stressing to her auditors the need to produce their own literature. Its scathing opening attack upon past literary mischaracterizations of black people rendered it forensic as well. Matthews, in the concluding section, pointed to this threefold structure, describing the speech as a "cursory glance at what I may call the past, present and future of our Race Literature" (147).

The first section, then, focused on the past, judging harshly the negative representations of black people in literature by white authors and journalists. These negative representations, which she enumerated in detail, strongly resemble Anna Cooper's discussion of portrayals of blacks in "The Negro as

Presented in American Literature," a chapter in *A Voice from the South* (1892). Cooper commented primarily on the polemic writings of white authors, including Harriet Beecher Stowe, who, she writes, approached the subject with "humility and love" (Cooper, "The Negro" 186), with high praise for the prose of Albion Tourgée ("His caustic wit, his sledge hammer logic, his incisive criticism, his righteous indignation, all reflect the irresistible arguments of the great pleader for the Negro" [189]) and more reserved praise for local colorist George Washington Cable, who, according to Cooper, "embodies and represents that Christian conscience and enlightened self-interest of the hitherto silent South; he vocalizes and inspires its better self" (191). Matthews had certainly read Cooper's work, and her use of many of the same examples confirmed their continued grating effect.

Matthews exposed the prejudice of color embedded in such writings as Washington Irving's *Life of Columbus*, in which Las Casas, a Spanish missionary, proposed that Africans be enslaved to relieve the maltreatment of the South American Indians; in the depiction in *Harper's* of pathetic characters labeled typical "Darkies"; and in *The Tragedy of Pudd'nhead Wilson*, in which Samuel Clemens—whom she described as the "Negro-hating Mark Twain"—portrays an "educated octoroon" unfavorably. She also pointed to John Ridpath's degrading representation of blacks in his historical accounts of the great races of mankind and reviewed for them the romance between Dr. Olney and Rhoda in William Dean Howells's *Imperative Duty*, where he agonizes over "how a white man came to love a girl with a remote tinge of Negro blood!" Cooper had also cited this novel as one prime example of offensive prose, objecting in particular to Howells's depiction of the congregants in a certain church as "representing *the best colored society*." Cooper concluded, "One feels that he had no business to attempt a subject of which he knew so little, or for which he cared so little" ("The Negro" 202–3; emphasis in original). Matthews also pointed to Arthur Conan Doyle's portrayal of the educated but savage and bloodthirsty black man. She took her final negative example from Marie Therese Blanc's 1895 volume titled *The Condition of Women in the United States: A Traveller's Notes*. In a book approaching three hundred pages, fewer than one hundred words were devoted to black women. These one hundred words apparently consisted of a description of a "'Black Damsel' in New Orleans engaged in teaching Latin" and "a class of little Negro girls with faces like monkeys studying Greek," leading Blanc to conclude that "the disgust expressed by their former masters seemed quite justified" (Matthews 135–6).

After placing these compelling examples of literary abuse on display, Matthews concluded that the only defense against such portrayals was that black people must produce their own literature to serve as "counter-irritants." This defensive posture, assumed by post-Reconstruction black writers, attached to their productions heavy extraliterary baggage. Not only were they called to present more accurate accounts of the black experience in America, but by doing so they were also to demonstrate their own intellectual potential to skeptical readers. Matthews proclaimed that any people without a literature is "valued lightly the world round. Who knows or can judge of our intrinsic worth, without actual evidences of our breadth of mind, our boundless humanity" (136). Matthews was appealing to the widely held belief among her auditors that literature was the ultimate mark of civilization, providing tangible proof of this "boundless humanity" (136).

Appearing well and weighted with many degrees of titles, will not raise us in our own estimation while color is the white elephant in America. . . . [I]f [America] ever produces a race out of her cosmopolitan population, that can look beyond mere money-getting to more permanent qualities of true greatness as a nation, it will call this age her unbalanced stage. (136)

Matthews had set the stage for this argument in the speech's epigraph, a quote from Ralph Waldo Emerson's 1844 lecture titled "On the Emancipation of the West Indies," about the need for blacks to write themselves into citizenship:

If the black man carries in his bosom an indispensable element of a new and coming civilization, for the sake of that element, no money, nor strength, nor circumstance can hurt him; he will survive and play his part. . . . If you have *man*, black or white is an insignificance. The intellect—that is miraculous! who has it, has the talisman. His skin and bones, though they were the color of night, are transparent, and the everlasting stars shine through with attractive beams.[7]

At the same time, Matthews did not deny that much had already been produced, launching the epideictic portion of her address. In this section, Matthews chronicled black achievements in a wide array of professions—education, journalism, writing, music, and science. By so doing, she followed in the tradition of journalist Gertrude Mossell's celebratory volume titled *The Work of the Afro-American Woman* (1893), which itself features the writing of Matthews. As Claudia Tate points out, this tradition grew out of a need to refute the retrogressionist views put forth by white conservatives of the post-Reconstruction era. According to these views, blacks, without the restraints of slavery, had regressed to an earlier savage state, making them dangerously unsuited to function as fully entitled citizens. Tate writes that "repudiating the racist sexual discourse of retrogressionism at the heart of white Southern ideology was crucial to black people's changing their subjugated social status" (10). Cataloguing literary accomplishments was part of this repudiation project. Not immune to prevailing concerns about any black accomplishment reflecting "the highest credit on the race," Matthews cited essays, sermons, and addressees by Alexander Crummell and Edward Blyden, both close associates of Anna Cooper, and Richard Greener, first black Harvard graduate, as "high specimens of sustained English, good enough for any one to read" (138). The autobiographies, essays, and novels of William Wells Brown and Frederick Douglass, Phillis Wheatley's poetry, William Nell's histories, T. Thomas Fortune's and I. Garland Penn's journalistic work, and Paul Laurence Dunbar's and Frances Harper's poetry and prose are all mentioned.

After listing the literary accomplishments of scientists and churchmen, along with an extended discussion of journalistic writing, Matthews digressed into a refinement of her definition of race literature, pointing out that it "does not mean things uttered in praise, thoughtless praise of ourselves, wherein each goose thinks her gosling a swan. We have had too much of this, too much that is crude, rude, pompous, and literary nothings, which ought to have been strangled before they were written much less printed" (144). Matthews discussed the inferior quality of much that had been written generally, cautioning, however, that all good race writing must be preserved for future generations.

In the closing section, Matthews considered the specific contributions of black women to race literature, opening it with the question, "What part shall we women play in the Race Literature of the future?" She answered by pointing to past journalistic performances in the columns of the *Woman's Era*. But in the tradition of the times, she assigns as woman's most important role that of nurturing future generations by engaging her influence. This was the same kind of "influence" Maria Stewart called upon the women of the Afric-American Female Intelligence Society to exert over their husbands and children in 1832.

Anna Cooper spoke of this influence in her 1886 address to the black Episcopalian clergy, where she presses the importance of "woman's influence on social progress." It was also similar to the influence about which Frances Harper spoke in her 1893 address to the World's Congress of Representative Women, an influence combined with power at the ballot box. Even as nineteenth-century Victorian women advanced in various professions outside the home, as doctors, educators, journalists, and lawyers, their discourse remained grounded in the domestic. Matthews recognized women's roles as producers of poets, statesmen, and historians, using the example of Napoleon's mother, who worked on Homeric tapestry while "bearing the future conqueror or the world." Tate, in her discussion of the prose of Matthews's contemporaries Anna Cooper and Gertrude Mossell, observes that their writing evoked domestic rather than public or civil images of a people by "drawing on the currency of the reformist discourse, equating domestic efficiency with political, economic, and moral vitality" (132). Domestic discourse also took the form of social feminism, a discursive strategy that gained prominence after 1875, especially in the rhetoric of the Woman's Christian Temperance Union. Social feminism claimed that women were more naturally virtuous and sympathetic and were therefore more suitable for effecting social change through their domestic influence. Karlyn Campbell explains that by accepting traditional roles for women while arguing that their "distinctive influence should be extended to areas outside the home," social feminism provided a way for women to enter the public sphere without challenging masculine authority (*Man* 121). Matthews concluded, "When living up to her highest development, woman has done much to make lasting history, by her stimulating influence and there can be no greater responsibility than that, and this is the highest privilege granted to her by the Creator of the Universe" (146).

Interwoven deliberative features admonish blacks to produce their own "race" literature throughout the address. In the closing section, however, Matthews specifically urged further research and writing in such "neglected fields" as art, neurology, mechanical science, and the African origins of ancient civilizations, still a contested area. She closed by repeating her earlier plea that past accomplishments be preserved for "the generations that shall come after us" (148). Matthews herself maintained a library of such materials. As one biographer wrote, "Long before the interest in Race Literature became general, she was an enthusiast on the subject and placed in the White Rose Home a choice collection of books written by and about the Negro in America, forming, as a white reporter wrote, 'One of the most unique special libraries in New York.' The books of this library were used by Mrs. Matthews as a basis for her class in Race history" (H. Brown 215).

The Audience

Now according to Bitzer, the best measure of a fitting response is whether the audience addressed has an interest in and is capable of mediating change or taking the action that the speaker advocates. This audience does not necessarily include everyone who has access to the message. As addressed communication, the message must be aimed at certain hearers or readers able to respond in a certain way. But the rhetor's role often is also to enable audiences to recognize their ability to respond or to invoke in them the desire to respond rather than to address them as fixed, fully empowered, and fully able and willing to respond. In many instances the hearers need to be made aware of their potential to respond in the way desired by the rhetor. The audience then becomes invoked as much as addressed, invited to participate reciprocally in the rhetorical act.[8] In Matthews's audience were many of the contributors to race literature, named in the speech's epideictic portions, who would have known the various cited literary works. They functioned within the black public sphere, a sphere clearly different from the exclusionary and idealized Habermasian bourgeoisie public sphere occupied by a white male elite.[9] Instead it can be thought of as an alternative public sphere, in this instance, a "black counterpublic" (Dawson 203).[10] The conference itself served as one of many nineteenth-century sites for black counterpublic critique. Venues like the National Baptist Conventions and the Hampton Negro Conferences, local gatherings at the Richmond, Virginia, First African Baptist Church, the pages of the various newspapers, and meetings of the Tuskegee Woman's Club also served this same purpose. The empirical audience, those physically present, also, then, constituted the target audience, those Matthews wanted to reach because of their potential as agents of change. One can imagine that in addition to the empirical audience, Matthews also had in mind typical readers of the *Woman's Era*, like the members of the Woman's Loyal Union of New York and Brooklyn, the Woman's Club of Omaha, and the Tuskegee Woman's Club. Challenging them to produce more race literature, Matthews invited her auditors to extend their intellectual activities; audience addressed became audience invoked.

Earlier women writers had stressed the need for black self-definition through literature. Frances Harper invoked the same sentiment, less critically, in her didactic novel *Iola Leroy, or Shadows Uplifted* (1892), when Frank Latimer encourages the title character, Iola, to write a book: "Miss Leroy, out of the race must come its own thinkers and writers. Authors belonging to the white race have written good racial books, for which I am deeply grateful, but it seems to be almost impossible for a white man to put himself completely in our place. No man can feel the iron which enters another man's soul" (263). Gertrude Mossell, in "A Sketch of Afro-American Literature," a chapter from her book titled *The Work of the Afro-American Woman*, summarized a list of contributions to race literature with the claim that the "race is making history, making literature; he who would know the Afro-American of this present day must read the books written by this people to know what message they bear to the race and to the nation" (60). As one example of such literature, Mossell devoted several pages to a discussion of Matthews's "Aunt Lindy."

The Constraints

The other component of a rhetorical situation is its constraints or the opportunities and limitations associated with the situation. One can imagine that for Matthews such a gathering presented more opportunities than limitations. She faced an audience of her peers, certainly roused and ready to respond and already responding in a variety of ways. There was no reason to expect resistance or hostility—she was indeed preaching to the converted. She could comfortably allude to a variety of literary works confident that most in her audience had read or were at least familiar with them, for after all, these were the best and brightest of "race women." In a way then the range of evidence she offered served as reminders, rehearsals of the literary abuses of their day. And it was logical that she would invoke this kind of plea, a plea to produce a body of literature, because of her own background as a writer and journalist. Further, it was natural for her to speak on a subject in which she held a deep and abiding interest.

One salient psychological constraint on this occasion may have been

Matthews's prior ethos—the opinions held about her before the speech event. Aristotle believed that a favorable view of the speaker's character was the most persuasive appeal. In Book I of *The Rhetoric of Aristotle*, he wrote: "It is not true, as some writers on the art maintain, that the probity of the speaker contributes nothing to his persuasiveness; on the contrary, we might almost affirm that the character [ethos] is the most potent of all the means to persuasion" (9). While Aristotle was primarily concerned with character "as created by the speech itself," it is important, in this instance, to consider possible residual persuasive influence emanating from her prior ethos as well. By all accounts, Matthews, the consummate scholar, was a forceful if impatient leader. Frances Keyser, one of her closest associates, remembered her as follows:

Perhaps because in her ideas she was far in advance of the times in which she lived, possibly no woman was more greatly misunderstood. Her enthusiasm and quick grasp of any situation, together with a certain dramatic quality gave her a forceful, decided manner of speaking that was not always understood. Urged on by her eager, restless spirit and that foresight which enable her to see the end, she could not always wait for others to see, but seemed impelled to carry out her plans immediately, as if there might not be time enough to do all that had to be done. (H. Brown 215)

The Conference Souvenir edition of the *Woman's Era* included no mention of reactions to Matthews's speech but does comment on her participation in general, declaring, "To many minds Mrs. Matthews was the 'star' of the convention; so devoted was she to the interests of the Conference that Boston saw comparatively little in a social way of this gifted woman." The same issue later described her as "full of fire and intensity, with natural gifts as a speaker and writer" (*Woman's Era* August 1895, 15, 19). These comments suggest generally high regard for Matthews's abilities, her intellect, and her organizational skills, which no doubt enhanced her persuasive appeal.

If there is anything surprising about this speech, it is the breadth and depth of knowledge it displays. Matthews probably had less formal education than most of the women who addressed the conference. Margaret Murray Washington, who spoke on the same night, had completed both the preparatory and college courses at Fisk University in Nashville, Tennessee; Anna Cooper, who spoke on the opening day, was an 1884 graduate of Oberlin College; Josephine Ruffin, conference organizer, finished her education in the Boston public schools; and Selena Sloan Butler, who spoke the following morning, was graduated from the Spelman Seminary in Atlanta.[11] Matthews, in contrast, was forced after a successful start to drop out of the New York public schools and go to work because of family problems. Still, as the March 14, 1907, *New York Age* obituary pointed out, this limited formal schooling "by no means gives an adequate idea of the education of the woman who was a great reader and thinker, being one of the best read women in the country" (Keyser 6).

As a public intellectual, fiercely dedicated to "race" work, Matthews preferred the term "Afro-American" over "colored" or "Negro." In this speech, Matthews alluded to one source of her objection to "colored": "But all this impious wrong has made a Race Literature a possibility, even a necessity to dissipate the odium conjured up by the term 'colored' persons, not originally perhaps designed to humiliate, but unfortunately still used to express not only an inferior order, but to accentuate and call unfavorable attention to the most ineradicable difference between the races" (128). The objection here was to a focus on physical features. In 1896, during merger negotiations between the NFA-AW and the National League of Colored Women, Matthews strongly objected to the chosen name, the National Association of Colored Women. According to the conference minutes, Matthews stated that

she had African blood in her veins and was of African descent, which entitled her to the name Afro. While this was true, having been born in America, she was an American citizen and entitled to all the privileges as such, although many of these rights are constantly denied, she was entitled to the name American, therefore she claimed that the Negro in America was entitled to the name Afro-American as much as the French, Franco-American, or the English, Anglo-American; as for the name "colored," it meant nothing to the Negro race. She was not a colored American, but an Afro-American." (*History* 45)

Matthews justified her preference in arguments that resonate in still unresolved late-twentieth-century debates about what Americans of African descent should call themselves.

When we consider the speech's strong emphasis on defining and defending race history, addressed to an audience of women, and a few men, clearly in a position to produce just the kind of material Matthews called for, her response seems entirely fitting. She was speaking to the pressing issues of her time, issues not limited to those raised by one disparaging letter. It was addressed to an audience in a position to act, with a desire to act, and certainly with the ability to act. Many had, in fact, already begun to meet the challenge she put before them. Yet the historical context, the rhetorical structure, and the fit of Matthews's speech may be less significant than its present-day implications. Matthews's exhortations to produce a race literature are just as urgent today; it is still the case that those who hold the pen tell the story and shape the consciousness of a nation.

Two weeks prior to the 1895 conference in Boston, the Society of Christian Endeavor held its fourteenth annual convention in the same city. The Society, organized in Maine in 1881, evolved into an international interdenominational youth movement with a membership of over 1.5 million by 1893 (Chalmers 45). Regarding this convention, Josephine Ruffin wrote in her "Call of Meeting of '95":

The Christian Endeavor Society brings to Boston fifty thousand delegates in July, railroad rates all over the country are consequently reduced. Many colored women come to Boston at that time as delegates to this Convention. The assured presence in this city of so many representative women is too good an opportunity for a coming together to be missed. (*History* 4)

While it is not clear how many women actually stayed over for the Conference of Colored Women, Ruffin's observation tells us something about the attendance at these conventions and the level of participation among black women. Matthews was subsequently invited to "represent the Negro Women of America" at the Society's Sixteenth International Convention in San Francisco in 1897 (Keyser 6). In celebration of what was apparently considered to be a prestigious speaking invitation, a special program was held, prior to Matthews's departure, at St. Mark's Methodist Episcopal Church in New York, attended by prominent race leaders, including Booker T. Washington, at which letters of congratulations were read (Keyser 6). Since this was the sixteenth consecutive gathering of this body, there was no precipitating exigence as with the Boston conference of black women. It is not clear why Matthews was chosen over other likely candidates to fill this role of woman race representative—perhaps someone heard her Boston speech—but considering the recognition Matthews received from her peers, having been selected must have been a significant accomplishment. That she was chosen "to represent the Negro Women of America" suggests that few, if any, other black women were slated to speak. Speaking on Sunday, July 11, the day before the close of the conference, Matthews followed a Dr. Kin Eca da Silva, whose address titled "How to Reach the Hearts of Oriental Women" asked the audience to pray that "God will send his spirit to women in Oriental lands ("Society" 200).

Returning, then, to Miller's definition of exigence, one can ask how Matthews seized upon this "socially recognizable way" to make her private views public. The speech she delivered, "The Awakening of the Afro-American Woman," presents a contrasting rhetorical performance by Matthews. On this occasion, she addressed a predominantly white audience of Christian women concerning the progress of the race, particularly its women. As a rhetorical situation often repeated in postbellum America, it elicited responses that revealed—harking back to Simons's phrase—"distinctive and recurring patterns of rhetorical practice." While individual speakers filled certain generic slots with a particular cause or special interest, each remained, at the same time, within a predictable frame. Thus, "The Awakening of the Afro-American Woman" assumed features of previous responses designed to highlight what black women had accomplished since emancipation. Typically, the speaker first reminded the listeners of past slavery horrors, with indirect references to enslaved women's sexual exploitation. We find in this speech the same tendency exhibited by other speakers to discuss this subject obliquely. Fannie Williams's 1893 address—"The Intellectual Progress of the Colored Woman of the United States Since the Emancipation Proclamation"—to the World's Congress of Representative Women in Chicago is one earlier example of this genre, delivered under similar circumstances—black woman speaking to white women about black women's postbellum progress. Nearly halfway through her speech, Williams broached the subject with the following opening phrase of apology: "I regret the necessity of speaking to the question of the moral progress of our women." She later used this language to attribute "moral imperfection" to the former enslaved: "While I duly appreciate the offensiveness of all references to American slavery, it is unavoidable to charge to that system every moral imperfection that mars the character of the colored American" (703). As in "The Awakening of the Afro-American Woman," the abuses are couched in an indirect language crafted to protect Victorian and Christian sensibilities.

Describing the plight of black women to the San Francisco audience, Matthews proclaimed: "They had no past to which they could appeal for anything. It [slavery] had destroyed, more than in the men, all that a woman holds sacred, all that ennobles womanhood. She had but the future" (151). Such circumlocutions as "the caprice of brutal power and passion," a womanhood "locked in . . . moral eclipse," "the shame," "the debasement," and "despoiled attributes" provided Matthews with a set of verbal filters through which to portray the reality of the sexual abuse of slavery. Even in "Some of the Dangers Confronting Southern Girls in the North," Matthews's speech to black women about black women being led into prostitution, Matthews never used the word, referring instead to "sin-stained years of city life," use for "immoral purposes," making "money out of their helplessness and ignorance," "entertaining promiscuous company," and becoming "part of [a] circle of wickedness and depravity." In "The Awakening of the Afro-American Woman," Matthews's most explicit reference was deflected somewhat in a section that looked ahead to a Christian future: "I believe the God who brought them out of the Valley of the Shadow, who snatched them from the hand of the white rapist, the base slave master whose unacknowledged children are to be found in every hamlet of the Republic, guided these women, and guides them in the supreme work of building their Christian homes" (152). She had reminded them earlier in the speech of her own previous enslavement: "As I stand here to-day clothed in the garments of Christian womanhood, the horrible days of slavery, out of which I came, seem as a dream that is told, some horror incredible" (150). This personal reference, one of only a few in Matthews's public discourse, reminded her auditors of slavery's many contradictions—a former slave now addressing them in her "garments of Christian womanhood" and, additionally, looking very much like them.

In such responses, next came the wonder that given their low beginnings, black women had accomplished as much as they had, in large part, with little help from those being addressed. Matthews stated: "She has done it almost without any assistance from her white sister; who, in too large a sense, has left her to work out her own destiny in fear and trembling. . . . The marvel is not that they have succeeded, not that they are succeeding, but that they did not fail, *utterly fail*" (152; emphasis in original). With this pattern, exceptions were generally made for those white women who traveled South after the war to help educate the masses: "I am not unmindful, however, of the Northern women who went into the South after the war as the missionary goes into the dark places of the world" (152). Then there was the final admonition that much more remained to be done and the closing appeal to their common Christianity. Matthews concluded, "I feel moved to speak here in this wise for a whole race of women whose rise or fall, whose happiness or sorrow, whose degradation or exaltation are the concern of Christian men and women everywhere" (155).[12]

Declaring that "home is the noblest, the most sacred spot in a Christian nation," Matthews pointed to black women's role in home building as a miraculous accomplishment, claiming:

> From such small beginnings she was compelled to construct a home. She who had been an outcast, the caprice of brutal power and passion, who had been educated to believe that morality was an echo, and womanly modesty a name; she who had seen father and brother and child torn from her and hurried away into everlasting separation—this creature was born to life in an hour and expected to create a home. (151)

She crafted this occasion into an opportunity to present black women as having achieved nearly the impossible. Perhaps to make their progress appear even more amazing, Matthews created the impression that prior to emancipation, black women had no sense of home or family. Fannie Barrier Williams had used the same argument in 1893:

> In the mean vocabulary of slavery there was no definition of any of the virtues of life. The meaning of such precious terms as marriage, wife, family, and home could not be learned in a school-house. The blue-back speller, the arithmetic, and the copy-book contain no magical cures for inherited inaptitudes for the moralities. Yet it must ever be counted as one of the most wonderful things in human history how promptly and eagerly these suddenly liberated women tried to lay hold upon all that there is in human excellence. ("Intellectual" 697)

Studies of slave culture clearly indicate that this was not the case.[13] The heroic and successful efforts of Matthews's own mother to regain legal custody of four of her children in the face of numerous legal difficulties serve as one among many examples of slave women's drive to recreate and reconstruct family units. But for these audiences the sharp before-and-after contrasts may have had a stronger impact.

Proclaiming to be "clothed in the garments of Christian womanhood," Matthews dressed her speech in the language of Christian discourse. She appealed to the common Christianity shared by her auditors and black women. The adjective "Christian" is applied to various concepts—including nation, womanhood, homes, work, virtues, law, opinion, and government—over twenty times in what was probably a twenty-minute speech. This too is in marked contrast to "The Value of Race Literature," a much longer speech, with only five references to Christianity. Clearly, Matthews was aware of the differing appeals needed to reach an audience of prominent black women assembled in response to continued disparagement, on the one hand, and a group of white Christian men and women, far removed from such a crisis, on the other.

Striking as well was Matthews's development of the growth metaphor, comparing the progress of the black woman after emancipation with the budding of a flower. This was the same metaphor Anna Cooper invoked in "Womanhood a Vital Element in the Regeneration and Progress of a Race" (see chapter 5). Cooper, also extolling the black woman, described her as a "delicate plantlet," declaring that there must be "life in the plant germ" if the race is to thrive. Matthews's plant imagery was also structurally similar to Chalmers's *The Juvenile Revival; or The Philosophy of the Christian Endeavor Movement* (1893), which develops around this growth metaphor. Chapters are titled "The Soil," "The Season," "The Seed," "The Blade," "The Ear," and "The Full Corn"; Matthews may have been familiar with the work. Building upon this metaphor, Matthews retraced the accomplishments of women whose roots stemmed from the soil of slavery and who, in spite of these degrading beginnings, could be credited with establishing Christian homes, contributing to economic stability and educational advancement, supporting black church memberships, and motivating a new generation of educated black women to establish organizations like the NFA-AW.

To fill the generic slot of special concern, Matthews took this rhetorical opportunity to make what was perhaps one of the most direct appeals for changes in the laws forbidding interracial marriages during this era. Wells, in her 1892 Lyric Hall address, "Southern Horrors," had also discussed the miscegenation laws of the South, in the context of lynch law, pointing out that "they only operate against the legitimate union of the races; they leave the white man free to seduce all the colored girls he can, but it is death to the colored man who yields to the force and advances of a similar attraction in white women" (6). Speaking the language of domestic discourse, Matthews, in contrast, focused on the consequences of such laws to families: "As long as the affections are controlled by legislation in defiance of Christian law, making infamous the union of black and white, we shall have unions without the sanction of law, and children without legal parentage, to the degradation of black womanhood and the disgrace of white manhood" (154). Drawing on her own social reform work and information gathered during her travels in the South, Matthews closed by requesting support for proper care of old and incapacitated persons and for improved conditions in Southern penal institutions. Williams chose to focus special attention on discriminatory employment practices, pointing out that "except teaching in colored schools and menial work, colored women can find no employment in this free America" (705).

Both Williams and Matthews returned to the anticipated closing appeal to common Christian sentiments. However, they transformed this traditional closing supplication, associated with religious address, into an opportunity to claim their right to citizenship by reminding their white auditors that they too observed the basic tenets of civilization's alleged foundation, Christianity. Williams placed her most explicit use of this tactic in an earlier portion of her speech: "It has always been a circumstance of the highest satisfaction to the missionary effort of the Christian church that the colored people are so susceptible to *a religion that marks the highest point of blessedness in human history*" ("Intellectual" 699; emphasis added). Matthews's supplication served also as the last sentence of her 1897 address:

I feel moved to say in conclusion that in all Christian and temperance work, in all that lifts humanity from its fallen condition to a more perfect resemblance of Him in whose image it was made, in all that goes to make our common humanity stronger and better and more beautiful; the Afro-American women of the Republic will "do their duty as God shall give them light to do it." (155)

While over fifty thousand delegates attended these conventions, we can imagine that Matthews spoke to some smaller component of that body, perhaps a women's gathering. Frequent references in the speech to the organization's "Christian womanhood" suggest that Matthews anticipated such a collective. On this occasion, Matthews delivered a lyrical speech filled with plant metaphors and the contrasting imagery of darkness and light, and snatches of poetry from Henry Wadsworth Longfellow, Lord Byron, and William Cowper, to engage the audience, along with high praise for the accomplishments of black women, presented in the language of domestic discourse. Matthews followed the pattern of speeches given on similar occasions but shaped it to her purpose of elevating black women. She took advantage of this rhetorical opportunity to achieve the goal (a goal that also serves as the title of this chapter) expressed in the following passage from "Awakening of the Afro-American Woman":

If there had been no other awakening than this, if this woman who had stood upon the auction block possessed of no rights that a white man was bound to respect, and none which he did respect, if there had been no other awakening of the Afro-American woman than this, that she made a home for her race, an abiding place for husband, and son, and daughter, it would be glory enough to embalm her memory in song and story. (153)

In closing, I want to return to my opening claim that Victoria Matthews served as a prototype of the emerging black woman public intellectual. Incorporating portions of Dyson's definition, I characterize the public intellectual as one who, addressing various publics, draws on considerable critical resources to help resolve complex public problems. Of course, what constitutes a "public problem" is determined, to some extent, by the rhetor herself. For example, Matthews was able to demonstrate to the Society of Christian Endeavor audience that antimiscegenation laws resulted in general family degradation, not just shame to those involved. Further, as Nancy Fraser notes, the term "publics" rejects the "class- and gender-biased notion of publicity, one that accepts at face value the bourgeois public's claim to be *the* public" (116). These various publics, to the extent that they push against and offer alternative perspectives to the bourgeois public, can be thought of as counterpublics. But as the black counterpublic of the late nineteenth century became predominantly male and patriarchal, in imitation of bourgeois norms, black women public intellectuals like Matthews and Ida Wells found themselves in the position of having to create discursive spaces within a range of exclusionary oppositional counterpublics (Dawson 200–207). As a journalist, Matthews met this challenge particularly though letters, columns, and articles in the *Woman's Era*, addressing such public problems as the need for black women to form a national organization and the Atlanta "Lynch Law Resolution." As a writer, she reached various reading publics through her short fiction, all extant work published in the *AME Church Review*, which depicted enduring black characters. As a speaker, she reached various publics through lectures to black and white women's groups on the "public problems" of young black women's sexual exploitation, misrepresentations of blacks in literature, and antimiscegenation laws. Matthews ultimately reached various publics through her activism, organizing the testimonial for Ida

Wells, founding the Woman's Loyal Union, helping to launch the National Association of Colored Women, investigating the treatment of youth on the chain gang, and establishing the White Rose Industrial Association. For public intellectual Victoria Matthews, each rhetorical opportunity represented an occasion for social action and a chance to demonstrate the humanity of the race.

7

"Can Woman Do This Work?"
The Discourse of Racial Uplift

We would prescribe: homes—better homes, clean homes, pure homes; schools—better schools; more culture; more thrift; and work in large doses; put the patient at once on this treatment and continue through life. Can woman do this work? She can; and she must do her part, and her part is by no means small.

—Lucy Laney, "The Burden of the Educated Colored Woman" 1899

The late 1880s saw a marked deterioration in the status of blacks throughout the South, a resurgence of mob violence, and repression of civil rights. Out of fear, economic competition, frustration, and the drive to control came the numerous provisions that made this a low point in American history. The Supreme Court's 1883 declaration that the civil rights bill was unconstitutional spawned legislation that attempted to ban practically all activities that would bring black and white people into close proximity: living, riding, drinking, marrying, playing sports—including checkers in Birmingham, Alabama—going to school, and dying; even prisons and asylums were segregated. As Ida Wells pointed out in the introduction to her lynching report, *A Red Record*, when blacks were no longer enslaved, they posed a threat to the political and economic supremacy that whites had claimed for their own. In 1884, when Grover Cleveland became the first democratic president elected since the Civil War, there was much concern among the black leadership. But President Cleveland steered "dead center" with respect to black civil rights, making few changes at all (R. Logan 61). It was during the term of Republican president Benjamin Harrison, the second term of Cleveland, and the first term of William McKinley—the period from 1889 to 1901—that blacks felt most severely the Southern Democrats' counterattacks against legislative efforts to improve their condition. In 1896, with *Plessy* v. *Ferguson*, the Supreme Court made legal the doctrine of separate but equal. Mobile, Alabama, established a 10:00 P.M. curfew for blacks. Black people were disfranchised through grandfather clauses attached to literacy and property tests. George H. White, the last black congressman of the post-Reconstruction era, completed his term in 1901, at the end of McKinley's first administration.

As one of the respondents to the query "The Democratic Return to Power—Its Effect?" in the fall 1884 issue of *AME Church Review*, Frances Harper advised that black people concentrate less on external politics and more on developing internal moral and spiritual resources: "If for the next twenty years the colored people take no feverish interest in the success or failure of either party, but will do all they can to build up an intelligent and virtuous manhood, and a tender, strong and true womanhood, we can afford to wait for political strength while developing moral and spiritual power" (223). Harper's was not a call for accommodation but an appeal for self-improvement in the midst of adversity.

As if in response to such advice, black public intellectuals turned inward, partially in the belief that middle-class respectability would eventually make the masses more acceptable to whites. But racial uplift's inward gaze also developed out of the belief that through education, economic independence, and sanitary living conditions, black people could thrive. As this chapter makes clear, the audience for their persuasive discourse was rarely white; although a dominant white society serves as ground, black empowerment emerges as figure. In speeches to their black sisters during this period, prominent women educators and religious leaders also responded by advancing the agenda of racial uplift. While the term "uplift" carried with it the assumption that those being lifted occupied inferior positions and that they needed to be elevated to a more socially acceptable level, these speeches acknowledge inferiority only as a direct consequence of slavery, not as an innate and indelible trait. To remove this taint of an inferior and "downtrodden" race, black intellectuals argued for improvement in the material conditions of black people.

In 1894, the Woman's Era Club of Boston chose as its slogan "Make the World Better." Representatives of the NACW organized and spoke under the motto "Lifting As We Climb." The commitment to uplift was evident as well in informal discourse. Josephine Silone Yates, who later served as second president of the NACW, signed an August 1894 letter—"Yours for the race"—to the *Woman's Era* (9), echoing a similar closing used by Mary Ann Shadd Cary forty-five years earlier in a letter—"Yours for a better condition"—to Frederick Douglass (Cary, Letter 33). Both expressions were common letter closings, indicative of the prevailing commitment to the racial uplift work of improving conditions for black people in nineteenth-century America.

These prominent activists cast themselves as race women, privileging their reform activities over their wage-earning activities. Historian Sharon Harley, writing about black women workers in the late nineteenth and early twentieth centuries, points out that they often took greater pride in their home and community work than in the work they performed for pay (47). Racial uplift was their real work, the work that held their passion. Victoria Matthews, a leading organizer of black women, issued a circular in 1896 called "Work Before Our Women," encouraging them to form local clubs. Matthews was concerned that the newly formed NACW become a "truly National Association, representing all conditions of our women" ("An Open Appeal" 2), a concern indicating the organizers' desire to be representative rather than elitist. The club women were surely aware of their apparent duplicity as models of what society assumed all black women could become, given opportunity, on the one hand, yet also spokespersons for those women who had been denied opportunity, on the other. They were reaching out to other black women and seeking strength from unity, circling the wagons, so to speak, in defense against the ill will of this period.

In educator Lucy Laney's 1899 speech at the third Hampton Negro Conference, "The Burden of the Educated Colored Woman," she raised the question that serves as the title of this chapter, "Can woman do this work?" For Laney and the women to whom she spoke, this "work" was racial uplift. While concerned with the improvement of conditions for both women and men, these "race women" viewed racial uplift as having a great deal to do with educating black women to assume the traditional roles defined by the cult of true womanhood. The cult of true womanhood proclaimed "homemaker" the true vocation for woman. In this view, her true feminine, spiritual nature was fulfilled by creating a peaceful home, separated from the struggles of the marketplace. But we will see that while these women argued for this kind of training for homemaking, their public discourse also addressed the urgency of improving working conditions for black women in public spaces. They already knew what Elisabeth Fiorenza would write a hundred years later: "This praise of femininity conveniently overlooks that poor and unmarried women cannot afford to stay 'at home'; it overlooks the violence done to women and children in the home, and it totally mistakes patriarchal dependency for Christian family" (348). Further, it assumed that staying at home was always preferable.

While this chapter focuses on the rhetorical activities of black women during the last two decades of the nineteenth century, it should be remembered that discussions about the improvement of employment options and working conditions for black women prevailed throughout the century. As early as 1832, before there were nationally organized women's groups, Maria Stewart articulated employment concerns in her Franklin Hall address, when she described the difficulty black Boston women had gaining other than domestic work:

I have asked several individuals of my sex, who transact business for themselves, if providing our girls were to give them the most satisfactory references, they would not be willing to grant them an equal opportunity with others? Their reply has been—for their own part, they had no objection; but as it was not the custom, were they to take them into their employ, they would be in danger of losing the public patronage. (45)

The impact of Mary Ann Shadd Cary's rhetoric in support of women's labor rights was felt at the Colored National Labor Union Convention in 1860. After her address to the body, a resolution was passed that "as unjust discrimination in the departments of labor is made against women . . . colored women be cordially included in the invitation to further and organize cooperative societies" (Foner and Lewis 55). In a speech to the Women's Congress, published in the January 1878 issue of *Englishwoman's Review*, Frances Harper recalled the many independent black working women she had met during her travels throughout the Reconstruction South. She described women who raised poultry and hogs, farmed, sold baked goods, manufactured sugar, and engaged in bookkeeping, many of them using their income to buy their own homes without the assistance of men (Harper, "Coloured" 10–15).

Writing about Baptist women who lectured to Northern white women during the last two decades of the century, historian Evelyn Brooks Higginbotham observes that "[t]hese black women articulated eloquently through their words and example the merit of 'woman's work for woman' " (*Righteous* 102). Their words advocated for broader definitions of work that honored the dignity of all honest labor and, at the same time, challenged audiences to engage in what they deemed the most honorable work of all—the work of race uplift.

The persuasive discourse selected for analysis was produced in this context, much of it presented at church and educators' conferences convened in the late 1880s and the 1890s, specifically to discuss problems of blacks in the nadir. I selected church discourse since the church served a central role in black women's racial uplift work. Darlene Clark Hine reminds us that black women, through various church clubs, performed numerous services, even though, especially in Baptist churches, they did not hold official leadership positions. She writes that "[w]hen disasters of economic depression, bankruptcy, and disease struck the black communities in each decade from the collapse of Reconstruction to the Great Depression in the 1930s, black church women were there to keep communities functioning. They created orphanages and launched philanthropies to help widows and the aged. They taught Sunday schools, did missionary work, and participated in endless fund-raising drives to pay off church mortgages. The church rests most securely upon the backs of black women" (57). Two speeches delivered at the 1886 and 1887 meetings of the American National Baptist Convention (ANBC) by Lucy Wilmot Smith and Mary Cook, Kentucky churchwomen, are considered, along with an essay by Cook, as examples of racial uplift discourse addressed to black church women. These texts carry the expectation that every women will contribute what she can to the common goal. They do not so much argue for racial uplift as for support of its various manifestations. At the same time, both Smith and Cook were educators.

Speeches and essays from the publications of educational institutions were chosen in acknowledgment of the long-standing value placed on literacy as a means to freedom and opportunity. Education, in the view of black women, also expanded employment options and freed them from the sexual harassment too frequently associated with domestic work. Selected addresses to the second Atlanta University Conference for the Study of Problems Concerning Negro City Life of 1897 reveal the extent to which racial uplift for women was interpreted as education for home uplift. Speeches by Lucy Laney, Adella Hunt Logan, Georgia Swift King, and Selena Sloan Butler serve as sources of evidence. The final section is an analysis of two papers presented at the Hampton Negro Conferences of 1898 and 1899—Matthews's "Some of the Dangers Confronting Southern Girls in the North" and Laney's "The Burden of the Educated Colored Woman"—and an article by Anna Julia Cooper in the August

1899 *Southern Workman and Hampton School Record*, "Colored Women as Wage-Earners."[1] At the time that they wrote and spoke, these women were already committed to racial uplift work. This chapter as a whole considers the distinctive persuasive features of these texts as they argue support for the racial uplift work of black women and for the uplift of black women's work. The chapter points to the strengths and limitations of a discourse that—while it demands respect for the work of women—still views it essentially as supportive of and subordinate to the real work performed by men. At the same time, it considers the extent to which these women engaged language to promote empowerment from within.

Women's Work: Racial Uplift and Church Work

Lucy Wilmot Smith was only twenty-five years old when she delivered her address called "The Future Colored Girl" to the newly formed ANBC, gathered in St. Louis on August 25–29, 1886. Although women delegates attended the meetings, the majority of those present were men. The president of the Convention, the Reverend William J. Simmons, was also president of the State University at Louisville, Kentucky, where Smith taught. Further, Simmons was the chief male supporter of organized black Baptist Kentucky women, although he was opposed to a separate national organization. Women were more prominent in the ANBC than in the other two national black Baptist conventions—the Baptist Foreign Mission Convention and the national Baptist Educational Convention (Higginbotham, *Righteous* 64). They served on committees, delivered speeches to the convention, and held offices. Smith was elected ANBC historian in 1887.

Smith was born in Lexington, Kentucky, on November 16, 1861. At sixteen, when she was graduated from the Normal department of the State University at Louisville, Smith was already supporting herself and her mother. During her short life, Smith taught at State University, worked as a journalist, and, along with Mary Cook, was a leading organizer of the Baptist Women's Educational Convention of Kentucky. Dying in 1890, at the age of twenty-nine, Smith did not witness the formation of the national women's convention, which she helped to bring into existence.

An exploration of wage-earning options for black women in the late 1880s, "The Future Colored Girl" moves from the general to the specific. Starting on the banks of the Rhone and Arno rivers with an analogy, Smith compared the confluence of the rapidly rushing Arno and the steady, placid Rhone with the two approaches to black uplift education. Smith applauded the declining obsession with "the cramming of heads" to the neglect of the "other members of the body," emerging from the ongoing debate, most often associated with Booker T. Washington and W. E. B. Du Bois, around the kind of education most needed by black people during this period. She expressed dismay that at one time, "[h]onest toil was shunned and the highest ambition of those who had educational affairs in control seemed to be in cheating the humbler paths of labor of their rightful heritage to fill the pulpit and the teacher's chair" (L. Smith 68). A teacher herself, Smith stressed the need to educate hand as well as head, a need she argued was as important for young women as for young men. Smith's emphasis on training for manual labor and for intellectual work set the stage for her later iteration of employment options.

Exhibiting her knowledge of history, Smith explored with her audience varying attitudes toward women across time and cultures: French, Hindu, Korean, Greek, Hebrew, Roman, Sioux, and Russian. Smith was, after all, addressing a group of her intellectual peers. She landed her narrative in nineteenth-century America when women who deviated from expected behavior were labeled "strong-minded or masculine by those who forget that 'new occasions make new duties' " (69). Women, she pointed out, had always demonstrated leadership ability in such fields as science, political economy, politics, literature, philanthropy, oratory, and the fine arts. Smith here pulled away from conventional views of women as submissive, voiceless objects of affection.

Smith reminded her audience that women had always been conceded the right to an occupation but that they especially needed respectable occupations when so many had to support themselves and when employment options remained limited. At that point, she addressed black women's labor conditions in particular. Funneling to the specific concerns of black women was a tactic of arrangement adopted by other black women speakers of the century. Rather than begin immediately with the central concern, speakers like Fannie Barrier Williams and Anna Cooper (discussed in chapter 5) employ this big history approach, locating black women within the larger universal realm. Fifty-four years after Maria Stewart's Franklin Hall Speech, Smith pointed again to the limited career options for the black woman. She wisely recognized that while much discussion centered on her moral, physical, and intellectual status, few were paying attention to "how she makes her way as a laborer" other than in domestic work (70). In her 1832 call for fair hiring practices, Maria Stewart did not belittle domestic work: "I do not consider it derogatory, my friends, for persons to live out to service" (47). Smith, as well, argued merely for more options. Further, Smith proposed that black girls avoid the city, a proposition repeated most emphatically by Victoria Matthews in her 1898 speech titled "Some of the Dangers Confronting Southern Girls in the North" (discussed below). Instead of traveling North, Smith recommended, young women should earn money through independent self-employment in such trades as poultry-keeping, small-fruit raising, dairying, lecturing, photography, and medicine.

Smith revealed what some might interpret as feminist leanings in the section supporting work in journalism, when she wrote, "We need papers and magazines edited *by* women *for* women," and in the section supporting work in medicine, when she wrote, "I think all surgical operations on women should be performed only by women" (73), lending her support to a medical school founder's claim that women were best suited to take care of women. Nonetheless, as Higginbotham writes, "Smith could subordinate easily, almost imperceptibly, her feminist consciousness to that of race" (*Righteous* 144). For example, in an article first published in the February 23, 1889, *Indianapolis Freeman*, she generously praised black men for their support of black women:

The educated Negro woman occupies vantage found over the Caucasian woman of America, in that the former has had to contest with her brother every inch of the ground for recognition, the Negro man, having had his sister by his side on plantations and in rice swamps, keeps her there, now that he moves in other spheres. As she wins laurels he accords her the royal crown. This is especially true in journalism. Doors are opened before we knock, and as well equipped young women emerged from the class-room the brotherhood of the race, men whose energies have been repressed and distorted by the interposition of circumstances, give them opportunities to prove themselves; and right well are they doing this by voice and pen. (Dann 61)

Smith's own career as a journalist began in 1888, when William Simmons founded *Our Women and Children*, with Smith as head of the woman's department, Mary Cook as editor of the educational department, and Ida B. Wells as editor of the home department. Although Wells writes in her autobiography that the "lavish" salary of one dollar weekly Simmons offered would be her first as a journalist, Smith did not stress wage-earning potential in her discussions of newspaper work, lecturing, and medicine (*Crusade* 32). Shifting instead to an imperative, racial uplift mode, Smith emphasized the necessity for women in these professions: "We *need* papers," "Our girls *must* play the part of healer," "Our girls *must* qualify themselves to rectify these evils," "reform in the home-life of our people *must* be agitated" (emphasis added). This seamless shift to racial uplift imperatives indicates the extent to which nineteenth-century black women speakers frequently blurred the distinction between work for the race and work for wages. Through such claims, Smith made clear that any form of honest work uplifted the race as a whole but that certain professions lifted a heavier load.

Smith closed this speech expressing dismay that a girl is advised differently regarding the value of work, being told that since she will ultimately be supported by a husband, her labor outside the home is not important. Smith lamented that by "teaching her that . . . whatever field of labor she enters she will abandon after a few years [one] is teaching her to despise the true dignity of labor" (74). Her speech to the predominantly male audience, then, after an opening argument in support of broad occupational endeavors for all black laborers, ends on a strong feminist note, stressing the right of women to provide services for one another and to be trained for the same types of work, with the same expectation to work as men. This argument's persuasive force resides in its ability to promote more favorable working conditions and more varied working opportunities for black women ultimately within the context of racial uplift. It argues for the uplift of woman's work and for the work of racial uplift.

Smith's speech and the immediate rhetorical context are similar to a more expansive speech delivered on a parallel occasion that same year by Anna Julia Cooper. Cooper's "Womanhood A Vital Element in the Regeneration and Progress of a Race" (discussed in chapter five) was addressed to another body of black church men. At the age of twenty-eight, just two years after earning her bachelor's degree from Oberlin College, Cooper was invited to speak before the Convocation of Colored Clergy of the Protestant Episcopal Church held in Washington, D.C. Cooper also opened her speech with a general discussion of women's history, leading to a discussion of black women of the South and their special needs. Less interested in specific occupational options than Smith, Cooper, a lifelong Episcopalian, criticized the clergy for its failure to insist that the church act to protect young Southern black women. Here were two young black women challenging groups of older male church leaders to engage in man's work for woman. Both had been mentored by prominent leaders in their denominations—Cooper by Alexander Crummell; Smith by William J. Simmons—and both men had probably extended the invitations to speak. Cooper's arguments, however, were less grounded in practical needs and actions. Her black women are passive, belonging to "that large, bright, promising fatally beautiful class that stand shivering like a delicate plantlet before the fury of tempestuous elements," waiting to be lifted up and led (Cooper, "Womanhood" 61). Mary Helen Washington, in her introduction to *A Voice from the South*, talks about Cooper's apparent lack of identification with the ordinary black women for whom, but not to whom, she spoke: "Nothing in her essays suggests that they [Southern black women] existed in her imagination as audience or as peer" (xxx).[2] Cooper's discourse in this speech belongs squarely in the category of advocacy for the work of racial uplift rather than for the uplift of woman's work. Concerned that most of the true "workers for the race" had abandoned the Episcopalian Church, Cooper urged women and men with "unselfish souls" to "go into the highways and byways, lifting up and leading, advising and encouraging with the truly catholic benevolence of the Gospel of Christ" (*Voice* 33). Smith's women, conversely, are challenged to start their own businesses and forge a way for themselves. Speaking to rather than about the black women of the South, Smith endowed them with agency and proposed more progressive action, pressing for self-determination and self-employment: "Give the girl the same freedom in exercising as the boy, the same liberty of wearing loose clothes, the same mental food and she will accomplish the same work. I do not want the boys to have all the labor, the girls all the rest. Place them on the same footing by giving them the same education" (74). Cooper lived to be 106, with numerous opportunities to apply and refine her rhetorical skills and her thinking about black women and work. Smith died in 1890, four years after delivering this speech. In her eulogy for Smith, Mary Cook succinctly characterized her life of service and her persuasive style:

She was connected with all the leading interests of her race and denomination. Her pen and voice always designated her position so clearly that no one need mistake her motive. . . . Her highest ambition, and that to which she bent her energies, was to elevate woman to a moral, Christian standard, that better homes might be established, a higher type of boys and girls might be reared, and that the world might be made better by having good and noble women in it. (Cook, "Eulogy" 4–5)

Mary V. Cook, born in 1862 in Bowling Green, Kentucky, was also prominent in the black Baptist women's movement. Having limited resources, Cook attended the State University at Louisville, with support from Northern white Baptist churchwomen, and, like Smith, upon graduation from the Normal department, in 1883, she became a teacher at the institution.[3] In 1887, the same year that she received her bachelor's degree from the University, she spoke at the ANBC. Like Smith, Cook was also twenty-five when she spoke to the convention, presenting the first lecture in a symposium titled "Woman's Place in the Work of the Denomination."[4] The title of the symposium suggests to many a separate and perhaps marginalized role for women in the Baptist Church. For Cook, however, this distinct role emerged as a consequence of the prevailing nineteenth-century perception of intrinsic differences between male and female identities.

As did Smith and Cooper the previous year, Cook began her lecture by tracing changing perceptions of women throughout history—before and after the spread of Christianity. Cook described the low opinion held of women in most societies, concluding that conditions were the same for women "except where Christianity has emancipated her" ("Place" 46). She argued that Christian cultures, unlike ancient and contemporary non-Christian cultures, emancipated and elevated women, making women's work a prevalent topic of late nineteenth-century feminist discourse. Smith stops short of ascribing to Christianity the leading role in the uplift of women. But Anna Cooper, after giving partial credit to the Feudal System for this "ennobling ideal" in her 1886 speech to the Episcopalian clergy, concludes:

It seems not too much to say then of the vitalizing, regenerating, and progressive influence of womanhood on the civilization of to-day, that, while it was foreshadowed among Germanic nations in the far away dawn of their history as a narrow, sickly and stunted growth, it yet owes its catholicity and power, the deepening of its roots and broadening of its branches to Christianity. ("Womanhood" 18–19)

Of course, there were women who flatly disagreed with this view of Christianity; Elizabeth Cady Stanton's collection of essays titled *The Woman's Bible* rejects Christian teachings on the basis that they promote subordination of women. The controversy centered on whether this so-called elevation of women resulted in equality or simply a gender difference based on feminine qualities. Gender parity also fueled the controversy surrounding suffragists' arguments. Should women have the vote because they are the same as men or because of the unique qualities they bring to the political process?[5] Higginbotham, in *Righteous Discontent*, reminds us that black Baptist men themselves were not entirely clear about the proper "work" for churchwomen, as was indicated in an 1894 issue of the black newspaper, the *Virginia Baptist*. Two articles declared woman's roles in the church to be singing and praying and that teaching and preaching were in contradiction to divine authority. In an August 1894 editorial, the *Woman's Era* responded:

The writer of this article is evidently in earnest but sadly in need of enlightenment. . . . It is according to law, gospel, history and common sense that woman's place is where she is needed and where she fits in and to say that the place will affect her womanliness is bosh; womanliness is an attribute not a condition, it is not supplied or withdrawn by surroundings. . . . ("Editorial" 8)

Complicating the definition of women's church work even further was the influence of romantic racialism, a belief that African peoples were more suited to Christianity, allegedly because of their more humane nature, their "cheerfulness, sympathy, [and] willingness to serve" (Fredrickson 70). Since these attributes tend also to be associated with women, the belief led to the assigning of essentialist "feminine traits" to African people, both male and female, and the assigning of "masculine traits" to all white people. Theodore Tilton, white abolitionist, once called blacks the "feminine race of the world" (qtd. in Higginbotham, *Righteous* 146). Doubly constrained, black churchwomen who wanted to participate in traditionally "masculine" leadership roles had to overcome both gender and racial stereotypes of their proper place. Even Lucy Laney, in her 1899 speech to the Hampton Negro convention, invoked the argument that women were more naturally fitted for uplift work, because "their maternal instinct makes them patient and sympathetic" ("Burden" 343). Black women produced an apparently bifurcated persuasive discourse during this period because they understood that work for the race had to be cast in the mold of the cult of true womanhood. Shaping uplift work to fit this mold allowed them to propose and perform it within the sphere of appropriate behavior for women. In her 1887 speech titled "A Woman's Place in the Work of the Denomination," Mary Cook wrote, "There is no necessity for a woman to step over the bounds of propriety, or to lay aside modesty, to further the work, and she will not, if God be her guide" (55).

Cook carefully negotiated the apparently contradictory roles for women in this address. After singing Christianity's praises, she pointed to the fact that much still needed to be corrected in nineteenth-century America. The government had done nothing, she charged, to correct infidelity, immorality, and indecency. These evils demanded the work and humanizing influence of Christian women: "It must come by woman's unswerving devotion to a pure and undefiled Christianity, for to that alone, woman owes her influence, her power and all she is" (46). To bolster this claim, Cook traced the role of women through biblical history, again following a standard arrangement for these speakers. She began with Eve, Miriam, and Deborah, pointing not just to their conventional work as women but to their roles as leaders, for, she continued, God "recognizes in His followers neither male nor female, heeding neither the 'weakness' of one, nor the strength of the other, but strictly calling those who are perfect at heart and willing to do his bidding" (47). Quoting Denis, a third century patron saint of France, and St. Ephiphanius, Cook described Mary, the mother of Jesus, as having Eurocentric features: a "dazzling beauty," whose "hair was blond; her face oval; her eyes bright and slightly olive in color; her eyebrows perfectly arched, her nose aquiline and of irreproachable perfection and her lips were ruby red" (48). This description foregrounds the extent to which Cook had accepted not only the tenets of the cult of true womanhood but also its standards of beauty. Cook then described other examples of woman's work in the New Testament. She challenged men, stating, "Emancipate woman from the chains that now restrain her and who can estimate the part she will play in the work of the denomination?" (49). As would Lucy Smith in her 1889 Indianapolis *Freeman* article, Cook reserved high praise for the treatment of women in the Baptist Church, declaring, "Every woman in the world ought to be a Baptist" (49).

In the next section, she turned her attention to the role of women in the denomination, inviting those without formal training or public speaking experience to take part in this effort. Black Baptist women's work appealed to women of every economic and class condition. Unlike the secular black women's organizations, formed in part because of rejection by white women's clubs, the Baptist women's convention emerged partially in resistance to an already established male hegemony with the church. Cook rebuts Paul's injunction in the New Testament (I Corinthians 14:34) that women keep silent in church, on the grounds that Paul was addressing a specific group of women at a specific point in the history of the church.[6] She wrote, "I know Paul said 'Let the woman keep silence in the churches' but because he addressed this to a few Grecian and Asiatic women who were wholly given up to idolatry and to the fashion of the day is no reason why it should be quoted to the pious women of the present" (50). She was optimistic about the increasingly prominent role women played in church work, predicting that "a change is coming; it has already commenced and God is shaking up the church—He is going to bring it up to something better and that, too, greatly through the work of the women. Already the harvest is great. Can ye not discern the signs of the times?" (50).

Throughout this speech, Cook blended traditional feminine roles with more activist roles: In one sentence she prescribed, "A good pastor should have a good wife. . . . She is to beautify his home and make it a place of peace and cheerfulness" (50). But in the same section, she also located the woman outside of the house, sending her into the "highways and hedges," compelling "sinners to come in," and still returning home in time to exert influence over her children. Cook later described the work of child rearing as "the most important" for women in the denomination (50–51, 54). The work of churchwomen for Cook, then, is expansive within the framework of nurture. Women should assist the pastor, teach Sunday school, care for the sick, and train their children. This is racial uplift work appropriately within the sphere of true womanhood.

In a section on women and newspaper work, Cook again placed women in limited public roles. She argued that as newspaper editors, women could reach large numbers of other women and children. She pointed out that as of 1887, no religious paper especially edited for black children existed. In the following year, William Simmons established *Our Women and Children*—specifically with the purpose of inspiring black women and children to achieve—with Cook as editor of the educational department. The work of women is defined then in a larger context of newspaper editing, but it is newspaper work essentially to support women's primary roles as caregivers.

In the section called "The Educational Work of the Denomination," Cook, in the context that black women held most of the precollege teaching positions, provided a historical overview of the contributions of women educators. Cook concluded that black Baptist women educators needed to teach church creed because "[n]ot one-half of the members of our churches can give a doctrinal reason why they are Baptists (52). Cook then argued that since woman can think, she should not be confined to the home: "The possession of mind," she asserted, "affords the strongest evidence that God created her for society" (52). So Cook here once again located her working black Baptist woman in "society," using as justification the fact that she possessed a mind. It seems clear at this point in the lecture that Cook will definitely leave her there. In one of the speech's most eloquent passages, Cook presses her point that women must carry out *public* work:

> It was when Christianity and infidelity were wrestling in Europe, that Hannah More came from retirement to take part in the contest.[7] It was when slavery was at its highest, that Phillis Wheatly [*sic*], Francis Ellen Harper, and Harriet Beecher Stowe, gave vent to the fullness of their souls in beautiful lines of poetry and prose. (52–53)

Cook also acknowledged the increasing importance of the "written voice" over the human voice and pushed for more women to write, at the same time that she echoed Lucy Smith's appeal for more women lecturers. She poignantly reminded the predominantly male audience that in some European cultures from the fifteenth to the nineteenth centuries, "it was not esteemed indiscreet for women to give lectures in public to crowded and admiring audiences" (53).

Cook continued the argument for women's right to participate in public discourse. She praised the reformist role women have played throughout history, mentioning in particular the temperance work of Frances Harper and Francis Willard, but argued again under the assumption of an essentialist, caregiving, nurturing role: "It belongs to woman's tender nature, sympathy, and love, to uplift the fallen. A home can not be raised above the mother, nor the race above the type of womanhood, and no women are more ready to respond to the call than the women of the Baptist church" (53). Minus its advocacy for black Baptist women, Cook's statement sounds much like an axiomatic statement from Cooper's speech to the Episcopalian clergy, when she writes, "A stream cannot rise higher than its source. The atmosphere of homes is no rarer and purer and sweeter than are the mothers in those homes. A race is but a total of families. The nation is the aggregate of its homes" ("Womanhood" 29). This clustering of maxims grounds both propositions in established wisdom.

It seems then that the church work of Cook's black woman radiates out from the home. Having located woman in the public sphere—advising, leading, teaching, lecturing, writing—Cook always attributed the source of ultimate satisfaction to her work in the home. Higginbotham points to the way in which black Baptist women "continually shifted back and forth from feminine to masculine metaphors," expressing "a dual gendered consciousness—defining themselves as both homemakers and soldiers," resulting in a destabilization and blurring of meaning of race and gender work roles (*Righteous* 142). These shifts represent their attempts to define a work space that best served other black women and the race as a whole. Cook ended her speech with a direct plea to the men and women in her immediate audience for acceptance: "The pulpit, the pew, the choir, the superintendent's chair, the Sunday School teacher's place, the Bible student, the prayer circle, the sick bed, the house of mourning, the foreign mission field, all these are her place" (55).

One observer remarked after hearing Cook speak on the history of the Baptist Women's Educational Convention that "[s]he left the well-beaten tracks of most of the lady speakers, and dealt entirely with facts, and without sentiment traced the Convention from its incipiency until the present time. . . . Miss Cook is never more in earnest than when saying a word for the women's work" (Penn 372). The remark highlights two contemporary perceptions of women speakers and women's work. According to the spectator, the speech was effective because it presented the facts "without sentiment," unlike most speeches by women. Sentiment and emotion, associated with women, were considered weaknesses and were, therefore, to be avoided. Papers read by Lucy Smith before national church gatherings are described as showing "carefulness of thought, as well as logical arrangement of her subject matter" (Penn 378). This rejection of emotionalism prefigures Ida Wells's similar annoyance several years later when during her first public speech she gave way to "woman's weakness" and began to cry when narrating the lynching of her three Memphis friends. Such reactions remind us that these women were speaking out of a tradition attributing intellect to men and emotionalism to women. Further, the observer's claim that Cook was most earnest when speaking of "women's work," signifies the value attached to that activity.

In his introduction to *The Negro Baptist Pulpit: A Collection of Sermons and Papers by Colored Baptist Ministers*, Edward M. Brawley, editor, defined the book's exigence: "Much has been done by the living voice to train and lead the people, but the time has come when the pen must also be employed. Our trained leaders must write" (7). Published in 1890, the collection contained twenty-eight original essays, explaining the confessions of faith generally held by black Baptists and recording black Baptist church history. Cook wrote the one essay by a woman, "The Work for Baptist Women," three years after her address to the ANBC. Written for publication rather than delivery and addressed to the established converted, the essay is an epideictic for the black Baptist denomination. Perhaps it would have been more appropriately titled "The Organizational Work of Black Baptist Women," chronicling as it does the formation of women's church groups in Kentucky, Alabama, Texas, Georgia, South Carolina, and other Southern states. The groups were all founded to do something "for the elevation of the race."

In line with the standard arrangement for persuasive discourse of this kind, the essay opens in the Bible. She began this essay with the New Testament and the women surrounding Jesus, to show that there had always been "work" for Christian women. Cook seemed to have assumed here primarily male readers as she described the activities of these various groups. She stressed in general terms the advantages of having women as helpmeets, assisting the men in all aspects of church work. Cook closed with an appeal that women be allowed to do more and be "made to feel that they too are personally responsible for the salvation of the world, and are enlisted to labor *by the side of the men*" (285; emphasis added). Cook was more interested here in writing a history that would establish the work of black Baptist women than in pushing ahead into new frontiers.

The texts coming out of the black Baptist women's movement centered on women and work represent only a small portion of the persuasive discourse from the organizational activities of church women at the turn of the century. For example, at the 1890 Convention, Virginia Broughton from Tennessee delivered a speech titled "The Ideal Woman," in which she argued for a separate women's convention (Broughton 100). Many other black Baptist women spoke at conventions, eventually organizing themselves into the Woman's Convention, auxiliary to the National Baptist Convention in 1900, under the leadership of Washington, D.C., born Nannie Helen Burroughs, and Broughton.

Women's Work: Racial Uplift as Home Uplift

Toward the end of the century, a number of conferences were organized to discuss "the Negro problem" or "the Negro question" in America. Among these were the conferences held at Hampton and Tuskegee Institutes in the 1890s; they focused on rural issues such as farming and the needs of the one-room schoolhouse. The Atlanta University conferences were different in that they investigated problems associated with the 12 percent of blacks who had moved to urban areas by 1890. Under the direction of George Bradford, a university trustee, and university president Horace Bumstead, the second Atlanta University Conference on Problems of Negro City Life convened in Ware Memorial Chapel on May 25, 1897.[8] With the exception of Adella Hunt Logan's speech titled "Prenatal and Hereditary Influences," the speeches considered here were delivered at the separate Women's Meeting, to discuss issues designated of special concern to them. As one historian writes, this "invisible wall assumed to exist between men's and women's duties kept the two groups from working together on causes of direct importance to both" (Neverdon-Morton 113). Taken together these addresses reveal a great deal about perceptions of woman's work and the extent to which racial uplift was home uplift.

Lucy Laney presided over the Women's Meeting and delivered the introductory address. By the time she spoke to the women at this 1897 conference, she was already an accomplished "race woman." Laney was born in Macon, Georgia, and grew up in a large and deeply religious family. She was one of the first women to receive degrees from Atlanta University in 1873.[9] After teaching for several years in the Georgia public schools, Laney, in 1886, opened in Augusta what would later be named the Haines Normal Industrial Institute. It was a private school for black children, funded in part by the Presbyterian Church of the United States. One comment made when she traveled to the General Assembly of the Presbyterian Church to solicit funds gives indication of her oratorical skills: "There was jealousy regarding her speaking for fear that her eloquence might win friends that were counted on for other causes" (Daniel 6). Her ability to apply this eloquence in speeches to Northern benefactors enabled her to keep the school nearly solvent with contributions alone. Like many of the "race women" of this period, committed to the cause rather than to public performance, she was known for her simple manner and common sense. Nannie Helen Burroughs made these remarks regarding her own speaking style: "I speak from sketchy notes or extemporaneously when I think I'm full enough to surcharge the listeners. I am in earnest, and I have no axe to grind. I do not speak when I'm lukewarm on a subject. I do not speak to show off" (Boulware 104).

It is perhaps appropriate to begin a discussion of persuasive discourse, crafted to cultivate home uplift, with a speech by Lucy Laney, because of her belief that racial uplift began in the home, with the woman in the most privileged position, as mother and teacher, to regenerate and uplift. In her "Address Before the Women's Meeting," Laney extolled the virtues of motherhood, stressing the importance of children being brought up in a home watched over by "a manly and God-fearing husband" and "a womanly and God-fearing wife," declaring motherhood the highest achievement of woman and the "crown of woman-hood" (56).[10]

She denied that politics, education, or religion alone was the answer but argued rather that all three combined would ensure improvement. Calling the Negro citizen "the youngest child of civilization," Laney devoted the speech to considering what this child needed to do if she expected to grow up and "claim the boon" (55). While she emphasized the role of women and girls, Laney also requested that boys be brought up with as much attention as girls, not reared according to a false double standard that assumes "boys will be boys." The appeal parallels one made by Mary Ann Shadd Cary in a March 21, 1872, letter to the editor of the *New National Era*, the Washington newspaper published by Frederick Douglass. While the paper was unsuccessful, "many of the ablest colored men of the country," according to Douglass, "made it the medium through which to convey their thoughts to the public" (Douglass, *Life and Times* 400). By 1872 Cary would surely have been counted among those able "men," being an agent for the *New National Era* who contributed occasional articles. In the letter, Cary expressed her annoyance with "the death-like silence of colored women" who fail to speak out in support of trades "to get the boys started properly in life," later adding, "I want our poor tongue-tied, hobbled and 'scart' colored women . . . to let the nation know how they stand (Cary, "Trades" 177). Although writing nearly twenty-five years earlier, Shadd, in her typically direct style, proposed a more aggressive way to assure meaningful employment for sons. Laney challenged the women to consider children "with the spirit of the true and loving mother" (57). For Lucy Laney the chief racial uplift work for women was the work of motherhood.

Georgia Swift King expressed this same opinion of the importance of motherhood in her brief remarks to the women. King was one of several black women active in the Women's Christian Temperance Union in Atlanta. King opened with the rhetorical syllogism that if home has the greatest influence on individual development and mothers have the larger share in making the home, "then it follows that the destiny of the Negro race is largely in the hands of its mothers" (61). Sustaining a strong rational appeal, King cited statistics showing that the birthrate barely exceeded the death rate, with infant deaths increasing among the literate and the illiterate. As a solution to the absence of informed homemaking, King proposed a series of "mothers' meetings," during which knowledge would be dispensed on such subjects as "care of infants," "economic cooking," "proper and wholesome dress," and "the laws of sanitation" (62).

In Selena Sloan Butler's address, "Need of Day Nurseries," she described a scenario played out in many homes today, 100 years later, of a tired parent coming home at the end of a long day to children who have practically been tending themselves—except that in 1897, few support systems had been established. Butler herself established a kindergarten in her own Atlanta home to accommodate her son and his peers. She remained an advocate for parental involvement in early education, establishing in 1926 the National Congress of Colored Parents and Teachers. In the speech, Butler pointed out that in many deprived circumstances, mothers die early, leaving orphaned children to be brought up on the streets. Day nurseries, she insisted, would provide a place for children to go while their mothers worked. In the speech, Butler spoke of absent parents but clearly focused on absent mothers "obliged to be away from home in order that they may earn an honest living." Butler argued not that these mothers should be at home with their children but that working mothers needed the societal support of day nurseries. Rosa Morehead Bass, during that same session, argued for the establishment of kindergartens not only to provide a place for young children to be but also to give them training in their formative years (66–67). These proposals represented a shift in focus from the in-home role for women prescribed by Laney and others to institutionalized uplift.

Adella Hunt Logan's speech, "Prenatal and Hereditary Influences," was presented that evening at a joint session presided over by President Bumstead. As had the papers during the women's session that afternoon, Logan's lecture argued for attention to early development of children and even to in utero influences that could shape personality. Logan had completed the normal course at Atlanta University in 1881 and eventually taught at Tuskegee Institute. She was active in the Tuskegee Women's Club, the National Association of Colored Women, and the National American Woman Suffrage Association, supporting education and health care for children. In this speech Logan ascribed a great deal to heredity, reaching back several generations to account for physical, social, and moral inadequacies: "We are to-day reaping what was sown, not by our fathers alone, but by their fathers and grandfathers" (38).[11]

Logan strongly urged early prenatal care, even recommending that the expectant mother monitor her thoughts lest they have a negative influence on the unborn child. The speeches delivered at this second Atlanta University Conference centered on the important work of mothering both boys and girls and began to pay attention not only to the racial uplift work of motherhood but also to the support of working mothers.

The Uplift of Women's Work

The persuasive discourse on women's racial uplift work and the uplift of women's work in this last section comes out of the Hampton Negro Conferences of 1898 and 1899 and out of a Hampton publication. The Hampton, Virginia, conferences, first held in 1897, were presided over by Hollis Burke Frissell, principal of the Hampton Normal and Agricultural Institute from 1893 to 1917. Victoria Earle Matthews's address, "Some of the Dangers Confronting Southern Girls in the North,"[12] was delivered at the second summer conference, July 20–22, 1898. "Colored Women as Wage-Earners," an article by Anna J. Cooper, appeared in the August 1899 *Southern Workman and Hampton School Record*. Lucy Laney's speech, "The Burden of the Educated Colored Woman," was delivered at the Third Hampton Summer Conference in July 1899.

Matthews, a year before she delivered her speech on the exploitation of Southern girls, had already established the White Rose Mission for young women who had traveled to New York City looking for work and a respectable place to stay. The mission also served as a gathering place for women in the community. Titles of other conference papers during that session, "Some Observations of Farms and Farming in the South," "The Importance of Sewing in the Public Schools," and "How to Hold Young People in the Church," indicate an emphasis upon rural and domestic issues. Matthews's speech to the Woman's Conference, however, followed the young women out of the homes and out of the South into the big cities in the North. Matthews painted a bleak picture of young women's sexual exploitation, describing the recruitment tactics in the South, the high wages offered initially in the North, and the incurred indebtedness that could never be repaid. She made the point that these atrocities occurred not only in New York but also in other cites including Boston, San Francisco, and Chicago. In 1905, Matthews established the White Rose Traveler's Aid Society, with agents posted in Norfolk, Virginia, near Hampton, and in

New York, to watch for the arrival of potential victims. Matthews recognized that it was not worth the time and money to ferret out the culprits. It was better, she claimed, to enlighten the women to the dangers that awaited them and to teach them how to search for jobs intelligently. Most, she pleaded, should stay at home. For those present at the 2:00 P.M. session, the solution seemed to have been "keep them down on the farm." The discussion that followed the speech, as reported in the *Southern Workman and Hampton School Record*, centered on how best to prevent young black girls from going North to seek work, with one participant concluding, "I think our girls ought to learn that it is no disgrace to stay at home, even on a farm, to pick cotton and peas, and see after the chickens" (174). One conference recorder indicated the impact of Matthews's bleak message: "In pleasant contrast to the dark picture presented by Mrs. Matthews, was the bright one given by Mrs. Titus, of the work done in Norfolk and other cities . . . classes in cooking and sewing have been in operation for some time" (173). Other follow-up discussions also emphasized education for domestic science so that the girls and women would find enough work to do at home.

The speech and the discussion that followed it reveal a discourse still very much directed toward restraining, confining, and limiting the work options of women rather than preparing them to take advantage of a range of job options. Matthews does stress as one solution informed decisions about jobs in the North: "Let women and girls become enlightened, let them begin to think, and stop placing themselves voluntarily in the power of strangers. Let them search into the workings of every institution under whose auspices they contemplate traveling North" (Matthews, "Dangers" 69). But essentially racial uplift work here means working to make home more appealing, and black women's work remains confined to those activities that will keep them in the community.

While there is no doubt that such exploitation occurred, Elsa Barkley Brown offers an additional metadiscursive perspective on the causes and effects of black women's interest in the subject. She points out that many middle-class black women, like those at the Hampton Negro Conference, in an effort to create political space in which to function, began to present themselves as protectors of working-class women. Attempting to militate against their own disparaged manhood, black male leaders of the 1880s participated in this project by developing, she writes, "a narrative of endangered black women. Urban areas, once sites of opportunity for women, became sexually dangerous places for

the unprotected female, easy prey to deceitful and barbarous white males."
Eventually, however, sexual violence became a woman's issue to be discussed at
Women's Meetings such as this one. Brown adds that "[b]y increasingly claiming sexual violence as a women's issue, middle-class black women claimed a
political/public space for themselves but they also contributed to an emerging tendency to divert issues of sexual violence to a lesser plane and to see them
as the specific interest of women, not bound up in the general concerns and
struggles for freedom" (143–45). Still, the serious nature of what these young
women faced should not be minimized, even though it seems to have become
a woman's issue.

Anna Cooper's essay titled "Colored Women as Wage-Earners" was placed
in the "Contributed Articles" section of the August 1899 issue of the *Southern
Workman*, a section headed with the disclaimer: "The editors of the *Workman*
do not hold themselves responsible for the opinions expressed in this department. Their aim is simply to place before their readers articles by men and
women of ability without regard to the opinions held." Of the two other articles
included in this section of the *Southern Workman*, one critiqued the participation of "colored American soldiers" in the Spanish–American War, and the
other described a growing resentment among the "Indian of the Plains" living
on reservations, in line with the paper's purpose, stated in the masthead, to report "work for and progress of the Black and Red races of our country." In 1878,
Hampton had assumed the education of Native Americans captured and held
as prisoners of war by the United States following an 1875 uprising; thus the
"red" race was incorporated into the school's general uplift project.

In her article, Cooper analyzed the changing perceptions and roles of black
working women by considering four significant points. She first brought to
light current Atlanta University research revealing that of 1,137 black families,
650 or 57.17 percent were supported wholly or in part by women and that since
women were already principle wage earners, they were entitled to the rights of
all other workers (Cooper, "Wage-Earners" 295). The second and longest section of the piece is an argument for a broader definition of the term "wage
earner" that would clearly include women working in the home. Cooper
claimed that women should be considered the "indoor partner of the firm," just
as truly a contributor to the product gained as the "outdoor manager," and as
a contributor, the woman was entitled to a share of the wages. Anticipating

the objection that perhaps one should not attach a price tag to mothering and homemaking, Cooper countered that as noble as this work is, the woman should not have to ask for doles; her partner should remember that she "earns a definite part of the wage that he draws; and that, though she has never figured it out and presented the bill, his account is greatly in arrears for simple wages" (292). In the third section, Cooper also argued for women wage earners outside the home, stressing the importance of providing them with as much education as possible. Cooper, while opposed to what she called the "woman with elbows," pointed out that black women needed to demand fair compensation. Speaking generally of black workers, she defined the disadvantages of a 250-year lag in educational opportunities. Finally, to make up the deficit, Cooper discouraged contemporary efforts by some black families to imitate middle-class white society with costly weddings, funerals, clothing, and other material objects. She returned to her opening claim that women are invaluable wage earners, whether working in the home or outside, and that a "prudent marriage is the very best investment that a working man can make" (298). Cooper argued here, as she did in *A Voice from the South*, for woman's difference as a special advantage.

In Lucy Craft Laney's 1899 opening address to the Woman's Conference of the third Hampton Negro Conference, she called this challenge of racial uplift a "burden," not resentfully but with despair that the times had created in fact a triple burden of "shame and crime and prejudice" ("Burden" 341). The "shame" Laney saw as a consequence of nonlegalized slave marriages, poor parenting skills, and ignorance of hygiene. Twentieth-century scholars who write about slave family life paint a less bleak picture of that environment. Angela Davis, for example, in *Women, Race and Class*, discussed the pride with which enslaved men and women "manifested irrepressible talent in humanizing an environment designed to convert them into a herd of subhuman labor units" (15), with many couples choosing to remain together in the absence of legality. If not entirely accurate as to cause, Laney was clear as to the effects to be addressed. The large numbers of young men and women incarcerated provided evidence of the "crime"; the crime, however, was not one they had committed but the crime of a system that forced young black men and women to work on road gangs for alleged misdemeanors. At the 1896 meeting of the National Federation of Afro-American Women in Washington, D.C., Victoria Matthews had reported on the effects of the chain gang laws she had observed during her travels in the South. She noted that children were serving fifteen- and twenty-year sentences for minor offenses (*History* 41). For Laney, the "prejudice" came from those in power, who made it difficult to overcome the other two burdens.

What appears to be an elitist appeal to a specific class of black woman, "the woman of culture and character," is strong here. Throughout the address, Laney stressed the importance of having a certain type of woman do this uplift work. Laney, no doubt, viewed hers as a call to those who had acquired education and other valuable experiences to be involved in lifting not because it was fashionable but because it was a responsibility, a duty, and, in fact, a heavy burden. Laney targeted a specific category of women, variously referred to as "the educated colored woman," "the intelligent women," "educated Negro women," "the woman of character and culture," "Negro women of culture," "the refined and noble Negro woman," "our cultured women," and "cultured Negro women." Laney stressed that "only those of character and culture [could] do successful lifting, for she who would mould character must herself possess it" (343). In a section discussing church work, she drew a clear distinction between the women designated for this work and other women: "The less fortunate women, already assembled in churches, are ready for work. Work they do and work they will; that it maybe effective work, they need the help and leadership of their *more favored sisters*" (344; emphasis added). But Laney was more interested in including than excluding here. She felt a strong personal obligation to help those less fortunate members of the race, as demonstrated in her work at the Haines Institute, and was concerned that many of her "favored sisters" did not feel this obligation.

Reinforcing this sense of obligation, Laney's speech more than any others considered in this chapter exudes the imagery of uplift, beginning with the question in the second sentence, "how may it [the burden] be lifted?" and recurring as leitmotif throughout: "lend a hand to the lifting of those burdens," "forces to lighten and finally to lift this and all of these burdens," "successful lifting," "a very sore burden," "start its people on the upward way," "the weight of which will sink us unless it is at once made lighter and finally lifted," "suffers under the weight of this burden," "she must help to lift it," and "the negro woman may lift much with this lever." This strong imagery of lifting a downtrodden race at times seems to place black people in such dire straits as to cause a level of despair surely not intended by Laney. The women of this period attributed this descendent state to slavery and felt that with the united energies of the "better women" of the race most of the ills could be corrected in a short time. Laney's call to action was in fact filled with an optimism about social work and collective effort not frequently articulated today.

During the last decades of the century, black women were speaking out in a number of venues about women's work and the work of racial uplift. For example, at just one evening session of the 1896 Convention of the National Federation of Afro-American Women, speeches were delivered on the following topics: training women for domestic service, woman's work in general, "defects" in the training of girls, and the ideal home. In the words of the convention recorder, "All the papers were excellent, and it would be well if some method could be adopted to preserve these papers for the rising generation" (*History* 46).

Black women activists in the last two decades of the nineteenth century articulated the position that racial uplift for women would result from improved homes and improved working conditions outside the home. They placed black women among the chief agents in achieving these improvements. They argued, then, for the uplift of women's work and the work of racial uplift.

I have tried to display the broad range of rhetorical strategies black women employed in their public discourse throughout the nineteenth century. Much like the two-headed Janus, looking in opposite directions, these women occupied unenviable positions as ambassadors for and lecturers to their own people. Their discursive constructions negotiated the similarities and differences between themselves and other women and between their needs and the needs of black men. They looked to Africa for pride in origin and to America as a model of progress. This multiple positioning brings to mind Mae Henderson's comments on the heteroglossic nature of black women's discourse, enabling them to speak in multiple public languages. Henderson, drawing on the Bakhtinian notion of dialogism, observes that black women "enter into a competitive discourse with black men as women, with white women as blacks, and with white men as black women" (20). Claudia Tate describes this dilemma at the close of her volume on turn-of-the-century black texts: "Black expressive culture . . . seems to oscillate between two extremes: embracing or repudiating assimilation; redefining black identity or imitating white America; celebrating folk wisdom or bourgeois accomplishment" (230). But what ultimately distinguished these women speakers was not their verbal skills nor their ability to select appropriate discursive strategies. True eloquence does not reside in the words and phrases; it must exist in the speaker. The eloquence of these nineteenth-century women came from an earnest commitment to ensuring for their people a future with hope.

Appendixes
Notes
Works Cited
Index

Appendix 1

Need of Day Nurseries

Selena Sloan Butler

Among the important questions of to-day is the need of day nurseries in cities and towns where children of parents who, by force of circumstances, are obliged to earn a living by working in service, may receive good and wholesome influences during that period of life when impressions are easily made and character readily molded, either for good or bad.

Many parents in cities must do work which calls them away from home, and often they toil from early dawn till a late hour to keep the wolf from the door, and, because of their small wages, their children often are forced to do work too hard for them that their meager earnings may add to the support of the still smaller children left at home during the day without the care of a poor but loving mother; left alone during that most important period of their lives when good or evil principles will, by cultivation, become the ruling passion through life; left alone to grow up amid a multitude of unfavorable surroundings. With these existing circumstances, it does not need a prophet to tell what the result will be.

It is a daily experience to find a child of tender years left to tend the baby with but a scant meal of meat and bread, while the widowed mother is out at work. At a late hour the mother returns, tired and almost exhausted; she proceeds at once to satisfy the hunger of her unfortunate children, and then, in her humble way, as best she can, with their bowed heads at her side she teaches them to lisp the "Lord's Prayer"; then all are lost in sleep. The majority of the children who would be glad to find protection in a day nursery are not blessed with even this limited knowledge of a good moral training.

Butler, Selena Sloan. "Need of Day Nurseries." Atlanta U Publications no. 2. *Social and Physical Conditions of Negroes in Cities and Proceedings of the Second Conference for the Study of Problems Concerning Negro City Life.* Atlanta: Atlanta UP, 1897. 63–65.

Such circumstances are not only unfavorable to the physical condition of the children, but detrimental to the parent, because such a state of constant activity and anxiety exhausts the vital force. Do you ask the result? Why, the mother dies at an early age, leaving little children in the hands of chance, to be brought up, quite likely, among the weeds of vice and sin, going from bad to worse, until they become a menace to society. If there had been a day nursery with good conscientious persons at its head, in which these children could have had their physical, mental and moral natures properly cared for at a small cost to the mother, they would have developed into characters with sufficient magnitude to lift humanity to a higher plane, instead of degrading it; and the mother would have no doubt lived out her three score years and ten.

If you will examine the records of the mortality of the Negroes of this city, you will find that about one-third of the deaths occurred among the children, and a closer investigation will disclose the fact that the majority of these deaths occurred in families where parents were obliged to work out and therefore could not detect disease in their little ones until too late to be relieved by medical aid.

I will relate only two of the many cases coming under my observation which make a strong appeal for the establishment of day nurseries. A widowed mother, who worked for a family in this city, had a boy about six years of age. This mother left her little boy alone, asking each morning the family in the adjoining room to have an oversight over him during the day. For several nights when the mother returned from her work between the hours of eight and nine, she found her boy with flushed cheeks, sleeping restlessly. Being tired she did not investigate the cause of this abnormal condition, but attributed it to exhaustion from play. Finally the child's condition became alarming, and one night about nine o'clock the mother took it to the office of a physician. After a careful examination, the mother was told that her child was in the third stage of typhoid fever, and recovery depended upon immediate attention and good nursing. Then the mother, with tears in her eyes, related her sad story.

The other case is that of a boy who went into a physician's office crying, and with his clothes covered with blood. What was the matter? Why, the same old story. The boy had had an artery cut with a stone that was thrown by another boy whose mother was obliged to work away from home, that she might be able to pay her house rent and feed and clothe her children: and but for the interest the physician took in the case, there might have been a dead boy, a lawsuit, and a juvenile criminal; all because of the need of day nurseries.

Another evidence of the need of day nurseries is the large number of boys, almost babies you might say, to be found not only loitering and making mischief in the alleys, but even in the chain-gangs. Many are there because in early childhood they have no one at home to hold them in check, and, yielding to the influences about them, their minds became steeped in sin and vice; and they grew wise only in the knowledge of petty crimes.

If the absence of day nurseries affected the physical nature only it might not be so alarming, but seeing the effect daily upon the mental and moral natures, and not knowing to what extent these natures may be transmitted to coming generations, we ought to see plainly the necessity of administering the ounce of prevention by establishing day nurseries.

We need an institution where mothers who are obliged to be away from home in order that they may earn an honest living may leave their children and have the satisfaction of knowing that their little minds are lifted above the miry slough and prepared to shun the pitfalls that have been the destruction of many a young life born to be useful.

Woman's Place in the Work of the Denomination

Mary V. Cook

How pleasant it is to wander over, and enjoy this beautiful world God has made. Its green meadows, its beautiful fields, its dense forests with wild flowers and rippling streams, its wide expanse of water and lofty mountains all delight us. But while charmed with its beauty, our joy is greater if we can comprehend that it "was without form and void" and contrast its present beauty with the roughness of its former state. So in viewing the wonders of divine grace, we need to note its results in connection with what might have been, and before attempting to describe woman's work in the denomination and the great blessings God has bestowed upon her, we will first consider her condition when His gospel found her, that we may better appreciate the grace which wrought the change. Among all nations woman was degraded. Besides being bartered or sold as a thing of merchandise, there were barbarous laws and customs among the Phoenicians, Armenians, Carthaginians, Medes and Persians, and all too revolting and indecent to be mentioned. Greece, whose land abounded in scholars, heroes, and sages where the sun of intellect illumined the world, looked upon her as an object "without a soul." Gibbon[1] says, "The Romans married without love, or loved without delicacy or respect."

In China, Japan and Africa the condition is the same except where Christianity has emancipated her. And wherever the religion of the true Messiah has spread its snowy white pinions and lighted up the deep dark recesses of man's heart, woman has been loved, adored, respected. I will not affirm that all virtue and joy were unknown: There are some fertile spots in the most arid deserts; there is light in the darkest places amid all this wickedness and infidelity. God had preserved the spark of faith, purity, and love. Though we live in the Nine-

Cook, Mary V. "Woman's Place in the Work of the Denomination." American National Baptist Convention, Mobile, AL. *Journals and Lectures* (1887): 45–56.

teenth century, and have it in its beauty and strength, our own beloved America is not free from the curse. Modern Athens is not totally unlike ancient Athens.

The leaven of infidelity is infesting this land. Immoralities, indecencies and crimes as revolting as ever withered and blighted a nation are of usual occurrence. They fearlessly maintain their hold and flaunt their wicked banners in the face of the government which is either too corrupt to care, or too timid to oppose. Who is to wipe these iniquities from our land if it be not Christian women? A reform in these things can not be effected by the ballot, by political station, or by mere supremacy of civil law. It must come by woman's unswerving devotion to a pure and undefiled Christianity, for to that alone, woman owes her influence, her power and all she is. To establish this truth we will recount history as its light comes to us from the pages of the Bible. Fortunately the records of the past present an array of heroic and saintly women whose virtues have made the world more tolerable; and chief among these are the wives, mothers and daughters of the Holy Scriptures.

In the formation of the world when the beasts of the field, the fowls of the air, the fish of the sea and the beautiful garden of Paradise were made for the happiness of man, and when man himself was made in the image of his Creator, God plucked Eve from the side of Adam "without childhood or growth" to be "a helpmeet for him." When Adam first looked upon her he was enraptured with the perfectness of her form, the splendor of her beauty, the purity of her countenance and in this excess of joy he exclaimed: "Bone of my bone, flesh of my flesh; therefore shall a man leave his father and mother and shall cleave unto his wife."[2] They knew naught but divine happiness. Their hearts were filled with pure love unsullied by sin, but alas! in a short time the scene was changed—Eve was tempted—partook of the forbidden fruit and gave to Adam and he did eat. In this fallen state they were driven from the garden, yet she proved still a helpmeet for her husband, sharing his sorrow as she had shared his joy. Many have been the reproaches uttered against her—few have been her defenders. Dr. Pendleton[3] says: "Eve acting under a mistake and a delusion was by no means excusable, but Adam was far more inexcusable than she for he acted intelligently as well as voluntarily. He knew what he was doing." There is much to admire in the character of Sarah, wife of Abraham: her reverence for her husband; her devotion to her son; her faithfulness to duty; her willingness in its performance. She was beautiful, chaste, modest and industrious—all these she sacrificed for the good and welfare of those around her. It was in this family

God preserved the seed of righteousness. Also we find Miriam cheering on the hosts of Israel with her timbrel in her hands as she uttered the songs of praise "Sing, sing ye to the Lord, for he has triumphed gloriously, the horse and his rider hath he thrown into the sea."[4] God's thought and appreciation of woman's work appears when he appoints Deborah[5] to be a warrior, judge and prophet. Her work was distinct from her husband's who, it seems, took no part whatever in the work of God while Deborah was inspired by the Eternal expressly to do His will and to testify to her countrymen that He recognizes in His followers neither male nor female, heeding neither the "weakness" of one, nor the strength of the other, but strictly calling those who are perfect at heart and willing to do his bidding. She was a woman of much meekness and humility, but of great force of character. Her song of praise, when Israel overcame the enemy, has only been excelled by the Psalms of David: "and Israel had rest forty years." Mention might also be made of Huldah,[6] wife of Shallum, who dwelt in Jerusalem in a college, to whom went Hilkiah, the priest, and Ahikam, and Achbor and Shapham and Asaiah to inquire concerning the words of the book that was found in the house of the Lord. It was a woman whom God had chosen as a medium between Him and His people who would faithfully report all that he desired. Huldah's dwelling in college shows that she was anxious to become familiar with the law—to better prepare herself for the work of Him Who had called her. Woman's faith and devotion are beautifully illustrated by the touching scene between Ruth and Naomi, when Naomi besought Ruth to return to the home of her birth, thinking that the pleasure of childhood days had endeared it to her, and when Ruth with that pathos of devotion, and firmness said: "Entreat me not to leave thee, or to return from following after thee: For whither thou goest, I will go; and where thou lodgest, I will lodge; thy people shall be my people and thy God my God; where thou diest I will die, and there will I be buried; the Lord do so to me and more too if aught but death part thee and me."[7] We cannot forget the maternal tenderness of Hagar,[8] the well kept promise of Hannah,[9] the filial devotion of Jephthah's daughter,[10] nor the queenly patriotism of Esther.[11] But no woman bore such recognition as Mary the mother of Jesus, who was chosen to bear a prominent part in human regeneration. After the fall of our first parents, God promised that a virgin should bear a son who should be the Redeemer of the human race. The memory of this promise was preserved through all nations, and each was desirous of the honor. The story of the birth of Romulus and Remus coincides with the miraculous birth of Jesus Christ. Silvia became their mother by the God Mars, even as Christ was the son of the Holy Ghost. An effort was made to take the life of these boys by throwing the cradle which contained them into the river Arno, whence it was carried into the Tiber. The cradle was stranded at the foot of Palatine and the infants were carried by a she-wolf into her den where they were tenderly cared for. This escape is likened to the flight into Egypt, and while this story has become a myth, the birth of Christ becomes more and more a reality. There are others who claim this mysterious birth. The most revered goddess of the Chinese sprung from the contact of a flower. Buddha was claimed to have been borne by a virgin named Maha-Mahai, but none realized the power of the words spoken by the angel, "Hail full of grace, the Lord is with thee! Blessed art thou among women," save Mary. History and tradition tell us she excelled all her young companions in her intelligence and skill. Denis, the Areopagite[12] says: "She was a dazzling beauty." St. Epiphanius,[13] writing in the fourth century, from traditions and manuscripts says: "In stature she was above the medium, her hair was blonde; her face oval; her eyes bright and slightly olive in color; her eyebrows perfectly arched, her nose aquiline and of irreproachable perfection and her lips were ruby red. The ardent sun of her country had slightly bronzed her complexion; her hands were long, her fingers were slender." As a virgin she honored one of the most beautiful virtues of woman; as a mother she nourished a Redeemer. She gave to the world an example of non-excelled maternal devotion; of the most magnificent grief which history affords. The life of Christ furnishes many examples of woman's work, love and devotion. They took part in the Savior's work, followed Him on His journeys, believed on Him and loved Him. They were "last at the cross and first at the grave." Christ did certainly atone for the sins of man, but His mission to woman was a great deal more; for He has not only saved her soul, but actually brought out and cultivated her intellect for the good of His cause. He was her friend, her counselor and her Savior. She bathed His feet with her tears and wiped them with the hairs of her head. He found comfort in the home of Mary and Martha when burdened, or tired from a day's journey. At the well of Samaria He converses with a woman which was unlawful for a man of respect to do, but He not only talked with her but permitted her to do good for mankind and the advancement of His cause. Filled with enthusiasm she leaves her water pot and hastens to proclaim her loyalty to One Who had won her heart and spoken to her of "living water." She testified that she had seen the true

Messiah and invites others to see Him for themselves. To Mary Magdalena was the commission given to bear the joyful intelligence that Jesus had risen. It was the women more than men whose faith ventured to show Jesus those personal kindnesses which our Lord ever appreciated. In the lives and acts of the Apostles women are discovered praying, prophesying and spreading the gospel. Prominent for good works and alms deeds which she did was Dorcas. Like her Savior she went about doing good, but in the midst of this usefulness she died and so great was the grief of the widows unto whom she had ministered that the Lord again restored her to them.[14] Paul placed much value on the work of Phebe and commends her to the churches as "our sister." Phebe was a deaconess of the church of Cenchrea and was, no doubt a great helper of Paul's "in the gospel." In the letter she carries to Rome, mention is made of quite a number of women who had been co-workers with the apostle. One of the first on the list was Priscilla, the wife of Aquila who had with her husband laid down her neck for him. She possessed high qualities and did active work in the cause which she espoused. Lydia was the first European convert—after she received the word into her heart, at once opens her house and offers a home to the apostle who had been instrumental in her conversion.[15] At Thessalonica we find "the chief women not a few" among the workers of the church.[16] The church to-day wants more Priscillas,[17] Phebes,[18] Chloes, Elizabeths, Marys, Annas, Tryphenas,[19] Tryphosas,[20] Julias[21] and Joannas[22] to labor in the gospel; to give of their substance; to follow Jesus; to be willing to sacrifice their lives for the love they bear their Lord. It is not Christianity which disparages the intellect of woman and scorns her ability for doing good, for its records are filled with her marvelous successes. Emancipate woman from the chains that now restrain her and who can estimate the part she will play in the work of the denomination? In the Baptist denomination women have more freedom than in any other denomination on the face of the earth. I am not unmindful of the kindness you noble brethren have exhibited in not barring us from your platforms and deliberations. All honor I say to such men. Every woman in the world ought to be a Baptist, for in this blessed denomination men are even freer than elsewhere. Free men cannot conscientiously shut the doors against those whom custom has limited in privileges and benefits. As the vitalizing principles of the Baptists expand and permeate the religious principles of the world women will become free. As the Bible is an iconoclastic weapon—it is bound to break down images of error that have been raised. As no one studies it so closely as the

Baptists their women shall take the lead. History gives a host of women who have achieved and now enjoy distinction as writers, linguists, poets, physicians, lecturers, editors, teachers and missionaries. Visit the temples of the living God and there you will find them kneeling at His shrine as ready now as in centuries past, to attest their faith by their suffering and if need be by the sacrifice of life. As they by their numbers, who followed Christ up Calvary's rugged road, caused the cowardice of man to blush, so in the crowds of worshippers who do Him honor to-day put to shame the indifference and the coldness of man's allegiance to God. But to the limited subject,

What Is Denominational Work?

I deem it to be the most honorable, the most exalted and the most enviable. It strengthens the link between the church militant and the church triumphant— between man and his Creator. All women who are truly Christians are candidates in this broad field of labor. It calls for valiant hearted women who will enlist for life. None whose soul is not overflowing with love for Christ and whose chief aim is not to save souls need apply. Success need not necessarily depend on learning, genius, taste, style, elegant language, nor a rapid use of the tongue, but it is the earnestness of the soul, the simplicity of the Word accompanied by the Spirit of the living God. The Maker of all has wisely distributed these talents and whatever characterizes the individual He has commanded "to occupy till I come" and to use well the talent entrusted to your care. It often happens that some humble woman bent on her staff full of fervor yet unlettered, does more by her upright living, her words of counsel, her ardent prayers "that go up to God as a sweet smelling savor" than many who pick their words and try to appear learned. This denominational work demands active labor in and for the churches. It does not demand that every woman shall be a Deborah, a Huldah, a Dorcas, or a Phebe—It simply asks that every woman be a woman—a Christian woman who is willing to consecrate all for the cause of Christ. A story is told of a woman who when she was unable to express intelligently and satisfactorily what the Lord had done for her and when the anxious crowd was about to turn away disappointed she exclaimed: "I cannot talk for Him, but I can die for Him." Whosoever will lose his life for my sake, the same shall save it." To serve the church we must die daily to selfishness, pride, vanity, a lying tongue, a deceitful heart and walk worthy of the calling in Christ Jesus.

We are to pray without ceasing—to be fervent in season and out of season—"to present our bodies a living sacrifice, holy and acceptable before God which is our reasonable service." We are to speak as the spirit shall give utterance, that He may work in us to will and to do His good pleasure. I know Paul said "Let the woman keep silence in the churches"[23] but because he addressed this to a few Grecian and Asiatic women who were wholly given up to idolatry and to the fashion of the day is no reason why it should be quoted to the pious women of the present. A woman may suffer martyrdom, she may lift her voice in song, she may sacrifice modesty to collect money for the church, for her work in this particular is considered essential and it matters not how prominent a place she occupies in fairs, festivals, sociables, tea parties, concerts and tableaux, but to take part in the business meeting of the church is wholly out of place because Paul said so. We are too apt to quote Paul and shut our eyes and ears to the recognition and privilege Christ, his Master, gave us, and not only did the apostle appreciate the labors of the women, and show towards them the greatest care and tenderest affection, but we find him in some places greatly dependent upon them, for co-operation in the foundation of the churches. But a change is coming; it has already commenced and God is shaking up the church—He is going to bring it up to something better and that, too, greatly through the work of the women. Already the harvest is great. Can ye not discern the signs of the times? Do you not see how wickedness and crime are flooding our country—how tares are growing up in the midst of the wheat? See the foothold the Catholics are getting in our Christian land. They are taking our children, putting clothes on their backs, food in their mouths and educating them that they may swell their number and represent their claim. See how nations, every where, are opening to the reception of the gospel. Listen to the cry of Africa's heathen sons—note the rush of other denominations to offer their faith, their belief, to satisfy the hunger of their souls and quench the thirst of their spirits. Can ye not discern the signs? It is quite time Christian soldiers were taking the field for Christ. The doctrines of our denomination must be so thoroughly diffused that a man though he be a fool need not err. A good pastor should have a good wife. He should find in her rest from care; comfort when distressed; his depressed spirits must be lifted by her consoling words; she must be his wisdom; his courage; his strength; his hope; his endurance. She is to beautify his home and make it a place of peace and cheerfulness—she is to be an example worthy of pattern for the neighborhood in which she lives—she is to take the lead in all worthy causes. Women are to look after the spiritual interest of the church as well as the men. Let them be punctual at services and make the prayer meeting interesting. Woman's power of song, her heartfelt prayer, her ability to go into the highways and hedges and compel sinners to come in, have marked her as proficient in revivals. A praying mother exerts more influence over the minds of the youth than all else. The recollections of such seasons when the tender plants were garnered in can never be effaced. The voice of that sainted mother still lingers upon them, and memory can never relinquish the priceless treasure she holds. Some of our best men owe their conversion and all that they are to the influence of a sainted mother, a devoted sister or some dear female friend. For money raising women have no equals.

Our churches are largely supported by her financial efforts, but she should discountenance many of the plans to which she and her daughters are sub-jected—they are gates of vice that lead to destruction—this begging money from any and every body only invites and encourages insults and it must be stopped. Our churches must have some system in money raising and there-by save the girls. Many a girl with good intent got her start downward by this very act of soliciting money. A woman's place is to assist the pastor, work in the Sabbath school, visit the sick, to care for the sick and lift up the fallen. She has a conspicuous place in

The Newspaper Work of the Denomination,

which is a powerful weapon for breaking down vice, establishing virtue, spread-ing the gospel and disseminating a general knowledge of the work of the de-nomination. Here she can command the attention of thousands. She can thun-der from the editor's chair and make the people hear. It has a wider circulation and as has been said "penetrates the most remote corners of the country." In this field we need strong intellectual women. We need women of courage, who dare defend the faith and make the truth felt. As an editor a woman can better reach the mothers, daughters and sisters. Let her be a regular correspondent, let the articles be strong and vigorous, let them show thought, learning and an earnestness for the cause represented. If she cannot be a regular correspondent she should write occasionally such articles as will give the people something to think and talk about. She should make them so plain and attractive that chil-dren will read them with eagerness and let some be especially to them; make them feel that some one else is interested in them besides mother and father and endeavor to impress them with upright living. Assist the editor in getting subscribers and see that a Baptist paper is in every home. See that the Baptist family reads your denominational paper.

The field of juvenile literature is open. I said recently before the National Press Convention, held in Louisville, Kentucky, there are now published 24 secular papers and magazines in the United States for the children with a circulation of 775,934—the largest of which is the "Youth's Companion" with a circulation of 385,251. Of the religious journals there are 47 with 678,346 circulation. "The Sunday School Journal" (Methodist) claims 81,090; "The Sunday School Times" 77,500; and "Our Young People" 47,000. Of this number, 71 secular and religious papers, there is not one so far as I know, edited especially for colored children. There is a little paper whose name does not appear on the list that is written for the colored youth, being edited and controlled by Miss J. P. Moore of Louisiana.[24] It is known as "Hope" and though of humble pretensions, in its silent way it is sowing seed from which shall spring up an abundant harvest.

The Educational Work of the Denomination

belongs principally to woman. Three centuries ago women were almost universally uneducated and a half century ago found American women shut out from all places of learning. Ignorance seemed a bliss while wisdom was a foolish idea. A young girl in Italy and a young widow in France almost simultaneously conceived the idea of educating young girls. It was the beginning of an institution that was destined to reform the world and this they comprehended, for they said "This regeneration of this corrupt world must be accomplished by children, for children will reform the families, families will reform the provinces and the provinces will reform the world." Mademoiselle de Sainte-Beuve, foundress of the "Ursilines"[25] of France, purchased a house at the Faubourg St. Jacques where she had two hundred pupils. It was her delight to watch them in their sport and as she looked upon them with maternal gaze she charmingly said: "They sprung not from her loins, but from her heart." At her death her portrait represented her before a window, her eyes fixed with intent devotion upon a garden full of beehives, with the legend "Mother of Bees." Mary Lyons, in our own century, opened the way, and established Mount Holly[26] Seminary, the first institution established for girls. This is what woman has done, and may not our women do even more for the denomination with the surrounding advantages? May they not found more "Spelman" and "Hartshorn" seminaries, more "Vassars?" The women have been promoted from mere kitchen drudgery, household duties, and gossiping from house to house—they can teach not as subordinates merely, but as principals, as professors. Woman has not only the art of inspiring the affections in her pupils, but also in keeping them interested in the tasks to be performed. I think the duty of our women is to impressibly teach the Scriptures and the doctrines of our denomination to the young under their care. I think we talk and preach baptism, "The Lord's Supper," and the "Final Perseverance of the Saints" too little. Not one-half of the members of our churches can give a doctrinal reason why they are Baptists. We are too fearful of feelings, when we have the Bible that makes the Baptist churches on our side. They should instill in the child's mind love toward God, his Creator, his Benefactor, his Saviour, and respect for all mankind.

As an author, woman has shown rare talents. The possession of mind affords the strongest evidence that God created her for society. As the fragrance which is in the bud will, when the bud expands, escape from its confinement and diffuse itself through the surrounding atmosphere, so if forms of beauty and sublimity are in the mind, they will exhibit themselves, and operate on their minds. The genius of woman was long hidden. Greece had a Sappho[27] and a Carina; Israel had a Miriam. Antiquity turned a deaf ear to the cultivation of woman's talent. The home of Cicero and Virgil neglected her intellect, but the revolution of ages and the progress of the present century have wrought a new change of affairs, and now woman has the pen, and participates in the discussions of the times. It was when Christianity and infidelity were wrestling in Europe, that Hannah More[28] came from retirement to take part in the contest. It was when slavery was at its highest, that Phillis Wheatly [*sic*],[29] Frances Ellen Harper,[30] and Harriet Beecher Stowe,[31] gave vent to the fullness of their souls in beautiful lines of poetry and prose. The human voice is fast receding; the written voice predominates. Since this is true, let the women see that the best and purest literature comes from them. Let them feel that they are called upon to consecrate all to truth and piety. Lecturers address the people through the sense of hearing; writing through the sense of sight. Many persons will pay goodly sums to hear a good talk on some subject, rather than spend the time investigating books. As public lecturers women have been successful, and have secured good audiences. Rev. Mr. Higginson[32] says: "Among the Spanish Arabs women were public lecturers and secretaries of kings, while Christian Europe was sunk in darkness. In Italy, from the fifteenth to the nineteenth century, it was not esteemed unfeminine for women to give lectures in public to crowded and admiring audiences. They were freely admitted members of learned societies, and were consulted by men of prominent scientific attainments as their equals in scholarship."

All good causes owe their success to the push of woman. The temperance cause had its origin in her, and to-day finds noble advocates in the persons of Frances E. Harper and Frances E. Willard.[33] Indeed, the place of woman is broad, and of the vocations of life none are so grand, so inspiring, as that of being a missionary. Long before the organization of any general missionary society of our denomination in this country, Christian women were actively engaged in prosecuting the work of home missions. Little bands of women organized in the churches to help the pastors in the poor churches, by sending clothing and other supplies needed. When the Foreign Mission Enterprise was begun, it found in these women ready and powerful allies—they sent up contributions annually for both Home and Foreign work. The first missionary society ever organized in the country was by the women in 1800. It was composed of fourteen women. From this many branches sprang. The women of to-day are realizing that in the homes among the degraded there is a great work to be done. It belongs to woman's tender nature, sympathy, and love, to uplift the fallen. A home can not be raised above the mother, nor the race above the type of womanhood, and no women are more ready to respond to the call than the women of the Baptist Church. They feel the necessity of meeting the responsibility with organized forces in the field. Many have been effected, and great has been the result.

This work is not exclusively confined to the churches, but to orphans, asylums, hospitals, prisons, alms-houses, on the street, in the home, up the alley, and in all places where human souls are found, has woman, with her love for Christ and fallen humanity, found her way, amid the jeers and scorn of those who were too selfish to care for any other save self and household.

Woman sways a mighty influence. It began with Eve in the Garden of Eden, and is felt even now. It has not been exaggerated nor exhausted. She exalts man to the skies, or casts him beneath the brutes. She makes him strong or she makes him weak. Under her influence nations rise or fall. In the dark days of Rome, when woman received her most cruel treatment from the hand of her lord, Cato said: "Even then the Romans governed the world, but the women governed the Romans."

Bad women sometimes have great power with men. It was Phryne[34] who inspired the chisel of Praxiteles. Cotytto[35] had her altars at Athens and Corinth under the title of "Poplar Venus." Aspasia decided peace or war, directing the counsel of Pericles. Demosthenes, the great orator, cast himself at the feet of Lais, and history gives scores of instances where women governed the passions of men for good or evil. It was Delilah who, by her words, persuaded Sampson to tell wherein his strength lay, and which Milton has so beautifully portrayed in these words:

> "Of what [now] I suffer
> She was not the prime cause, but I myself,
> Who, vanquished with a peal of words (Oh, weakness!),
> Gave up my fort of silence to a woman."[36]

It came to pass when Solomon was old, that his wives turned away his heart after other gods, and his heart was not perfect with the Lord his God, as was the heart of his father, David. There was none like unto Ahab, who did sell himself to work wickedness in the sight of God, whom Jezebel, his wife, stirred up. There are good women like Volumna, the mother of Coriolanus, who saved Rome by her influence over her son. The women of this country inspired the fathers and sons on to battle, and in all the affairs of life woman has encouraged or discouraged men; he is moved by her faintest smile, her lightest whisper. The Duke of Halifax says: "She has more strength in her looks than we have in our laws, and more power by hers than we have in our arguments." Though woman is a mixture of good and evil, be it said to her credit, that history has never recorded a single instance where she denied her Saviour. Her influence is entwined with every religion, and diffuses itself through every circle where there is mind to act upon. It gives tone to religion and morals and forms the character of man. Every woman is the center around which others move. She may send forth healthy, purifying streams, which will enlighten the heart and nourish the seeds of virtue; or cast a dim shadow, which will enshroud those upon whom it falls in moral darkness. Woman should consecrate her beauty, her wit, her learning, and her all, to the cause of Christ. She should put aside selfishness, for a selfish person is not only hideous, but fiendish, and destructive. She should not rest at ease, heedless of the perishing souls who need her prayers, her songs of praise, her words of counsel, her interpretations of the Scriptures for their salvation. Many a conversion has been attributed to some soul-stirring song; indeed, there is no music so penetrating, so effective as that produced by the human voice. Much good has been accomplished by a well written tract commending some word of God, which has certainly not returned unto Him void, but has prospered in the thing whereunto God sent it. Often a short article, setting forth some digestible truth, is like seed sown in good ground, which will bring forth a hundred fold, or like bread cast upon the water, that may be seen and gathered after many days hence.

Perhaps the most important place of woman in the denomination is to teach the children at home, and wherever she can reach them, to love God, to reverence His holy name, and to love the Baptist Church. The moral training of the youth is the highest kind, and it is of vast importance that the first opportunity be seized for instilling into the minds of children the sentiment of morality and religion, and the principles of the Baptist doctrine. The future of the denomination depends on the rising generation, and too much care can not be taken in the development of their characters. It requires constant, anxious watching to realize the embryo. Though the seed be long buried in dust, it shall not deceive your hopes—"the precious grain shall never be lost, for grace insures the crop."

The only foundation for all Christian graces is humility. Practice, as far as possible, Christ's meekness, his benevolence, his forgiveness of injuries, and his zeal for doing good. Woman is the hope of the Church, the hope of the world. God is slowly but surely working out the great problem of woman's place and position in life. Virtue will never reign supreme, and vice will never be wiped from the land, until woman's work of head, heart, and hand is recognized and accepted. No great institution has flourished without her support, neither has man succeeded without her, but the two must be unified. The work is not confined within the narrow limits of the church walls, not to the prayers sent forth or the songs sung. It extends far beyond this. Her work is in every cause, place, and institution where Christianity is required. The platform is broad, and upon it she must stand. Although the responsibilities to be met are great, the position is to be maintained. China, with her degraded millions, India, with her ignorance and idolatry, dark and benighted Africa, yea, the world, with its sin and wickedness, all have just and imperative claims on woman, such as she can and must meet.

Dear women, the cry comes to us from afar to bring the light of love, and to lead into the paths of peace and righteousness. From your ranks, as mother, wife, daughter, sister, friend, little as you have hitherto thought of it, are to come the women of all professions, from the humble Christian to the expounder of His word; from the obedient citizen to the ruler of the land. This may be objectionable to many, but no profession should be recognized that fails to recognize Christ, and all the Christians have a legal right where He is, for "with Him there is neither Jew nor Greek, there is neither bond nor free, there is neither male nor female, for ye are all one in Christ Jesus." There is no necessity for a woman to step over the bounds of propriety, or to lay aside modesty, to further the work, and she will not, if God be her guide. If, indeed, the King of all the Universe chooses a woman to kill a man who had opposed Israel for twenty years, it is all right, and who dare question God's right, if he raise up a woman who shall become a judge, and a leader of his people? God, at one time, used a dumb brute to do His service, and that alone is sufficient to convince any one that He can use whom He will, and glorify himself by whatever means he pleases to employ. Should woman be silent in this busy, restless world of missions and vast church enterprises? No! A long, loud No! Give place for her, brethren. Be ready to accept her praying heart, her nimble fingers, her willing hands, her swift feet, her quick eye, her charming voice, and the powers of her consecrated intellect. The pulpit, the pew, the choir, the superintendent's chair, the Sunday school teacher's place, the Bible student, the prayer circle, the sick bed, the house of mourning, the foreign mission field, all these are her place.

Dear brethren, point them out, direct my sisters, and help them to work for Christ. My dear sisters, wherever you are, and wherever this paper may be mentioned, remember that there is no department of your life that you can not bend your influence to the benefit of our blessed denomination. Let us take sharpness out of our tongues and put it in our pens; take the beauty from our face and put it into our lives; let us love ourselves less and God more; work less for self-aggrandizement, and more for the Church of Christ.

> "Do not then stand idly waiting,
> For some greater work to do,

Fortune is a lazy goddess—
She will never come to you.
Go, and toil in any vineyard,
Do not fear to do and dare;
If you want a field of labor,
You can find it anywhere."

Notes

1. Edward Gibbon (1737–1794) was a British historian and author of *The History of the Decline and Fall of the Roman Empire.*

2. Genesis 2:23–24.

3. Cook probably refers here to James Madison Pendleton (1811–1891), a strictly orthodox Baptist minister and author of numerous church treatises, including *Three Reasons Why I am a Baptist* (1853), *A Treatise on the Atonement of Christ* (1869), and *Christianity Susceptible of Legal Proof* (1885).

4. See Exodus 15:21.

5. See Judges 4, 5.

6. See 2 Kings 22:8–20.

7. Ruth 1:16–17.

8. See Genesis 21:9–21.

9. See Samuel 1–2.

10. See Judges 11:29–40.

11. See Esther 1–10.

12. Cook probably refers here to the writing of Pseudo-Dionysius the Areopagite (fl. c. 500) who wrote a series of treatises and letters on medieval Christian doctrine, rather than the biblical figure mentioned in Acts 17:34.

13. Saint Epiphanius (c. 315–403) was a zealous bishop in the early Christian church, who practiced monasticism and campaigned aggressively against heretics.

14. See Acts 9:36–43.

15. See Acts 16:14–40.

16. See Acts 17:4.

17. See Romans 16.

18. Ibid.

19. Ibid.

20. Ibid.

21. Ibid.

22. See Luke 8:3.

23. I Corinthians 14:34–35.

24. Joanna P. Moore (1832–1916) was a white missionary worker in the postbellum South and the first woman appointed to the American Baptist Home Mission Society.

25. Ursulines were members of the Roman Catholic religious order of Saint Ursula, dedicated to the Christian education of girls.

26. Mary Lyon (1797–1849) established Mount Holyoke Seminary in 1837.

27. Sappho (fl. c. 610–c. 580 B.C.E) was a celebrated lyric poet and writer.

28. Hannah More (1745–1833) was an English writer and evangelist, who established religious schools for poor children.

29. Phillis Wheatley (1753?–1784), a former American slave and accomplished poet.

30. Frances Ellen Watkins Harper (1825–1911), prominent poet, novelist, and lecturer.

31. Harriet Beecher Stowe (1811–1896), author of abolitionist novel *Uncle Tom's Cabin* (1852).

32. Cook probably refers here to Thomas Wentworth Higginson (1823–1911), Unitarian minister and author, with progressive views on women's rights and abolition.

33. Frances E. Willard (1839–1898) was founder of the Woman's Christian Temperance Union in 1883.

34. Phryne (fl. 4th century B.C.E) according to legend posed for Praxiteles' nude statue of Aphrodite and did not hesitate to use her beauty to her advantage.

35. Cotytto was a Thracian goddess associated with nocturnal orgiastic rites whose public worship thrived around 425 B.C.E.

36. Cook here quotes from John Milton's 1671 dramatic poem *Samson Agonistes* (ll. 233–36).

Appendix 3

Colored Women as Wage-Earners

Anna Julia Cooper

I shall not take time to discuss ideal situations on the speculative side. There may be those who think that woman has no business to enter the struggle for existence as a wage-earner; who think that she should be as the lilies of the field, and should toil not except to spin and array herself in gorgeous raiment to delight the Solomons in all their glory. The fact remains that a large percentage of the productive labor of the world is done by women; and also another fact, recently brought out through investigations under Atlanta University, that "of 1,137 colored families 650, or 57.17 percent, are supported wholly or in part by female heads."[1] So that in comparison with white, female heads of families and others contributing to family support, there is, by a house to house enumeration, quite a large excess on the part of colored women. Sentiment aside then, if men will not or cannot help the conditions which force women into the struggle for bread, we have a right to claim at least that she shall have fair play and all the rights of wage-earners in general, or, as Herbert Spencer puts it, "Justice demands that women, if they are not artificially advantaged, must not at any rate be artificially disadvantaged."[2]

I shall have to ask first, therefore, careful attention to a few of the dry but fundamental principles of economics, to which science our subject properly belongs. Wage-earning is the complement or proper corollary to the human element in the creation of wealth. Land, labor, and capital are the factors in the production of wealth. The term land includes all natural opportunities or forces; the term labor, all human exertion; and the term capital, all wealth used to produce more wealth. The whole produce is distributed in returns to these three

Cooper, Anna Julia. "Colored Women as Wage-Earners." *The Southern Workman and Hampton School Record* (28 Aug. 1899): 295–98. Reprinted by permission of University Archives, Hampton University.

factors. That part which goes to land owners as payment for the use of natural opportunities is called rent; the part which constitutes the reward of human exertion is wages; and the part which constitutes the return for the use of capital is called interest. The income of an individual may be made up from any one, two, or three of these sources according to the nature of his contribution to the product. But the laborer is always worthy of his hire. Should the owner of the land and the capital have the power and the greed to disregard the claims of the man who contributed the labor, and pocket the entire product, he is manifestly a robber whether the jailors can catch him or not.

In many thousands of homes the indoor partner of the firm, who undertakes to discharge the domestic and maternal duties within, is just as truly a contributor to the product gained, as the outdoor manager who conducts the business and controls the wages. The woman in the home has a right to a definite share in the wealth she produces through relieving the man of certain indoor cares and enabling him to give thereby larger effort to his special trade or calling.

But, say you, the highest services can not be measured by dollars and cents. It is sordid to talk about paying mothers to be mothers, and giving a wage to wife to be wife! True, there is a class of services transcending all rewards; but because the wife of your bosom does not take you by the throat saying, "Pay me that thou owest!" should she be made to feel like a pensioner on your bounty every time she needs a pair of gloves? The family tie is a sacred union—the most sacred on earth. It is full of mystery and God-appointed sanctity. But does it not at the same time recognize the existence of some very plain and practical rights founded on simple justice as between man and man? Two human beings have voluntarily contracted to unite their forces for mutual help and advantage. The fact that they pledged themselves to the partnership "Till death do us part" but adds solemnity to the duties and obligations on either side. That the partnership carries divine sanction makes all the more inviolable those duties and obligations. That the interests involved are the most precious to the state,—the building of homes and the rearing of its citizens, insures the guardianship of society over those duties and obligations.

Of this partnership, the one member goes forth in the morning, whether to dig ditches or to add figures. The world knows him as the bread winner for the firm. The silent partner toils in the home, whether to cook the dinners or direct little feet and hands. Her heart is in the work. Faithfulness and devotion are hers. At the end of her monotonous round of days' doings she prepares to welcome in the eventide the battle-scarred veteran of the outer life. She opens the door with a smile. That smile is an important part of her program. She leads him to the dinner that she has prepared; he eats with a right good relish, for he likes to be fed. Yes, she eats of the dinner too, for she has her food and her shelter and her clothes whenever she asks for them. But it never occurs to this "boarder" that his wife earns a definite part of the wage that he draws; and that, though she has never figured it out and presented the bill, his account is greatly in arrears for simple wages. On the other hand every right implies a duty, and woman on entering this partnership should see to it that she contributes a real increment to the stock of value.

When we pass from the home and enter the dusty arena of the world, we find women wage-earners shoulder to shoulder with men in the struggle in almost all the avenues of labor and here it may be well to repeat [that] this term labor with its correlate wage-earning, in the broad economic sense, includes all the capacities in man, intellectual as well as physical and moral, which have economic significance. Moral and intellectual qualities increase the productiveness of labor. "Temperance, trustworthiness, skill, alertness, perception, a comprehensive mental grasp—all these," says an eminent writer on political economy, "and other good qualities belonging to the soul of man are of chief importance in man. The economic value of intellectual training," he continues "is generally not sufficiently appreciated. It has been ascertained that with no exceptions, the higher in any part of the United States the per capita expenditure for schools, the higher is the average of wages, and the larger, consequently, the production of wealth." This is a fact I would like specially to emphasize for those who intend training either girls or boys for self support as laborers or wealth producers. The broadest and fullest development of all powers, though it cost a greater outlay, pays the best interest in actual returns of dollars and cents. It may be hard to do without your daughter's help while she studies a few more years in preparation for her labor, but the greater productiveness of that labor will more than repay your abstinence.

And now let us apply what has been said to the special class of women mentioned in our subject. The colored woman as wage-earner must bring to her labor all the capacities, native or acquired, which are of value in the industrial equation. She must really be worth her wage and then claim it. "Nature has made up her mind," says Emerson, "that what cannot defend itself shall not be defended," and if women enter the struggle for independent existence they should claim all the rights of advantage to men in the same positions. The world has a cold substratum of fair play and abstract justice, but it is so encrusted over with prejudices and favoritisms that the one who waits for its waters to bubble up spontaneously will die of thirst. No one deplores more than I do the "woman with elbows." Aesthetically, she pains me. But every wage-earner, man or woman, owes it to the dignity of the labor he contributes, as well as to his own self-respect, to require the rights due to the quality of service he renders, and to the element of value he contributes to the world's wealth.

As colored wage-earners, we are today under a double disadvantage destined sorely to try our fitness to survive if it does not overwhelm us in the very start. In the midst of a civilization the most brilliant on earth, in the very heyday of its ostentation and self-satisfaction, we are "let go" to start from zero—nay, from a chasm infinitely below zero, to build up our fortunes. As a consequence, the social wealth of the Negro is two hundred and fifty years behind that of the white American. You will understand what I mean by social wealth when you reflect on the many things owned by individuals which are really consumed by the society in which these individuals move. Take for example a child born in 1865 of emancipated parents. Leaving out hereditary drawbacks and losses, that child is born into a society without books, without pictures, without comforts, without homes. If he goes to school he has no dictionaries or cyclopedias to help him understand his lessons. His environment does not even furnish the language in which his books are written. Now, suppose he struggles to accumulate, secures a home, puts in it a few comforts, some books and pictures, carpets and curtains, a piano perhaps, a dictionary certainly; or he goes further and acquires orchards and lawns, a country seat and carriages—these things are not for himself alone. All who associate with him are made the richer by such acquisitions of his, and would be to that extent impoverished should he, on dying, take them away from the society in which he had moved by bequeathing them to a white man.

Colored society is today in available social wealth in the position of a company of pioneers, or where the white American was when he conned his solitary book by the light of a pine knot, and contended with bears and Indians for the possession of his potato patch and his one-story cabin. But the white American at that stage of his social accumulation worshipped God in a log hut and his wife went to meeting in her linsey-woolsey gown and brogan shoes. The black

American, however, comes up on the stage when his white forerunner is becoming blasé with luxury and surfeiting. He takes the white man's standard of living just where he finds it, rears and tries to support churches as magnificent, gives presents as costly, maintains in his weddings and funerals a style as lavish and idiotic. It is as if a little harpsichord with only middle and lower gamut were keyed up to a magnificent grand piano which stands with all its eight or more octaves already at concert pitch. A terrible strain results to all the strings of the little harpsichord. Its notes are but discordant shrieks and screams, ineffectual attempts to reach the easy, ringing tones of the grand; and a miracle it is if you do not hear a snap, a pop—resulting in utter ruin to what might have been a very sweet instrument, had it only been allowed to keep its range.

Economically considered, the colored people in this country are a society of wage-earners, but their standards of living and their judgments of one another are as if they were a race of capitalists.

Perhaps the severest trial of all for the colored wage-earner is the impossible height to which the standard of life is raised among us. "Standard of life," in the economic sense, "is the number and character of the wants which a man considers more important than marriage and family." Now I hold that not only does the strain from keying our life to the American pitch divert into the struggle to "keep up appearances" a large part of the wage which should go to physical comforts, such as sanitary housing and feeding and clothing our bodies, but worse yet, through this artificial and hopelessly high standard of living, many young men feel that they cannot support a wife and family; and so we lose the impetus toward a higher civilization that good homes would give us.

Our children make their first bow before the public in a dazzling shimmer of costly roses and laces; and however many pinches and sweat pounds it has cost the wage-earner to afford it, we somehow feel that our child ought to appear as fine as the rest, and so it goes. Wage-earners will have to learn to discriminate between wages and interest if we are ever to bequeath to posterity a capital out of our wages. Indeed, if we are ever to start homes and families at all that in the next generation our name be not blotted from the face of the earth, it will be necessary for us to have plain living and homely virtues in honest homes, built and banded by honest earnings. For it is here, as I conceive the matter and not, as Prof. Kelly Miller suggests in his review of Hoffman, in the "surplus" of women among us, that lies the real explanation of unnatural conditions in our large cities. Certainly the removal of the tension that comes from our effort to reach an extravagant and unattainable standard of life, by a return to simplicity of manners and naturalness of living, is a more facile remedy for increasing the number of honorable marriages and pure homes than by killing off the surplus women, the only remedy apparent as Prof. Miller depicts the situation.[3]

Surely the greatest sufferer from the strain and stress attendant upon the economic conditions noted among our people is the colored woman, and she is the one who must meet and conquer the conditions. She must be too wary to be lured on with the chaff of flattery. When her fine appearance or that of her daughter is commented upon let that be a signal for retreat. Study economy. Utilize the margins. Preach and practice plain living and high thinking. Let the wife come in as a sensible helper in building up the fortunes of the family. Let her prove that she can contribute something more than good looks and milliners' bills to the stock in trade. If her husband starts a business, let her study how she can be useful to him in it, and, shoulder to shoulder, let them plant and till, and then gather and garner the fruits of their united industry. So, by her foresight and wisdom, her calm insight and tact, her thrift and frugality, her fertility of resource and largeness of hope and faith, the colored woman can prove that a prudent marriage is the very best investment that a working man can make.

Notes

1. Cooper's figures correspond to those found in the publication *Social and Physical Condition of Negroes in Cities* (Atlanta: UP, 1897) Appendix p. 6.

2. Herbert Spencer (1820–1903) was an English sociologist and philosopher, who published his major work, *The Synthetic Philosophy*, in 1896. A social Darwinist, Spencer coined the phrase, "survival of the fittest," which supported a view of material dominance criticized by many black social scientists.

3. Kelly Miller (1863–1939), professor of mathematics and sociology at Howard University, was a founder of the American Negro Academy. The Academy published Miller's "A Review of Hoffman's *Race Traits and Tendencies of the American Negro*" in 1897. In the review, Miller critiqued Frederick Hoffman's 1896 treatise, which claimed to demonstrate the genetic inferiority of blacks. In response, Miller countered that "a greater than any cause yet assigned as leading to the social degradation of Negroes in cities is the excess of the female over the male element of the population" (p. 32). Miller further develops this notion in his 1908 essay "Surplus Negro Women" (*Race Adjustment: Essays on the Negro in America*. New York: Neale, 1908. 168–78).

Appendix 4

Mothers' Meetings

Georgia Swift King

If it is true, that of the three main factors in the make-up of the individual—the home, the school and the church—the greatest is the home, and since it is true that the home is what the parents make it, the mother by nature having the larger share in the making, then it follows that the destiny of the Negro race is largely in the hands of its mothers.

Statistics resulting from recent investigations indicate with respect to the Negro population of the United States, first, a general decrease in the birth-rate; second, an alarmingly excessive infant death-rate; third, because of inherited tendencies and defective education—physical, intellectual and moral—a greatly excessive death-rate among adults; fourth, that so little does the birth-rate exceed the death-rate that the race is doing little more than reproducing itself. These indications furnish food for thought, and reason for investigation and action.

The alarming increase of infanticide (without reference to the immoral, brutal class) seems to result from the overworked, discouraged, desperate state of many laboring mothers, upon whom the burden of family support so largely rests.

The large death-rate of both infants and adults, I believe, may be traced to poverty and ignorance of the laws of health; an ignorance not confined to the illiterate, for how many highly intelligent people there are who have almost no knowledge of the symptoms of ordinary diseases; who do not know when to send for the doctor, nor how to care for the sick. I recall several instances during the present year where promising lives in intelligent homes have been sacrificed

King, Georgia Swift. "Mothers' Meetings." Atlanta U Publications no. 2. *Social and Physical Conditions of Negroes in Cities and Proceedings of the Second Conference for the Study of Problems Concerning Negro City Life*. Atlanta: Atlanta UP, 1897. 61–62.

on the altar of ignorance and the most extravagant economy; what wonder that the illiterate and poor die in so great numbers!

Does this excessive death-rate indicate a corresponding mental and moral decay? What is the remedy for such conditions?

The blood of the fallen is required at the hands of the intelligent class. The demand is apparent for preachers who study the signs of the times and deal practically with the needs of the hour; for teachers, capable, conscientious, consecrated; for physicians, skilled, honorable, philanthropic. But these agencies alone can not meet the demands and should be supplemented by other methods.

Observation and experience lead me to conclude that a most excellent medium for effectual instruction of the masses is "Mother's Meetings," where all questions of human interest are pertinent and may be freely discussed; where all classes of women may become better informed; where even the illiterate, by regular attendance, may gain much essential knowledge of such vital subjects as the laws of sanitation; selection of foods; Economic cooking; proper and wholesome dress; care of infants; needs (physical, mental and moral) of childhood; care of boys and girls through the critical period between childhood and maturity; how to fortify young men against the follies of immorality and young women against the dangers of imprudence.

The science of health and heredity and prenatal influences, and all that pertains to household morality and economy, may be handled with such simplicity in these meetings, that not only the mothers but the whole people may receive real benefit.

When difficulty is experienced in getting the mothers to these meetings I have met with some success by taking the meetings to the mothers, that is, to their immediate neighborhood.

Address Before the Women's Meeting

Lucy C. Laney

Ladies: A little more than a quarter of a century ago this American Republic, after much painful travail, brought forth the youngest child of civilization—the Negro citizen. To-day we, the offspring of that birth, stand upon the entrance of a glorious future if we will accept and faithfully comply with the conditions upon which we may claim the boon.

To find out and to discuss some of these conditions is the object of this conference and the women's section of it. For a long time many were disposed to think that the condition of most importance was politics, and for years politicians, honest and dishonest, ignorant and wise, struggled in vain to bring about that consummation devoutly to be wished, true manhood in our race. Some vainly hoped that that miserable deformity wrongly called education, viz., the conning of a few facts from text-books, was *the* condition to be complied with. Still another class said honestly and devoutly that the condition and the only condition to be met was the development of our religious nature. A fourth class united the second and third conditions, and after some-what modifying the third, gave to the world as the watchword of Negro development "the Bible and the spelling-book." Any *one* of these made the rule of life, made the only condition to be met, has been to those who followed it an *ignis fatuus*, for it has misguided them and led them into dangerous places. Each by itself is but a part of a grand total.

No person is responsible for his ancestors; nor should he be held responsible for their sins and short-comings, though he bear about in his body the marks and scars of those sins; but every woman can see to it that she gives to

Laney, Lucy C. "Address Before the Women's Meeting." Atlanta U Publications no. 2. *Social and Physical Conditions of Negroes in Cities and Proceedings of the Second Conference for the Study of Problems Concerning Negro City Life.* Atlanta: Atlanta UP, 1897. 55–57.

her progeny a good mother and an honorable ancestry. I care not how humble may be the house in which two loving hearts may set up their household gods, if blessed with a manly and God-fearing husband, a womanly and God-fearing wife, intelligence and health, that place is a *home*, the nearest approach on earth to heaven. The chief joy of home is mother. You may place upon the brow of a true mother the greenest laurel or you may give into her keeping the highest civic honors, but these to her will be found wanting if weighed in a balance over against her home. To her the blessedness of motherhood is the greatest joy, a crown more costly than pearls of royalty.

Marriage, the beginning of home, is a matter of great importance and should not be carelessly entered into. It is the place to take the proverbial stitch in time. From this point a shadow may be cast which will darken the pathway of coming generations. This is not a question that can be settled on a basis of gain or convenience, but as has been said: "A tie that only love and truth should weave and nothing but death should part."

Motherhood, honored by our blessed Master, is the crown of womanhood. This gives her not only interest in the home and society, but also authority. She should be interested in the welfare of her own and her neighbors' children. To woman has been committed the responsibility of making the laws of society, making environments for children. She has the privilege and authority, God-given, to help develop into a noble man or woman the young life committed to her care. There is no nobler work entrusted to the hands of mortals.

Faithful mothers, mothers who know their duty and perform it, such must have been the mother of the Gracchi,—such a mother we read of in holy writ: "All nations shall rise up and call her blessed."

Will not the intelligent mother gather to her heart her sons and daughters and teach them to be pure in life and chaste in conversation, and see to it that there be no double standard set up in her home, and none in her community if she be able to tear it down?

Too often that mother who is careful of her daughter's environment, the formation of her girl's character, is negligent as to her son's. He may choose his own company,—be the molder of his own character. If the daughter should drag the robes of her womanhood in the dust that mother would be covered with shame and grief,—but the son of that mother may trample down his manhood and there will scarcely be a blush; only the old but false cry, and pernicious as it is false, "Boys must sow their wild oats."

Our boys need the careful, loving hand of mother; perhaps not more so that the girls—but certainly not less.

Shall the boys be left to the tender training of the saloons and the fascinations of women degraded by sin? God forbid it! Women of to-day, awake to your responsibilities and privileges.

The Mothers' Congress recently held at Washington was not only a most unique gathering, but as the years roll on and men and women study more carefully that most important of all questions,—the children of the nation,—it will be found to be the working out of the noblest ideas of the noblest minds and most loving hearts of the age. That vast assemblage of men and women discussing questions most vital to the welfare of their children shows how great is the lamentation in Rama[h], Rachel weeping for her children, refusing to be comforted because they are not.[1]

Shall we not catch inspiration from that Congress and in our literary societies, ladies' clubs, and even in our churches study our children by the searchlight of the new psychology and with the spirit of the true and loving mother?

Note

1. Jeremiah 31:15.

Prenatal and Hereditary Influences

Adella Hunt Logan

The boy takes his large nose from his grandmother, the small mouth from his father, and a quick temper from his mother. This is natural, for children always inherit the characteristics of their ancestors. But where does he get red hair? No one in the family has hair of that color. And how is it that the young man seems prone to the social sin? His father has always seemed upright, and his mother is regarded as a model of purity. To be sure, the grandfather sowed wild oats, and it is charged that a great-great-grandmother was born out of wedlock, but that was generations ago and this young man has never heard those family scandals of a hundred years past.

It is well if his ears have never listened to such unhappy stories. His parents were wise in withholding them from his knowledge. Alas! while they could easily keep the family skeleton in the closet and spare their son the humiliation of such ugly tales they could not so easily purify and change the blood that coursed in their veins; hence we see the son in spite of fine precept and example, on the downward grade in his social tendencies.

Again, they say this young man is not very strong. His mother fears he is going into consumption. The father says: "Have no fears along that line, my dear, for there is no consumption in my family nor in yours. No danger of that, although somehow our son is rather frail!"

That red hair is hard to account for, but, no doubt, this head is an exact reproduction of one in the same family generations ago. It may be so far back, indeed, that no living person remembers having heard of the peculiarity. In the

Logan, Adella Hunt. "Prenatal and Hereditary Influences." Atlanta U Publications no. 2. *Social and Physical Conditions of Negroes in Cities and Proceedings of the Second Conference for the Study of Problems Concerning Negro City Life.* Atlanta: Atlanta UP, 1897. 37–40.

same silent way influences which affect the morals and the health of the boy have been handed down.

How rarely in the every day ordering of our lives do we give any attention to that silent, but powerful, thing known as heredity! Although its power cannot be confined in time to the earthly life of man, nor in social contact to any one race, as long as we are not reminded in some very forcible or unpleasant way of its effects, we scarcely think of its operations. At any rate, the thought expended upon it rarely ripens into such action as will regulate its influence.

In respect to time the force of heredity cannot be checked by a generation. We are to-day reaping what was sown, not by our fathers alone, but by their fathers and grandfathers. "Unto the third and fourth generation of them" was the decree thundered from Mt. Sinai by the voice of Almighty God.

There can be no suspending of the influences of heredity until the human soul has had sufficient development to appreciate responsibilities; until it wills to be shaped by this or by that influence. No, there is no choice! Before the body is ready to begin life as a separate being, as a new personality, it is molded and cast by the combined traits of the father and the mother from whom this new creature must draw its individual existence. And the intellectual and ethical cast will follow as closely the law, "Like begets like," as will the physical. We do not expect to find the children of white parentage having black faces or kinky hair, nor the children of black ancestry having fair brows, blue eyes, and flaxen locks. It would be just as unreasonable to expect the intellectual and the ethical characteristics of children to be radically unlike those of their ancestors as it would be to expect their physical features to be radically different.

'Tis true that the progeny of some very good parents are very bad specimens of humanity, but such cases must be like our boy's red hair which fell to him despite the fact that no other such head had ever been seen in that family. In both cases the results came through blood. Both the red hair and the weak or vicious character were transmitted. Probably through a long stream of blood, but we must know that neither came as a matter of chance. The one was just as much a legacy as the other.

Placing an inheritance is often difficult for the reason that it may be the result of complex causes and combined forces.

Possibly no one in the preceding generations had red hair, but there must have been sufficient in the aggregate of that kind of pigment to produce one such head in the family. This same principle of transmission applies to the health, the brain and the morals of the descendants. The exact ailment of body or malady of mind may not be traceable to any one source, but it has been handed down.

Legacies of money seem to fall in most cases to those who are already fortunate. This may be on the theory that "To him that hath shall be given." Not so with the more enduring legacies of body and soul. Whether we will or no they come, and, like the dreaded bacteria, fix themselves in the most fertile soil. Where there is one weakness of body or mind another is the more apt to locate; hence, instead of having a general distribution of evil, it falls much more heavily in some places than in others.

To no one source more than the conditions attendant upon pregnant women can the cause of physical or moral evil be traced. The unborn child draws its physical and in large measure its intellectual and ethical make-up from its father and its mother. Not from the mother alone, as many suppose, but from both.

Both parents contribute to the possibilities for health, good or bad, and furnish the germs for character creation and development just as certainly as they together originate the physical life.

These are solemn truths! Yet how few people understand or regard them! The awful sacredness of procreation has never yet dawned upon any considerable proportion of mankind.

Sadly enough, the gratification of passion is too often the only thought, while the result is given little or no consideration. Too many children come into life as mere accidents. The father is irritated at the thought of an additional one to work for. He feels his present family to be quite as much as he can decently support. His moroseness is communicated to the already regretful mother, who reasons that she is not strong enough, that children worry her so she cannot do justice to those she already has, that her time and strength are too much divided, as she in many cases is also a bread-winner. Sad plight, we see, for there is reason in the objections offered. But prudential considerations come too late to be availing. Just think how the innocent offspring must reap the evil effects of these unholy feelings and expressions, and all the sympathy that you might have felt for the parents turns into disgust, and you exclaim: "In Heaven's name, call your will to the rescue and say, 'God helping me, I will not thus prejudice the cause of my own child!'"

Few women seem to appreciate the fact that the sensitive embryo receives the impressions made upon the mind of the mother. Very strange thoughtlessness, as the most ignorant believe in birthmarks and everything that affects the body. How is it that they do not realize that a mind also is being created?

All parents love their children and most love them to the very best of their understanding. Because of this love, which we believe to be the strongest known to the human breast, most parents are willing to be taught what is best for their offspring.

In making effort to give uplift to the vitality of the Negro race the best work needs to be put into the enlightenment of present and prospective parenthood. Not necessarily into general and extended learning,—that is more or less impracticable,—but the claims of prenatal and hereditary influences need to be brought to the direct and intelligent consideration of all classes.

In the women's meetings and in the men's meetings equally there should be set forth in a plain way the important teachings of science on this important subject. This instruction may be set forth in such language as the occasion demands and the instructor chooses to employ, but, above all, let it be distinctly understood that the development of germ life depends upon the original germ and equally upon the culture and treatment of that germ:—in short, teach that the prenatal development of a child depends largely upon whatever affects the mother. If the pregnant woman is constantly wishing that her unborn child were dead or that the man who has given her this burden,—as she has learned in her chagrin to regard the child,—were dead; who can wonder that out of such murderous thought there should come in very truth a murderer!

Should the material wants of the mother be denied her to such an extent that she feels the necessity and yields to the temptation of supplying them by theft or by prostitution, who shall think it strange that her child should be a thief or prostitute? If the father is a drunkard the son is apt to be a drunkard.

Criminals are often made years and years before they are sentenced to prison. Alas! too often made criminal before they are born.

The body may come into life as sorely doomed as the mind, unable to resist the ordinary diseases incident to childlife, because of the many neglects and abuses of the bodies of parents. This is very wrong: very unfair to the child and in many ways very hard on parents.

The creation of a strong public sentiment on these subjects seems to be an imperative necessity.

Appendix 7
Some of the Dangers Confronting Southern Girls in the North

Victoria Earle Matthews

If the majority of the girls who go North every year understood the condition of the labor market, the estimate in which the crowds are held, who are willing to adopt any method of transportation for the sake of getting to the North, and the kind of work they must expect to do, and an inkling of the many humiliations they must put up with after they get there from their so-called friends, it is reasonable to suppose that self-respect would deter hundreds from rushing into a life that only the strongest physically, spiritually and morally can be expected to stand. But the girls don't know. They feel stifled in the dead country town. Their very nature turns scornfully from the thought of supporting themselves in the home village by raising vegetables, chickens, making honey, butter, canning fruit or vegetables, putting up pickles and such like. And yet could they spend a few weeks with me, and hear the agonized moans of many a heart broken, disgraced young creature, from whom only a few short sin-stained years of city life has taken every vestige of hope, every chance of innocent happiness—could they hear as I have heard the one cry over and over,—"Oh, had I known—had I only staid down home," and seen the despair upon young faces when some sympathizing one would ask, "Why not go back?" "Go back! Never! I could not face the folks; I'd rather die." Could even some of the women see and hear these things, the condition of our people in the cities would soon change and many a life would be saved, many a home protected and blessed. But the girls don't know; it is simply a story of human nature—only "the burnt child really dreads the fire" it would seem, and until the truth is known in every

Matthews, Victoria Earle. "Some of the Dangers Confronting Southern Girls in the North." *Hampton Negro Conference*, no. 2, July 1898. Hampton, VA: Hampton Institute P, 1898. 62–69. Reprinted by permission of University Archives, Hampton University.

town and hamlet in the South, the youth of our race, educated and uneducated alike, will pay with their bright young lives, and the sacrifice of all that is noble, not only for our ignorance, but our sinful negligence in watching over and protecting our struggling working class against the hordes of unscrupulous money-making combinations that make the study of their needs and limitations for traps in moral and human life without a parallel in this country. So successful have been the operations of certain associations for the bringing of young innocent girls from the South for immoral purposes, that all southern girls are commonly adjudged to be weak morally. And the earnest young girl leaving her home for a northern city must expect to face this. So many of the careless, unneat, untrained, shiftless class have been brought out simply as blinds and imposed upon by ladies, for the purpose of lessening the demand among honest respectable people for colored help, that the demand has greatly fallen off. Combinations can't get as much money in the way of office fees from respectable people as from the disreputable class, hence every effort is made to increase trade among the latter, even at the expense of the innocence of ignorant and unprotected young girls.

Every week, from the early spring till the late fall, crowds arrive by the Southern Steamship Lines. They are spoken of as "crops." A "crop" will ordinarily last about five years. There are always new recruits and the work of death and destruction goes on without let or hindrance under the very eaves of the churches as it were. Never did the words of Jeremiah, the prophet, seem more fitting than at this time and in this connection: "Yet hear the voice of the Lord oh, ye women, and let your ear receive the word of his mouth and teach your daughter wailing and every one her neighbor a lamentation. For death is come up in our palaces to cut off the children from without, and the young men from the streets."—Jere. 9:20–21.

Many of the dangers confronting our girls from the South in the great cities of the North are so perfectly planned, so overwhelming in their power to subjugate and destroy that no women's daughter is safe away from home. And now that this honored institution has enabled the message to come to you, no women here can shirk without sin the obligation to study into this matter, to the end that the evil may be completely exterminated, and protection guaranteed to the lives and reputations of the generations yet to come.

In order that my meaning may be perfectly clear I will confine myself to one of the dangers confronting the southern girls, one designed expressly to make money out of their helplessness and ignorance, and of which innumerable dangers spring into existence in a way so bewildering as to make life in New York and other large centers a perfect net-work of moral degradation for the unknowingly unfortunate who may happen to fall into its toils. Black men and women are often the promoters of this vile scheme, but it is by no means confined to them, for on actual investigation as many white men will be found in it as black. The very necessities of the case demand that Afro-Americans be the figure heads at least, and the fact that men and women can be found of our race willing to aid such work but illustrates the extent of certain phases of racial deterioration.

As has been said, the sporting and otherwise disreputable class prefer green southern girls as servants. They pay higher wages and higher office fees than any other class. Their mode of living offers many inducements to untrained and inexperienced workers, considerable time, a chance to make extra money, and unrestricted opportunity for entertaining promiscuous company. Pretty girls are always in demand, but not at first as servants. In order to supply the demand made by this class of patrons safe, the interest of the public must be deflected. A general employment bureau is planned. The patronage and sympathy of the public is sought on the ground that in helping the earnest but almost despairing idle class of the south to better homes a grand work of humanity will be done. Agents are sent throughout the South. Great promises are held out to the people; many are helped, particularly those too wise to be fooled. The agent offers to send a certain number off on a certain day: he tells them that an "officer" from the "Society" will meet them and conduct them to the "office" and lodging house. Another officer will procure service places for them, and all they are to do in return is to sign a paper giving the company the right to collect their wages until traveling expenses are paid back.

As soon as they arrive in New York they find the company treats them as so many head of cattle. They are huddled in dirty ill-smelling apartments, many feeling lucky if a pallet is given them to sleep on the floor. Often girls are forced to sleep on their own clothes. The food provided is not only very scant but often of the most miserable quality. No privacy is secured to them. Men can pass out and in at will and not infrequently they sleep in the same room owing to over-crowding. Board and lodging is regularly charged against each one at regular city prices, also storage for trunks. The Society will collect wages until all debts are fully canceled according to their reckoning. Hundreds are provided with work, and if it were merely a question of an organized body charging first class fare for second class passage, extorting illegal rates of interest, herding the good, the bad and the indifferent into regular prescribed city dens making possible contact with every phase of vicious life, not excepting petty gambling, if this were all it would be simply a matter for the courts, but this is not all.

While the girls are waiting for work they are not permitted to see any lady who may call. All particulars are given and agreements are made in the "office." A girl will be sent to a place. Should she become dissatisfied with the character of the people and refuse to remain, the agent will threaten her with court proceedings, for broken contract, etc. Thoroughly cowed, she will remain with the determination to go on her own responsibility after she has worked out her debt. She does not know that no lady will care to employ her, will trust or even tolerate her in the family after she has had such contact; the girl does not know this; she determines to get out of the agent's debt and hunt for herself the kind of work she prefers. Hundreds mean this, but daily contact with depraved characters, daily association with friends (?) whose business it is to corrupt the mind of the subject by timely comments and subtle suggestions, destroys the good intention and many go down; their day is a brief one. They drift back to the "office" and become part of another circle of wickedness and depravity. Under the guidance of the officers various camps are countenanced, that is a man will be found who is willing to pose as husband. Innocent girls, tired of waiting day in and day out around the office will be decoyed, and soon they become regular members of the camp (a couple of rooms will be rented and the girls will pose as lodgers). From operating "traveling policy" and other petty gambling schemes they drift to the street. When any one of the camp is arrested the man appears and pleads for "my wife." Probably in the course of a month he appears before the same magistrate for four or five different women, each one claimed as "wife." In turn all the women of the camp share their earnings with him. When, by their combined efforts, a young and pretty girl is ensnared all will bunch their earnings, deck her out in fine clothes and diamonds—the "husband" becomes a sort of contractor—and in due time she is entered into some "swell set." Hundreds of dollars are made in this way, and distributed among the "company" the "camp" and the officers protecting both institutions. The poor butterfly finally drifts, a mass of disease and yearning for death, to the city hospital on Blackwell's Island!—begging piteously to be recorded as coming from anywhere but where she did come from, screaming in the abandonment of despair—"O! if I had only known! If I had only known!"

By various sophistries many refined, educated girls, particularly mulattoes and fair quadroons, are secured for the diversion of young Hebrews (the identity of their offspring is easily lost among Afro-Americans). These girls are led to believe they will get permanent work in stores and public service under the control of politics. So our "tenderloins" are filled. The public, seeing these women haunting certain portions of the city in such an unfailing stream, takes it for granted that all black people—all Afro-Americans—are naturally low. The trade which supplies southern girls as domestics to the disreputable has been carried to such an extent that many ladies refuse to employ colored help for no other reason than that they are associated in the public mind with that class, and the idea prevalent that they are "signs" or "badges" as to the whereabouts of these people. Thousands of Afro-Americans throughout the city are employed by this class, and the standard of the race is gauged by them. The small percentage, comparatively speaking, of the refined working girls is so hopelessly small that those in charge of desirable work unhesitatingly refuse to consider the application made by a nice Afro-American girl, until public sentiment has been created in favor of employing her along with respectable white girls. In other words the public must be convinced that there is another class than is represented by the depraved class commonly met with on the streets and in certain localities. The common standard of life must be elevated. The "tenderloins" must be purified. Corrective influences must be established in the infested centres. Torches must be lighted in dark places. The sending of untrained youth into the jaws of moral death must be checked. Any girl taking her chances in the cities in this stage of our history must expect in some way to be affected by the public repute of the misguided lives led by those preceding her. Unless a girl has friends whom she and her family know are to be trusted, unless she has money enough to pay her way until she can get work, she cannot expect to be independent or free from question among careful people.

These are hard truths, but truths they are. The conditions I have tried to present are not confined to any one city; by correspondence and personal investigation, I have found evidences of the system in such centres as New York, Boston, San Francisco, Chicago, and other cities of lesser note. You may ask what is to be done about this awful condition? Naturally the indignant mind would immediately suggest the bringing of the guilty ones to justice. That must be done, but not in the ordinary way. All employment systems are not necessarily combined against virtue. The wrong doers are not ignorant of the law. They know their limitations, and the loop-holes for their legal escape is simply a question of money. It would take the absorbing interest of more lives than one to ferret out all the real responsible culprits. Then the bringing of the guilty ones to justice is likely to blast the hopes of many a girl who now sees the light, and is building again slowly the ruined castle of honor. Such should be protected. This iniquitous system has the advantage of many years headway. It cannot be overthrown in a day. Let women and girls become enlightened, let them begin to think, and stop placing themselves voluntarily in the power of strangers. Let them search into the workings of every institution under whose auspices they contemplate traveling North. If they have no means of learning somewhat of every one connected with the business represented by a "traveling agent," let them stay at home. It is better to starve and go home to God morally clean, than to helplessly drag out miserable lives of remorse and pain in Northern tenderloins.

As Virginia seems to have been the starting point of the system (and its beginning dates shortly after the first honest intelligence office began operations in the South—just as soon as men saw there was money in it), it is meet that appeal should be made at this conference not only in behalf of Virginia's absent daughters, but the long-suffering cruelly wronged, sadly unprotected daughters of the entire South.

Appendix 8
The Future Colored Girl

Lucy Wilmot Smith

In Switzerland travelers are shown what is called "The Meeting of the Waters."
It is the conflux of the Rhone and Arno. It is said that as one stands looking at
the wild, rushing Arno, all thoughts of self are forgotten; and, for the time being,
the turbulence thrills and fills the soul. The two rivers, one steady and placid,
the other swift and maddening, flow side by side in the same bed without mix-
ing until a point several miles from the meeting-place is reached, then gradually,
drop by drop, they become one. So it was with the education of the colored
youth in the South. When the public school system was first established we
made a wild rush for the education offered. History will record that never since
the time of Frederick the Great was such a sudden waking up of zeal for the
education of a people. Here and there schools were started and enthusiastic
friends extolled the marvelous aptness of the colored child. It was thought by
many that the Anglo-Saxon standing as the proud monument of centuries
steady climbing, wrestling with kings, battling with priests and the conflicts of
ages, would be left far behind in the race of intellectual advancement. Everything was forgotten except the cramming of heads. All other members of the
body were given a long rest. Honest toil was shunned and the highest ambition
of those who had educational affairs in control seemed to be in cheating the
humbler paths of labor of their rightful heritage to fill the pulpit and teacher's
chair. As time rolled on, a few saw breakers in the distance and gave the alarm.
For a while the two branches of education, that of the head and that of the hand,
took the same direction but refused to become one. By degrees physical culture
was agitated, manual labor introduced in our best schools, and at this time no

Smith, Lucy Wilmot. "The Future Colored Girl." *Minutes and Addresses of the American National Baptist Convention*, St. Louis, MO, Aug. 25–29, 1886; Jackson, MS: Spelman, 1887.
68–74. Reprinted courtesy of American Baptist Historical Society.

education is considered complete unless the hand as well as the head can perform suitable labor. It is generally conceded that to educate one part of a child to the neglect of others is dangerous. Man has not only gone forward with time and the course of events, but taking it all in all his possibilities are greater than ever before; the same can be said with equal truth of women. The women of to-day are the girls of yesterday; if then I speak of women that are but grown up girls, and being heirs of all the ages, especially of our own day, we can truly be guided by past experiences and prevent many an ache and tear by saving the forest in the seed—the woman in the girl.

Observation will show that taking it as a whole men occupy vantage ground. I say, without fear of successful contradiction, that during the years of which we have record, the atmosphere in which women have moved has been fraught with repression, limitation and servitude. Now and then epochs in which she was considered the equal of man have dotted the annals of the past, but they were as short-lived as the meteors that shoot across the sky. The French have accorded her much latitude in the literary world. The Hindoos have such a contempt for women they do not allow them to speak the same language as their lords and masters. In Korea women really have no moral existence, have not even a name. They are either instruments of pleasure or machines of labor but never man's equal and companion. The Grecians said she was "an accidental production," and treated her as a child. The Hebrews said she was an "after thought of the Creator[.”] In the Apostolic times she was considered a "domestic peril," a "necessary evil"; they also admitted that she was a "desirable calamity." Among the Sioux she is a beast of burden. In Russia her voice is never heard in church; she is not considered worthy to sing the praises of God in the presence of men. Even in our own America, in this last quarter of the Nineteenth Century ablaze with the electric light of intelligence, if she leaves the paths made straight and level by centuries steady tramp of her sex, she is denominated strong-minded or masculine by those who forget that "new occasions make new duties."

Proof of Her Capabilities

are demonstrated by the great number that has taken front rank in the march of progress. It matters not in what walk of life you enter, foot-prints of women are found who have gone before, clearing forests, spanning rivers and making straight, in the desert of ignorance, a highway for the girls of to-day. We have representatives in science who have now world-wide renown. In political economy they have discussed every question which vexed the heads of sages, whether of government, labor, reform, slavery, peace, religion or temperance. In politics we have had some of the shrewdest the world has ever known; some who influenced the boldest intellects and the most ardent spirits of their times. Powerful and sagacious queens have wielded the sceptre, and, like Napoleon, the most illustrious were creators of kings. Scores of authors have done much with their pens to improve human society. To name the philanthropist would be to name the majority of American and English women who have been known by the public in the last fifty years. Painters, sculptors, poets, song-birds, orators and lecturers abound. Madam DeStaël[1] is the philosopher whom all women delight to mention. On one occasion she said: "I rejoice not so much that I have learning, but that there are ten occupations at which I could make a living. This brings us to the subject direct. After all the discussions and admissions concerning women and their 'rights,' all Christendom has conceded her the right of having something to do."

The great want of the Nineteenth Century is opening of pursuits where women can earn a respectable living. In no period of our Nation's history have so many women been thrown on their own exertions as now. How they are to wrest food, clothing and shelter from the world is one of the great problems of the day. What can she do in the economy of society? Women have been breadwinners since the birth of history and probably anterior to that date. When Miss Martineau[2] visited America forty years ago to study the condition of working women, she said that Massachusetts, one of the most liberal communities on the globe, had thrown open only seven doors of industry to her women. As time passed with no chronometer but a consciousness of being unjustly hampered, with no dial but a glimmering hope that the future held brighter things, 1886 finds in the same State 284 occupations employing 251,158 women who receive from $150 to $3,000 per annum.

History furnishes a clue to the condition of laboring women of other nationalities, but no pen can tell, no tongue describe how dearly earned is the bread of the majority of

Colored Women.

Her social standing, moral, physical and intellectual status is discussed, but how she makes her way as a laborer except in such positions as include scrubbing floors of offices, hotels and other public buildings, staggering under huge baskets of clothes to be laundried [sic], lugging petulant children, cooking or house cleaning is, in reality, a matter of conjecture. Recognizing the fact that we cannot reach the heights to which we aspire until we find new fields of labor for our girls, it is necessary that we who are interested in directing their future should search out other avenues and lend the weight of our influence in making openings. What our girls will do depends largely on the opportunity of getting the work. Many desire, and would do much, but the present financial condition of our people and the prejudice which closes the doors of four-fifths of the industries to us prevent. I would suggest, first, a change in the home life of our people so that the masses that live in the country where property is cheap and money can be saved, to start the girl in business. The city is not the place for the majority because the present state of affairs are [sic] against our children. While fair play is being agitated by our journals we should be accumulating money so as to be ready when the opportunity comes. In large cities hundreds of white girls whose acquirements and native ability are inferior in many instances to many of ours, are employed in stores and business houses after leaving school, while ours, whether they so desire or not, are forced to either teach, sew or become dependents on hard-worked parents. Of five hundred employments at which women are quoted as earning a living, there is none perhaps, that, with judicious management, will yield so large a profit as poultry-keeping.

Poultry Is King.

Throughout this country enterprising and industrious girls as well as men are engaged in this business. In 1882 the value of poultry products was $560,000,000. Statistics show that this exceeded the wheat crop by $92,000,000; of the hay crop by $124,000,000, and of the cotton crop by $150,000,000 or more than double their value. There is always ready sale for poultry products in large quantities at hotels, boarding houses and such places. The demand is greater than the supply. Within the last eleven years 101,173,835 dozen eggs, valued at $14,565,047, have been brought into the United States from foreign lands. Hundreds and hundreds could make a good living by selling eggs only, to say nothing of the price paid for feathers and poultry. A small capital is all that is necessary for beginners.

It is surprising how little ground is required for

Small Fruit Raising,

such as strawberries, currents, etc. I have a friend who, last year, realized $500 on a strawberry bed one-third of an acre large. Foreigners are growing wealthy at fruit-selling and our girls could do the same by selling early in the season when fruits are high-priced, and when cheap, preserve to fill winter contracts with caterers.

Milk, butter and cheese are so wholesome that

Dairying

ranks with the most important branches of industry wherein girls can succeed. Pure butter and milk are always in demand. One good cow will give several hundred gallons of milk in a year and an opportunity to make 900 pounds of butter. Regular customers are waiting. Every year millions of pounds of cheese are shipped from the United States to England.

Floriculture

is one of the most pleasant as well as the most healthy and profitable employments. Flower markets succeed in proportion to the refinement of the locality. Flowers of all kinds, roots, plants, and bouquets are in demand the year round. There is a young girl in New York who sometimes sends out $1,000 worth in one evening.

Bee Culture.

In many Southern States and in Great Britain many women have turned their attention to this work. The expense is a mere trifle; hives can be made at home and the bee furnishes its own board. Prudent and skillful management coupled with industry will bring success. In an article on labor, by Rev. W. J. Simmons,[3]

I find the following: "One hive of bees will teach more lessons of industry to the children than all the school masters. Give them a hive apiece; let them learn there are 20,000 to 40,000 little creatures to care for, that their hive has only one of 250 different kinds, and then let them collect and sell the honey and the wax, increasing their stock from year to year." The South supplies honey for the Northern market and sale is always certain.

Lecturers

There are hundreds of men and women who would like information on certain subjects but will not buy the books. These are willing to pay to hear a lecture. The field for competent female lecturers is a broad one. Our women and men are surprisingly ignorant about the laws of health. Herbert Spencer says: "To tens of thousands that are killed add hundreds of thousands that survive with feeble constitutions and millions that grow up with constitutions not so strong as they should be and you will have some idea of the curse inflicted on the offspring by parents ignorant of the laws of health." If our women of tomorrow are to be what we hope, intellectually, reform in the home-life of our people must be agitated. Many thoroughly qualified women have given to the world their knowledge of hygiene, but ours is not a reading people. Our girls must qualify themselves to rectify these evils.

One of the most desirable fields of labor is

Newspaper Work.

Proof-reading, type-setting, editorial work, &c. In every city of importance we have papers that would gladly give employment to competent colored girls. The aspirations of our people and their thirst for knowledge will create a heavier demand for editorial work in the future. We need papers and magazines edited *by* women, *for* women. Some have entered this field and are succeeding admirably. Others should do the same. Of late years the public has declared itself favorable to the art of

Photography.

Outfits are so cheap that a few dozen photographs will cover the bill. Very much of the art can be learned alone by one who desires to succeed. Photographic sceneries are very popular and a girl could make a living at it. Some of the greatest physicians of the age advise that more women devote their time to the study of

Medicine.

The mortality among the colored people in the South is alarming. Our girls must play the part of healer, and give special study to the diseases of women, and restore to her good health the birthright she has sacrificed at the shrine of fashion. The founder of the New England Female Medical College said: "The practice of male physicians in the department of diseases of women and children is not only dangerous but destructive of health." I think all surgical operations on women should be performed only by women. As long as there are people there will be sickness, and as long as there is sickness there will be a call for competent sick nurses. A good nurse is often more necessary than a physician. Thorough training is indispensable. Although the pay is good, only strong girls with patient, cheerful dispositions should think of fitting themselves for it.

Teachers of Fancy Needle Work

can earn from $5 to $10 per week; often, more. Until late years we knew nothing of this pleasant, profitable pastime. Lessons in embroidery, crochet, hair, wax, bead and paper work bring from 25 to 50 cents to $1.50 each. A skillful girl can, by placing work on exhibition, get as many pupils as she can teach. Together with this she could combine Lustre and Kensington Painting, Repousse or brass hammering, and the German Decorative Art, which, though simple, will doubly pay for all investments.

To the above list I could add telegraphy, stenography, agencies, hair dressing, bleaching and pressing of straw work, bird-raising, silk culture, typewriting, missionary labor, the work of the elocutionist, &c. A false notion of propriety in regard to the rearing of girls has so ruled the world that in most cases they are unable physically to compete in the same field of labor with boys the same age. It is not only unnecessary but a gross sin that so many girls are unhealthy. In many cases they are born with sickly bodies, but proper hygienic living will, in nine cases out of ten, overcome physical defects. Give the girl the same freedom in exercising as the boy, the same liberty of wearing loose clothes, the same mental food and she will accomplish the same work. I do not want the boys to have all the labor, the girls all the rest. Place them on the same footing by giving them the same education.

> "The honest, earnest man must stand and work,
> The woman also—otherwise she drops
> At once below the dignity of man,
> Accepting serfdom."[4]

It is one of the evils of the day that from babyhood girls are taught to look forward to the time when they will be supported by a father, a brother or somebody's [*sic*] else brother. In teaching her that in whatever field of labor she enters she will abandon after a few years is teaching her to despise the true dignity of labor. The boy is taught to fill this life with as many hard strokes as possible. The girl should receive the same lesson. In Mythology we read of a bird that has only one wing. When it desires to fly, the male and female come together as we do when clasping hands, and thus they soar above clouds and frosts to bathe in the clear sunlight. So with our men and women of to-morrow. They must

> "Rise or sink together
> Dwarfed or god-like, bond or free."

Let it be remembered that the Lord of harvests has said, "In all labor there is profit"; and in his sight there is neither male nor female.

Notes

1. Madame De Staël (1766–1817) was a French writer, who published political and literary essays, including *A Treatise on the Influence of the Passions upon the Happiness of Individuals and of Nations*.

2. Harriet Martineau (1802–1876) was an English writer. After a visit to the United States from 1834–36, she wrote *Society in America* (1837) and *Retrospect of Western Travel* (1838). Described by one biographer as "a radical Victorian," Martineau supported the Abolitionist Movement and other social reforms.

3. William Simmons (1849–1890) was pastor of the First Baptist Church in Lexington, Kentucky, and president of the State University at Louisville, where Smith taught.

4. Smith here quotes from Elizabeth Barrett Browning's *Aurora Leigh*, Bk. 8, ll. 712–15 (1857).

Notes

1. Black Women on the Speaker's Platform, 1832–1900: An Overview

1. Margaret Tate had also recited at the Congress of Colored Women of the United States, held in Atlanta, Georgia, in conjunction with the December 1895 Cotton States and International Exposition. Many of the same women, among them Frances Harper, Fannie Barrier Williams, and Victoria Matthews, attended this gathering leading to the formation of the National Association of Colored Women. Elizabeth Davis records that Tate, "a mere child," had been "voted honorary member of the Congress because of her excellence in recitation" (26).

2. I refer throughout this volume to various configurations of black women's associations that are identified in relationship to one another and in relationship to the black women intellectuals who were instrumental in their development. The national club movement, most active in Washington, D.C., New York, and Boston, ultimately evolved into the National Association of Colored Women (NACW) in 1896 with Mary Church Terrell as the first president. For an overview of the black women's club movement, see "National Association of Colored Women" (842–51) and B. Jones.

3. In her fictionalized revision of Margaret Garner's story, *Beloved* (1987), Toni Morrison focuses on the psychological impact of a bondage that drives one to infanticide.

4. Martin Robison Delany (1812–1885) was, among other occupations, a physician, lecturer, novelist, and journalist, who published his own newspaper and edited the *North Star* with Frederick Douglass. *The Condition, Elevation, Emigration, and Destiny of the Colored People of the United States* (1852) proposed a range of solutions to the problems of blacks in pre–Civil War America, including their emigration to predominantly black areas of the world, instead of to Canada (as Shadd Cary would propose in *A Plea for Emigration, or Notes of Canada West* [1852]). In this same sketch, Delany mentioned having read a prepublication version of Shadd Cary's 1849 pamphlet titled *Condition of Colored People*.

5. The most comprehensive discussion of the contradictions surrounding Sojourner's performance on this occasion is Nell Irvin Painter's *Sojourner Truth: A Life, A Symbol.* In this definitive biography, Painter points out that Gage's account of this speech was written on the heels of the publication of Harriet Beecher Stowe's April 1863 *Atlantic Monthly* article "Sojourner Truth, the Libyan Sibyl." Painter adds that Gage's extended profile, including her rendering of Truth's speech, printed in the April 23, 1863, New York *Independent*, is demonstrated to be essentially "Gage's invention" (171).

6. See, for example, Harper's 1866 speech at the Eleventh National Woman's Rights Convention, "We are All Bound up Together"; Foster (*Brighter* 217–19); and Wells's autobiography, *Crusade for Justice*, especially chapter 27.

2. African Origins/American Appropriations: Maria Stewart and "Ethiopia Rising"

1. Of course, we should not assume that Griaule's version or interpretation of Ogotemmêli is accurate and, even if accurate, that Ogotemmêli was necessarily representative of the Dogon culture. For further discussion of Griaule's study, see Clifford.

2. See Austin, for a discussion of the classes of utterances—the locutionary, the act of saying something, the illocutionary, the act performed in the saying, and the perlocutionary, the act achieved by the saying.

3. See Sundquist also for a detailed discussion of political and literary allusions to Ethiopianism by black male writers throughout the nineteenth and early twentieth centuries. Sundquist additionally discusses "the spell of Africa" in the novels of nineteenth-century novelist Pauline Hopkins.

4. See Nell Painter's critique of Stowe's portrayal of Truth as a "primitive objet d'art." Painter points out that Stowe uses such terms as "Africa," "Ethiopian," "Libyan," and "native" over twenty times in a nine-page article (*Sojourner Truth* 151–63).

5. For detailed accounts of the experiences and activism of blacks in the antebellum North, see Litwack, Horton and Horton, and Jacobs. My overview of this early period is indebted primarily to these three sources.

6. Also titled "Charge Delivered to the African Lodge at Menotomy."

7. See Horton and Horton's discussion of Prince Hall, the black Masons, and the prevailing African ties of Northern antebellum blacks (125–54).

8. Marilyn Richardson reminds us that Stewart was preceded by a number of oratorical and spiritual foremothers, known and unknown, including Lucy Terry (1730–1822), who delivered several court speeches, and Phillis Wheatley (1754?–1784), whose religious poetry appeared in the *Liberator* between February and December of 1832 (125n49). Ann Allen Shockley reports that Terry's three-hour argument for her son's admittance to Williams College, though unsuccessful, was "a brilliant speech spliced heavily with law and Gospel" and that her "gift for oratory gained national prominence" when she brought a property suit against a Vermont neighbor, pleading her case before the U.S. Supreme Court (14).

9. Among black women, two notable evangelistic predecessors of Stewart were Jarena Lee and Zilpha Elaw. Lee, after first being denied the opportunity to preach at Richard Allen's Bethel African Methodist Episcopal Church in Philadelphia, held prayer meetings in 1818 and went on to launch her own itinerant preaching career. Also from the Philadelphia area, Zilpha Elaw, during an 1817 camp meeting, was called by God to preach. Elaw proselytized for the rest of her life, traveling into slaveholding states, and eventually, in 1840, carried her message abroad to London. For more on these early evangelists, as well as Julia Foote, whose evangelistic activities began in the 1840s, see William Andrews.

10. See, for example, Frances Harper's "Woman's Political Future" and Anna Cooper's "Womanhood a Vital Element in the Regeneration and Progress of a Race" in S. Logan (*With Pen and Voice*). Both build arguments on the potential of woman's influence.

11. For a discussion of the way in which the structure of arguments surrounding equality in late eighteenth- and early nineteenth-century America led to the African colonization movement, see Condit and Lucaites.

3. "We Are All Bound Up Together": Frances Harper's Converging Communities of Interest

1. Foss, Foss, and Trapp explain that for Habermas, advancing capitalism collapsed the distinction between public and private domains. The public sphere "no longer existed as a place and space for rational discussion and consensus because all members of society no longer could participate equally. Those whose private interests were connected directly with political aims sought to influence how those aims fared in the public sphere, rather than allowing for open discussion about them" (255).

2. According to Robert Stepto, such appended matter as letters, prefaces, and guarantees validated or authenticated the existence and literacy of the writer, in most instances a former slave. Harper, in the poetry and prose that follows the preface, successfully reclaims authorship (3–5).

3. See chapter 6 for a discussion of Victoria Matthews's use of the term "race."

4. All quotations are taken from the excerpt as printed in the May 23, 1857, *National Anti-Slavery Standard*, unpaginated.

5. Vernon Loggins notes that the latest extant issue is dated March 1860 (393n72), although Penn states that the publication continued until 1861 (118–19).

6. See a discussion of Anna Julia Cooper's essay, "Colored Women as Wage-Earners," in chapter 7 of this volume. Cooper brought to light the fact that over half of the black families in an Atlanta University study were supported wholly or in part by women; hence, they were entitled to the same compensation as all other workers.

7. Henry Grady (1850–1889), in his famous 1886 speech titled "The New South," offered the hand of economic reconciliation to Northern whites under the condition that the South be left to handle its "race problem" unhindered. Harper, in her speech, was possibly quoting from a later Grady speech, "The Race Problem," delivered ten days before he died in 1889.

4. "Out of Their Own Mouths": Ida Wells and the Presence of Lynching

1. Although the term "lynching" was often associated with a variety of lawless punishments inflicted upon suspected persons, by the end of the nineteenth century, it had come to mean "summary and illegal capital punishment at the hands of a mob" (Cutler 12).

2. For excerpts from these testimonies, see Gerda Lerner (172–88).

3. See Karon for a discussion of the ways in which Perelman and Olbrechts-Tyteca's treatment of presence may be in conflict with other aspects of their theory of argumentation.

4. When the previous owner of the *Free Speech and Headlight* and pastor of the Beale Street Baptist Church, Reverend Taylor Nightingale, left the state in the heat of a controversy with the congregation, Wells and editor J. L. Fleming purchased Nightingale's shares, dropped the last part of the name, and expanded the newspaper's circulation to approximately four thousand (Suggs 326).

5. Maria Stewart grounded her speeches in biblical scriptures. Sojourner Truth, Frances Harper, and Anna J. Cooper all also invoked spiritual guidance and support to sanction their claims.

6. See Bederman's article for a discussion of how Wells's inverted discourse manipulated Northern middle-class fears about loss of manliness, an attribute closely associated with Eurocentric and therefore civilized behavior. Bederman traces the development of the concept "Victorian manliness," showing how Wells argued that by behaving like bloodthirsty savages, the lynchers had become more like the uncivilized barbarians from whom they claimed to be protecting white women.

7. For example, in her 1875 lecture, "The Great Problem to Be Solved," delivered during the Centennial Anniversary of the Pennsylvania Society for Promoting the Abolition of Slavery, Harper stated, "I do not believe there is another civilized nation under Heaven where there are half so many people who have been brutally and shamefully murdered, with or without impunity, as in this republic within the last ten years" (Foster, *Brighter* 220).

5. "Women of a Common Country, with Common Interests": Fannie Barrier Williams, Anna Julia Cooper, Identification and Arrangement

1. Wells offered her own explanation for this refusal in the pamphlet titled *The Reason Why the Colored American Is Not in the World's Columbian Exposition*, coauthored in 1893 with Frederick Douglass, I. Garland Penn, and Ferdinand Barnett.

2. I am indebted to Mary Helen Washington for calling this article to my attention.

3. I refer to these texts as speeches rather than essays or chapters because I consider their effectiveness as contextualized, situated, and delivered rhetorical acts.

4. Quotes from Cooper's speeches and essays are taken from *A Voice from the South*, Oxford 1988, with pages enclosed in parentheses, unless another source is indicated.

5. Nestor, in Homer's *Iliad*, is said to have placed his weakest military troops in the middle.

6. "To Embalm Her Memory in Song and Story": Victoria Matthews and Situated Sisterhood

1. Brown also calls into question the assumptions that women of the North and South operated in the same manner, that women of this period participated in politics chiefly through voluntary organizations, and that most of their participation took place at the national level. She describes the extensive post–Civil War political activity of Richmond women well before and in part leading to the national club movement of the 1890s (111–45).

2. See chapter 4 for a discussion of this testimonial.

3. Two of the best-known responses to Bitzer's definition come from Richard E. Vatz

and Scott Consigny. Vatz argues for situation as freely created by the rhetor; Consigny posits a setting in which the rhetor has control over certain "indeterminate matter" (185).

4. See chapter 7 for a discussion of reactions to this speech in the context of late nineteenth-century racial uplift discourse.

5. Quotations from "The Value of Race Literature" and "The Awakening of the Afro-American Woman" are taken from S. Logan (*With Pen and Voice*), with pages cited in text.

6. See chapter 3 for a discussion of Harper's "The Colored People in America."

7. The excerpt from Emerson, reproduced as quoted by Matthews in the epigraph to "The Value of Race Literature," is taken from the Moorland-Spingarn Research Center manuscript (2).

8. See the discussion of representations of audience in Ede and Lunsford and in Campbell (*The Rhetorical Act* 71–73).

9. In his essay titled "Critical Memory and the Black Public Sphere," Houston Baker points out that blacks would never have participated in Habermas's version of an egalitarian public sphere, clearly dependent on property ownership and literacy, since they had come to this country as property rather than property owners and had been denied the opportunity to acquire literacy. He adds, however, that "[f]ully rational human beings with abundant cultural resources, black Americans have always situated their unique forms of expressive publicity in a complex set of relationships to other forms of American publicity (meaning here, paradoxically enough, the sense of publicity itself as authority)" (13–14).

10. Michael C. Dawson points out that when blacks were formally expelled from mainstream post-Reconstruction public discourse at the end of the century, they developed a twofold strategy designed both to reinsert themselves into this discourse through political agitation and organizational protests and to cultivate a black counterpublic. Using as one example Ida Wells's antilynching campaign, he adds that many black leaders and organizations participated in both publics dialectically (204). The same dual roles were played by most of the women considered in this volume, addressing, as they did, both black and white publics.

11. It should be remembered, of course, that "formal education" for black women during this post-emancipation era included that delivered in a one-room schoolhouse, in a normal school, and, for a few, in a fully credentialed institution of higher learning. More important was the extent to which these early intellectuals made use of available resources. Both Frances Harper and Matthews are described as having been employed by owners of well-stocked libraries. Maria Stewart wrote of attending Connecticut Sabbath school classes until the age of twenty, where she, no doubt, received training in reading and religion.

12. Frances Harper adhered to a similar pattern in her 1891 speech titled "Duty to Dependent Races," addressed to the National Council of Women of the United States. She was also "representing the race" before a gathering of white women but concentrated on the past progress and future political power of black people generally. She also closed with an appeal to their common Christianity. For a further discussion of this speech, see chapter 3.

13. As one historian writes, the family "served the slaves as a mode of structuring sexual and kinship relations and the rearing of children, and as a focus for psychological loyalty and devotion. It was in the bosom of family that the young slave acquired much of his cultural

heritage, and it was through the medium of the family that the individual slave was related to the larger slave community" (Joyner 137). Black slave families developed into a variety of configurations, shaped by African traditions, Christianity, and slavery, but they did exist. See also A. Davis, who points out that enslaved families demonstrated "irrepressible talent in humanizing an environment designed to convert them into a herd of subhuman labor units" (15), and White.

7. "Can Woman Do This Work?": The Discourse of Racial Uplift

1. All texts selected for analysis in this chapter, except Laney's speech titled "The Burden of the Educated Colored Woman" and Cook's essay titled "The Work for Baptist Women," both currently available in anthologies (see Works Cited), are included in the appendixes to this volume.

2. See also Houston Baker's critique of Cooper's approach to racial uplift. He claims that it would be "overseen by a blackmale elite, who, in the preservation of a staid symmetry, will receive instruction in mercy from their college-bred wives" (*Workings* 34).

3. Although both Smith and Cook participated actively in Kentucky educational, religious, and political affairs during this period, neither is mentioned in George C. Wright's history of black Louisville—while both Simmons and Charles Parrish, who was married to Cook, are discussed at length.

4. Their ages seem less remarkable when we consider that Nannie Helen Burroughs, one of the chief founders of the Woman's Convention, auxiliary to the National Baptist Convention, was only twenty-one when she delivered her historic speech titled "How the Sisters are Hindered from Helping" to the Richmond, Virginia, convention in 1900.

5. See Kraditor (43–74) for a discussion of the change from natural rights to expediency as the chief suffragist argument.

6. See Fiorenza's exegesis of this passage, in which she claims Paul's intention to limit the activities of married women and to dissociate the new Christianity from orgiastic cults (226–35).

7. See Hobbs for a discussion of More's teaching working-class adults to read in English Sunday schools and of the way her "feminine benevolence model," educating women for motherhood and the promotion of Christianity, became the standard for female education in the United States (8–9).

8. W. E. B. Du Bois, with whom the Atlanta conferences are most closely associated, did not assume directorship until 1898, the summer after he took a teaching position at Atlanta University. See Lewis (211–25) for a discussion of conference changes under Du Bois's leadership.

9. I thank my colleague Francille Rusan Wilson for pointing out that, prior to 1895, Atlanta University and other black colleges made it difficult for black women to earn bachelor's degrees, tending to concentrate women's education in their Normal departments. Thus, Laney and Georgia Swift King were both graduates of the University's Normal school division and were discouraged from entering the college program.

10. References to speeches delivered at this conference are from Atlanta University and are cited in the text.

11. See Alexander (3–13) for an analysis of Logan's personal history as it relates to this speech.

12. The title of this speech is also listed in conference proceedings as "Dangers Encountered by Southern Girls in Northern Cities."

Works Cited

Alexander, Adele Logan. *Ambiguous Lives: Free Women of Color in Rural Georgia, 1789–1879*. Fayetteville: U of Arkansas P, 1991.

Allen, Richard, and Absalom Jones. *A Narrative of the Proceedings of the Black People During the Late Awful Calamity in Philadelphia in the Year 1793*. Philadelphia: Woodward, 1794.

Andrews, William, ed. *Sisters of the Spirit: Three Black Women's Autobiographies of the Nineteenth Century*. Bloomington: Indiana UP, 1986.

Aptheker, Bettina. "Woman Suffrage and the Crusade Against Lynching, 1890–1920." *Woman's Legacy: Essays on Race, Sex, and Class in American History*. Amherst: U of Massachusetts P, 1982.

Aptheker, Herbert, ed. *Documentary History of the Negro People in the United States*. Vol. 2. New York: Citadel, 1951.

———. *"One Continual Cry": David Walker's Appeal to the Colored Citizens of the World (1829–1830). Its Setting and Its Meaning*. New York: Humanities P, 1965.

Aristotle. *The Rhetoric of Aristotle*. Trans. Lane Cooper. Englewood Cliffs, NJ: Prentice Hall, 1932.

Asante, Molefi Kete. *The Afrocentric Idea*. Philadelphia: Temple UP, 1987.

Atlanta University. *Social and Physical Conditions of Negroes in Cities and Proceedings of the Second Conference for the Study of Problems Concerning Negro City Life*. Atlanta: Atlanta UP, 1897.

Austin, John L. *How to Do Things with Words*. Cambridge: Harvard UP, 1962.

Avery, Rachel Foster, ed. *Transactions of the National Council of Women of the United States*. Philadelphia: Lippincott, 1891.

Baker, Houston. "Critical Memory and the Black Public Sphere." *The Black Public Sphere: A Public Culture Book*. Ed. The Black Public Sphere Collective. Chicago: U of Chicago P, 1995. 3–14.

———. *Workings of the Spirit: The Poetics of Afro-American Women's Writing*. Chicago: U of Chicago P, 1991.

Barbour, John D. *Version of Deconversion: Autobiography and the Loss of Faith*. Charlottesville: UP of Virginia, 1994.

Bass, Rosa Morehead. "Need of Kindergartens." Atlanta U Publications No. 2, *Social and Physical Conditions of Negroes in Cities and Proceedings of the Second Conference for the Study of Problems Concerning Negro City Life*. Atlanta UP, 1897. 66–68.

Bederman, Gail. " 'Civilization,' the Decline of Middle-Class Manliness, and Ida B. Wells's Antilynching Campaign (1892–94)." *"We Specialize in the Wholly Impossible": A Reader in Black Women's History.* Ed. Darlene Clark Hine, Wilma King, and Linda Reid. New York: Carlson, 1995. 407–32.

Bitzer, Lloyd F. "The Rhetorical Situation." *Philosophy and Rhetoric* 1 (1968): 1–14.

Boulware, Marcus H. *The Oratory of Negro Leaders: 1900–1968.* Westport, CT: Negro Universities P, 1969.

Bragg, George F. *Afro-American Church Work and Workers.* Baltimore: Church Advocate Print, 1904.

Brawley, Edward M. *The Negro Baptist Pulpit: A Collection of Sermons and Papers.* 1890. Freeport, New York: Books for Libraries, 1971.

Broughton, Virginia W. *Twenty Year's Experience as a Missionary.* 1907. (Rpt. in *Spiritual Narratives.*) Ed. Henry Louis Gates. New York: Oxford UP, 1988.

Brown, Elsa Barkley. "Negotiating and Transforming the Public Sphere: African American Political Life in the Transition from Slavery to Freedom." *The Black Public Sphere: A Public Culture Book.* Ed. The Black Public Sphere Collective. Chicago: U of Chicago P, 1995. 111–50.

Brown, Hallie Quinn. "Frances Ellen Watkins Harper." *Homespun Heroines and Other Women of Distinction.* 1926. New York: Oxford UP, 1988.

Burke, Kenneth. *A Rhetoric of Motives.* Berkeley: U of California P, 1969.

Butler, Selena Sloan. "Need of Day Nurseries." Atlanta U Publications no. 2. *Social and Physical Conditions of Negroes in Cities and Proceedings of the Second Conference for the Study of Problems Concerning Negro City Life.* Atlanta: Atlanta UP, 1897. 63–65.

Calloway-Thomas, Carolyn. "Cary, Mary Ann Shadd." *Black Women in America: An Historical Encyclopedia.* Vol. 2. Ed. Darlene Clark Hine et al. Bloomington: Indiana UP, 1994. 224–26.

Campbell, Karlyn Kohrs. *A Critical Study of Early Feminist Rhetoric. Man Cannot Speak for Her.* Vol. 1. Westport, CT: Greenwood, 1989.

——. *The Rhetorical Act.* Belmont, CA: Wadsworth, 1982.

Campbell, Karlyn Kohrs, and Kathleen Hall Jamieson. "Form and Genre in Rhetorical Criticism: An Introduction." *Form and Genre: Shaping Rhetorical Action.* Ed. Karlyn Kohrs Campbell and Kathleen Hall Jamieson. Falls Church, VA: Speech Communication Assn., 1978. 9–32.

Carby, Hazel V. *Reconstructing Womanhood: The Emergence of the Afro-American Woman Novelist.* New York: Oxford UP, 1987.

Cary, Mary Ann Shadd. Letter to Frederick Douglass. 25 Jan. 1849. *The Black Abolitionist Papers.* Vol. 4. *The United States, 1847–1858.* Ed. C. Peter Ripley. Chapel Hill: U of North Carolina P, 1991. 31–34.

——. Sermon. 6 Apr. 1858. *The Black Abolitionist Papers.* Vol. 2. *Canada, 1830–1865.* Ed. C. Peter Ripley. Chapel Hill: U of North Carolina P, 1986. 388–91.

——. "Trades for Our Boys." Letter. *New National Era* (21 Mar. 1872). *The Black Worker*

During the Era of the National Labor Union. Ed. Philip S. Foner and Ronald L. Lewis. Philadelphia: Temple UP, 1978. 177–78.

Chalmers, Thomas. *The Juvenile Revival; or the Philosophy of the Christian Endeavor Movement.* St. Louis: Christian, 1893.

Cicero. *De Inventione, De Optimo Genere, Oratorum Topica.* Trans. H. M. Hubbell. Cambridge: Harvard UP, 1949.

[Cicero]. *Rhetorica Ad Herennium.* Trans. Harry Caplan. Cambridge: Harvard UP, 1954.

Clifford, John. *The Predicament of Culture: Twentieth Century Ethnography, Literature, and Art.* Cambridge: Harvard UP, 1988.

Condit, Celeste Michelle, and John Louis Lucaites. "The Rhetoric of Equality and the Expatriation of African-Americans, 1776–1826." *Communication Studies* 42 (Spring 1991): 1–21.

Consigny, Scott. "Rhetoric and Its Situations." *Philosophy and Rhetoric* 7 (1974): 178–86.

Cook, Mary. "Eulogy for Lucy Smith." *Home Mission Echo* 6.1 (1890): 4–5.

——. "Woman's Place in the Work of the Denomination." American National Baptist Convention, Mobile, AL. *Journals and Lectures* (1887): 45–56.

——. "Woman's Place in the Work of the Denomination." *Lift Every Voice: African American Oratory 1787–1900.* Ed. Philip Foner and Robert James Branham. Tuscaloosa: U of Alabama P, 1998. 663–76.

——. "The Work for Baptist Women." *The Negro Baptist Pulpit.* Philadelphia: The American Baptist Publication Soc., 1890. 271–85.

Cooper, Anna Julia. "Colored Women as Wage-Earners." *The Southern Workman and Hampton School Record* (28 Aug. 1899): 295–98.

——. "Discussion of the Same Subject by Mrs. A. J. Cooper of Washington, D.C." in Sewall 711–15.

——. "The Higher Education of Women." *A Voice from the South by a Black Woman of the South.* 1892. New York: Oxford UP, 1988.

——. "The Humor of Teaching." *The Crisis* Nov. 1930: 387, 393–94.

——, ed. *The Life and Writings of the Grimké Family.* 2 vols. I: *Personal Recollections of the Grimké Family,* II: *The Life and Writing of Charlotte Forten Grimké.* Privately printed, 1951.

——. "The Negro as Presented in American Literature" ("One Phase of American Literature"). *A Voice from the South by a Black Woman of the South.* 1892. New York: Oxford UP, 1988. 175–227.

——. "The Status of Woman in America." *A Voice from the South by a Black Woman of the South.* 1892. New York: Oxford UP, 1988.

——. *A Voice from the South by a Black Woman of the South.* 1892. New York: Oxford UP, 1988.

——. "Womanhood a Vital Element in the Regeneration and Progress of a Race." *A Voice from the South by a Black Woman of the South.* 1892. New York: Oxford UP, 1988.

Coopin, Fannie Jackson. "Discussion Continued by Fannie Jackson Coopin of Pennsylvania."

The World's Congress of Representative Women. Ed. May Wright Sewall. Chicago: Rand, McNally, 1894. 715–17.

Cromwell, Adelaide M. "The Black Presence in the West End of Boston, 1800–1864: A Demographic Map." *Black and White Abolitionists in Boston.* Ed. Donald Jacobs. Bloomington: Indiana UP, 1993. 155–67.

Crummell, Alexander. "The Black Woman of the South: Her Neglects and Her Needs." *Masterpieces of Negro Eloquence: The Best Speeches Delivered by the Negro from the Days of Slavery to the Present Time.* Ed. Alice Moore Dunbar. New York: The Bookery, 1914. 159–72.

Cutler, James Elbert. *Lynch-Law: An Investigation into the History of Lynching in the United States.* 1905. Montclair, NJ: Patterson Smith, 1969.

Daniel, Sadie Iola. *Women Builders.* Washington, DC: Associated Publishers, 1970.

Dann, Martin. *The Black Press, 1827–1890: The Quest for National Identity.* New York: G. P. Putman's Sons, 1971.

Davis, Angela Y. *Women, Race and Class.* New York: Random House, 1981.

Davis, Elizabeth Lindsay. *Lifting as They Climb.* New York: G. K. Hall, 1996.

Davis, H. "A Moses Wanted." *National Baptist World* 5 Oct. 1894: 1.

Davis, Simone W. "The 'Weak Race' and the Winchester: Political Voices in the Pamphlets of Ida B. Wells-Barnett." *Legacy* 12 (1995): 77–97.

Dawson, Michael C. "A Black Counterpublic?: Economic Earthquakes, Racial Agenda(s), and Black Politics." *The Black Public Sphere: A Public Culture Book.* Ed. The Black Public Sphere Collective. Chicago: U of Chicago P, 1995. 199–227.

DeBoer, Clara Merritt. *Be Jubilant My Feet. African American Abolitionists in the American Missionary Association, 1839–1861.* New York: Garland, 1994.

Delany, Martin Robison. *The Condition, Elevation, Emigration, and Destiny of the Colored People of the United States.* 1852. New York: Arno, 1968.

Douglass, Frederick. "Great Is the Miracle of Human Speech: An Address Delivered in Washington, D.C., on 31 August 1891." *The Frederick Douglass Papers.* Series 1: Speeches, Debates, and Interviews. Vol. 5. Ed. John W. Blassingame. New Haven: Yale UP, 1979. 474–77.

———. *Life and Times of Frederick Douglass.* 1892. New York: Collier, 1962.

———. *The Narrative and Selected Writings.* Ed. Michael Meyer. New York: Modern Library, 1984.

DuBois, Ellen Carol. *Feminism and Suffrage: The Emergence of an Independent Women's Movement in America, 1848–1869.* Ithaca: Cornell UP, 1978.

Dyson, Michael Eric. *Between God and Gangsta Rap: Bearing Witness to Black Culture.* New York: Oxford UP, 1996.

Ede, Lisa, and Andrea Lunsford. "Audience Addressed/Audience Invoked: The Role of Audience in Composition Theory and Pedagogy." *College Composition and Communication* 35 (May 1984): 155–71.

"Editorial." *Woman's Era* 1.6 (Sept. 1894): 8.

Fiorenza, Elisabeth Schussler. *In Memory of Her: A Feminist Theological Reconstruction of Christian Origins.* New York: Crossroad, 1983.

Foner, Philip S. *The Voice of Black America: Major Speeches by Negroes in the United States, 1797–1971.* New York: Simon and Schuster, 1972.

Foner, Philip S., and Ronald L. Lewis. *The Black Worker: A Documentary History from Colonial Times to the Present.* Vol. 2. *The Black Worker During the Era of the National Labor Union.* Philadelphia: Temple UP, 1978.

Foss, Sonja K., Karen A. Foss, and Robert Trapp. *Contemporary Perspectives on Rhetoric.* Prospect Heights, IL: Waveland, 1991.

Foster, Frances Smith, ed. *A Brighter Coming Day: A Frances Ellen Watkins Harper Reader.* New York: The Feminist, 1990.

———. *Written by Herself: Literary Production by African American Women, 1746–1892.* Bloomington: Indiana UP, 1993.

Franklin, John Hope, and Alfred Moss. *From Slavery to Freedom: A History of Negro Americans.* New York: McGraw-Hill, 1988.

Fraser, Nancy. "Rethinking the Public Sphere: A Contribution to the Critique of Actually Existing Democracy." *Habermas and the Public Sphere.* Ed. Craig Calhoun. Cambridge: MIT, 1992. 109–42.

Fredrickson, George M. *Black Liberation: A Comparative History of Black Ideologies in the United States and South Africa.* New York: Oxford UP, 1995.

Gabel, Leona C. *From Slavery to the Sorbonne and Beyond: The Life and Writings of Anna J. Cooper.* Northampton, MA: Smith College, 1982.

Garrison, William Lloyd. Preface. *Poems on Miscellaneous Subjects.* By Frances Ellen Watkins. Boston: Yerrinton and Son, 1854; Switzerland: Kraus-Thomson, 1971.

Giddings, Paula. *When and Where I Enter: The Impact of Black Women on Race and Sex in America.* New York: Bantam, 1984.

Griaule, Marcel. *Conversations with Ogotemmêli: An Introduction to Dogon Religious Ideas.* London: Oxford UP, 1956.

Gyekye, Kwame. *An Essay on African Philosophical Thought: The Akan Conceptual Scheme.* New York; Cambridge UP, 1987.

Hall, Prince. "Pray God Give Us the Strength to Bear Up under All Our Troubles." *The Voice of Black America: Major Speeches by Negroes in the United States, 1797–1971.* Ed. Philip S. Foner. New York: Simon and Schuster, 1972. 13–15.

Hamilton, Thomas. "Prospectus of the Anglo-African Magazine." *The Liberator* (31 Dec. 1858): 211.

Hansberry, William Leo. *Africa and Africans as Seen by Classical Writers: The Williams Leo Hansberry African History Notebook.* Vol. 2. Washington, DC: Howard UP, 1977.

Harley, Sharon. "When Your Work Is Not Who You Are: The Development of a Working Class Consciousness among Afro-American Women." *Gender, Class, Race and Reform in the Progressive Era.* Ed. Noralee Frankel and Nancy S. Dye. Lexington: UP of Kentucky, 1991. 42–55.

Harper, Frances E. W. "Coloured Women of America." *Englishwoman's Review* 9 (Jan. 1878): 10–15. (Rpt. in Foster, *Brighter* 271–75.)

——. "Could We Trace the Record of Every Human Heart." *National Anti-Slavery Standard* XVIII, No. 1, 23 May 1857: n. pag. (Rpt. in Foster, *Brighter* 100–102.)

——. "The Democratic Return to Power—Its Effect?" *African Methodist Episcopal Church Review* 1 (1884–1885) : 222–25.

——. "Duty to Dependent Races." *Transactions of the National Council of Women of the United States.* Ed. Rachel Foster Avery. Philadelphia: Lippincott, 1891. 86–91. (Rpt. in S. Logan, *With Pen and Voice* 36–42.)

——. *Iola Leroy, or Shadows Uplifted.* 1892. Boston: Beacon, 1987.

——. Letter to Jane E. Hitchcock Jones. 21 Sept. 1860. *The Black Abolitionist Papers.* Vol 5. *The United States, 1859–1865.* Ed. C. Peter Ripley. Chapel Hill: U of North Carolina P, 1992. 81–83.

——. "Our Greatest Want." *The Anglo-African Magazine* 1 (May 1859): 160. (Rpt. in Foster, *Brighter* 102–4.)

——. "We Are All Bound Up Together." *Proceedings of the Eleventh National Woman's Rights Convention.* New York: Robert J. Johnston, 1866. 45–48. (Rpt. in Foster, *Brighter* 217–19.)

——. "Woman's Political Future." *The World's Congress of Representative Women.* Chicago: Rand, McNally, 1894. 433–37. (Rpt. in S. Logan, *With Pen and Voice* 43–46.)

[Harper] Watkins, Frances Ellen. "The Colored People in America." *Poems on Miscellaneous Subjects.* Boston: Yerrinton and Son, 1854; Switzerland: Kraus-Thomson, 1971. 38–40. (Rpt. in Foster, *Brighter* 99–100.)

Hedin, Raymond. "The Structuring of Emotion in Black American Fiction." *Novel: A Forum on Fiction* 16 (Fall 1982): 35–54.

Henderson, Mae Gwendolyn. "Speaking in Tongues: Dialogics, Dialectics, and the Black Woman Writer's Literary Tradition." *Changing Our Own Words: Essays on Criticism, Theory, and Writing by Black Women.* Ed. Cheryl A. Wall. New Brunswick: Rutgers UP, 1989. 16–37.

Higginbotham, Evelyn Brooks. "African-American Women's History and the Metalanguage of Race." *Signs: Journal of Women in Culture and Society* 17 (1992): 251–74.

——. *Righteous Discontent: The Women's Movement in the Black Baptist Church, 1880–1920.* Cambridge: Harvard UP, 1993.

Hine, Darlene Clark. *Speak Truth to Power: Black Professional Class in United States History.* Brooklyn: Carlson, 1996.

A History of the Club Movement among the Colored Women of the United States of America. 1902. Washington, DC: National Association of Colored Women's Clubs, Inc., 1978.

Hobbs, Catherine. "Introduction: Cultures and Practices of U.S. Women's Literacy." *Nineteenth-Century Women Learn to Write.* Ed. Catherine Hobbs. Charlottesville: UP of Virginia, 1995. 1–33.

hooks, bell. *Teaching to Transgress: Education as the Practice of Freedom.* New York: Routledge, 1994.

Horton, James Oliver, and Lois E. Horton. *In Hope of Liberty: Culture, Community and Protest among Northern Free Blacks, 1700–1860.* New York: Oxford UP, 1997.

Howard-Pitney, David. *The Afro-American Jeremiad: Appeals for Justice in America.* Philadelphia: Temple UP, 1990.

"How to Stop Lynching." *Woman's Era* 1.2 (1 May 1894): 8–9.

Hutchinson, Louise D. *Anna J. Cooper: A Voice from the South.* Washington, DC: Smithsonian Press, 1982.

Jackson, Blyden. *A History of Afro-American Literature: The Long Beginning, 1746–1895.* Baton Rouge: Louisiana State UP, 1989.

Jacobs, Donald. "David Walker and William Lloyd Garrison: Racial Cooperation and the Shaping of Boston Abolition." *Courage and Conscience: Black and White Abolitionists in Boston.* Ed. Donald Jacobs. Bloomington: Indiana UP, 1993. 1–20.

Jahn, Janheinz. *Muntu: African Culture and the Western World.* New York: Grove Weidenfeld, 1990.

Johnson, James H. A. "William Watkins." *African Methodist Episcopal Church Review* 3 (1886–1887): 11–12.

Jones, Beverly Washington. *Quest for Equality: The Life and Writings of Mary Eliza Church Terrell, 1863–1954.* Brooklyn: Carlson, 1990.

Jones, Jacqueline. *Labor of Love, Labor of Sorrow: Black Women, Work, and the Family from Slavery to the Present.* New York: Basic, 1985.

Joyner, Charles. *Down by the Riverside: A South Carolina Slave Community.* Urbana: U of Illinois P, 1984.

Karon, Louise A. "Presence in *The New Rhetoric.*" *Philosophy and Rhetoric* 9 (1976): 96–111.

Keyser, Frances. "Victoria Earle Matthews." *New York Age* (14 Mar. 1907): 6.

King, Georgia Swift. "Mothers' Meetings." Atlanta U Publications no. 2. *Social and Physical Conditions of Negroes in Cities and Proceedings of the Second Conference for the Study of Problems Concerning Negro City Life.* Atlanta: Atlanta UP, 1897. 61–62.

Kraditor, Aileen. *The Ideas of the Woman Suffrage Movement, 1899–1929.* Garden City, NY: Doubleday, 1971.

Laney, Lucy. "Address Before the Women's Meeting." Atlanta U Publications no. 2. *Social and Physical Conditions of Negroes in Cities and Proceedings of the Second Conference for the Study of Problems Concerning Negro City Life.* Atlanta: Atlanta UP, 1897. 55–57.

———. "The Burden of the Educated Colored Woman." *The Southern Workman and Hampton School Record* 28 (Sept. 1899): 341–44. (Rpt. in Walker 167–74.)

Lauter, Paul. "Is Frances Ellen Watkins Harper Good Enough to Teach?" *Legacy: A Journal of Nineteenth-Century American Women* 5.1 (1988): 27–32.

Lerner, Gerda, ed. *Black Women in White America: A Documentary History.* New York: Vintage, 1972.

Levesque, George A. "Inherent Reformers—Inherited Orthodoxy: Black Baptists in Boston, 1800–1873." *Journal of Negro History* 60 (Oct. 1975): 509.

Lewis, David Levering. *W. E. B. Du Bois: Biography of a Race 1868–1919.* New York: Henry Holt, 1993.

Lincoln, C. Eric, and Lawrence H. Mamiya. *The Black Church in the African American Experience*. Durham: Duke UP, 1990.

Lintin, Daniel Paul. "Shall It Be a Woman?": A Rhetorical Analysis of the Works of Maria W. Miller Stewart." Master's thesis. U of Minnesota, 1989.

Litwack, Leon F. *North of Slavery: The Negro in the Free States, 1790–1860*. Chicago: U of Chicago P, 1961.

Logan, Adella Hunt. "Prenatal and Hereditary Influences." Atlanta U Publications no. 2. *Social and Physical Conditions of Negroes in Cities and Proceedings of the Second Conference for the Study of Problems Concerning Negro City Life*. Atlanta: Atlanta UP, 1897. 37–40.

Logan, Rayford W. *The Negro in American Life and Thought: The Nadir, 1877–1901*. New York: Dial, 1954.

Logan, Shirley Wilson, ed. *With Pen and Voice: A Critical Anthology of Nineteenth-Century African-American Women*. Carbondale: Southern Illinois UP, 1995.

Loggins, Vernon. *The Negro Author: His Development in America to 1900*. Port Washington, NY: Kennikat, 1931.

Matthews, Victoria Earle. "The Awakening of the Afro-American Woman." 1897. (Rpt. in S. Logan, *With Pen and Voice* 149–55.)

——. "An Open Appeal to Our Women for Organization." *Woman's Era* 3.5 (Jan. 1897): 2–3.

——. "Some of the Dangers Confronting Southern Girls in the North." *Hampton Negro Conference*, no. 2, July 1898. Hampton, VA: Hampton Institute P, 1898.

——. "The Value of Race Literature." Unpublished manuscript. Moorland-Spingarn Research Center, 1895. (Rpt. in S. Logan, *With Pen and Voice* 126–48.)

McFeely, William S. *Frederick Douglass*. New York: Simon and Schuster, 1991.

Miller, Carolyn R. "Genre as Social Action." *Quarterly Journal of Speech* 70 (1984): 151–76.

Minutes of the Proceedings of the National Negro Conventions, 1830–1864. Ed. Howard Holman Bell. New York: Arno, 1969.

"The Monthly Review." *Woman's Era* 1.6 (Sept. 1894): 7.

Moses, Wilson Jeremiah. *Black Messiahs and Uncle Toms: Social and Literary Manipulations of a Religious Myth*. University Park: Pennsylvania State UP, 1993.

——. *The Golden Age of Black Nationalism, 1850–1925*. New York: Oxford UP, 1978.

——. *The Wings of Ethiopia*. Ames: Iowa State UP, 1990.

Mossell, Gertrude. *The Work of the Afro-American Woman*. New York: Oxford UP, 1988.

Mott, Lucretia Coffin. "Discourse on Woman." *Man Cannot Speak for Her: Key Texts of the Early Feminists*. Ed. Karlyn Kohrs Campbell. New York: Greenwood, 1989. 71–97.

National Anti-Slavery Standard (5 Feb. 1870; 23 May 1857).

"National Association of Colored Women." *Black Women in America: An Historical Encyclopedia*. Bloomington: Indiana UP, 1993. 842–51.

Nero, Charles I. "Oh, What I Think I Must Tell This World!" Oratory and Public Address of African-American Women. *Black Women in America*. Ed. Kim Marie Vaz. London: Sage, 1995. 261–75.

Neverdon-Morton, Cynthia. *Afro-American Women of the South and the Advancement of the Race, 1895–1925.* Knoxville: U of Tennessee P, 1989.

"News from the Clubs." *Woman's Era* (24 Mar. 1894): 2–5.

O'Connor, Lillian. *Pioneer Women Orators: Rhetoric in the Ante-Bellum Reform Movement.* New York: Columbia UP, 1954.

Omi, Michael, and Howard Winant. *Racial Formation in the United States: From the 1960s to the 1990s.* 2nd ed. New York: Routledge, 1994.

Painter, Nell Irvin. "Sojourner Truth in Life and Memory: Writing the Biography of an American Exotic." *Gender and History* 2 (Spring 1990): 3–16.

———. *Sojourner Truth: A Life, A Symbol.* New York: Norton, 1996.

Penn, I. Garland. *The Afro-American Press and Its Editors.* 1891. New York: Arno, 1969.

Perelman, Chaim, and L. Olbrechts-Tyteca. *The New Rhetoric: A Treatise on Argumentation.* Notre Dame: U of Notre Dame P, 1969.

Peterson, Carla L. *Doers of the Word: African-American Women Speakers and Writers in the North (1830–1880).* New York: Oxford UP, 1995.

Piersen, William D. *Black Yankees: The Development of an Afro-American Subculture in Eighteenth-Century New England.* Amherst: U of Massachusetts P, 1988.

Porter, Dorothy B. "The Organized Educational Activities of Negro Literary Societies, 1828–1846." *Journal of Negro Education* 5 (Oct. 1936): 555–76.

Quintilian. *Institutio Oratoria of Quintilian.* Trans. H. E. Butler. Cambridge, MA: Harvard UP, 1922.

Raboteau, Albert J. *A Fire in the Bones: Reflections of African-American Religious History.* Boston: Beacon, 1995.

Remond, Sarah Parker. Speech delivered at the Athenaeum, Manchester, England. 14 Sept. 1859. *The Black Abolitionist Papers.* Vol. 1. *The British Isles, 1830–1865.* Ed. C. Peter Ripley. Chapel Hill: U of North Carolina P, 1985. 457–61.

———. Speech delivered at the Music Hall, Warrington, England. 24 Jan. 1859. *The Black Abolitionist Papers.* Vol. 1. *The British Isles, 1830–1865.* Ed. C. Peter Ripley. Chapel Hill: U of North Carolina P, 1985. 435–44.

Richardson, Marilyn, ed. Introduction. *Maria W. Stewart, America's First Black Woman Political Writer. Essays and Speeches.* Bloomington: Indiana UP, 1987. 3–24.

———, ed. *Maria W. Stewart, America's First Black Woman Political Writer. Essays and Speeches.* Bloomington: Indiana UP, 1987.

Ripley, C. Peter, ed. *The Black Abolitionist Papers.* Vol. 1. *The British Isles, 1830–1865.* Chapel Hill: U of North Carolina P, 1985.

———. *The Black Abolitionist Papers.* Vol. 2. *Canada, 1830–1865.* Chapel Hill: U of North Carolina P, 1986.

Robinson, Fred Miller. Afterword. "The Value of Race Literature." By Victoria Matthews. *Massachusetts Review* 27 (1986): 186–91.

Scruggs, L[awson]. A. *Women of Distinction: Remarkable in Works and Invincible in Character.* Raleigh, NC: Author, 1893.

Sewall, May Wright, ed. *The World's Congress of Representative Women*. Chicago: Rand, McNally, 1894.

Shaw, Stephanie J. "Black Club Women and the Creation of the National Association of Colored Women." *Journal of Women's History* 3.2 (Fall 1991): 10–25.

Shockley, Ann Allen. *Afro-American Women Writers 1746–1933: An Anthology and Critical Guide*. New York: Penguin, 1989.

Simons, Herbert W. " 'Genre-alizing' about Rhetoric: A Scientific Approach." *Form and Genre: Shaping Rhetorical Action*. Ed. Campbell and Jamieson. Falls Church, VA: Speech Communication Assn., 1978. 33–50.

Smith, Arthur L. (Molefi Kete Asante). "Socio-Historical Perspectives of Black Oratory." *Quarterly Journal of Speech* 56 (Oct. 1970): 264–69.

Smith, Lucy Wilmot. "The Future Colored Girl." *Minutes and Addresses of the American National Baptist Convention*, St. Louis, MO, Aug. 25–29, 1886; Jackson, MS: Spelman, 1887. 68–74.

"Social Notes." *Woman's Era* (Aug. 1895): 18–19.

Society of Christian Endeavor. *Official Report of the Sixteenth International Christian Endeavor Convention*, San Francisco, July 7–12, 1897.

Southern Workman and Hampton School Record 27 (Sept. 1898): 174.

Spear, Allan H. *Black Chicago: The Making of a Negro Ghetto, 1890–1920*. Chicago: U of Chicago P, 1967.

Stanton, Elizabeth C. *The Woman's Bible, 1895–1898*. New York: Arno, 1972.

Stanton, Elizabeth Cady, Susan B. Anthony, and Matilda Joselyn Gage. *History of Woman Suffrage*. Vol. 2. 1881. New York: Source, 1970.

Stepto, Robert. *From Behind the Veil: A Study of Afro-American Narrative*. Chicago: U of Illinois P, 1991.

Sterling, Dorothy. *Black Foremothers: Three Lives*. Old Westbury, NY: The Feminist, 1979.

———, ed. *We Are Your Sisters: Black Women in the Nineteenth Century*. New York: Norton, 1984.

Stewart, Maria. "Address Delivered at the African Masonic Hall." (Rpt. in Richardson 56–64.)

———. "Address Delivered Before the Afric-American Female Intelligence Society of Boston." (Rpt. in Richardson 50–55.)

———. "Lecture Delivered at the Franklin Hall." (Rpt. in Richardson 45–49.)

———. "Mrs. Stewart's Farewell Address to Her Friends in the City of Boston." (Rpt. in Richardson 65–74.)

———. "Religion and the Pure Principles of Morality, the Sure Foundation on Which We Must Build." (Rpt. in Richardson 28–42.)

Still, William. *The Underground Rail Road*. Philadelphia: Porter and Coates, 1872.

Stowe, Harriet Beecher. "Sojourner Truth, the Libyan Sibyl." *Atlantic Monthly* 11 (Apr. 1863): 473–81.

Stuckey, Sterling. *Slave Culture: Nationalist Theory and the Foundations of Black America*. New York: Oxford, 1987.

Suggs, Henry Lewis, ed. *The Black Press in the South, 1865–1979.* Westport: Greenwood, 1983.

Sundquist, Eric. *To Wake the Nations: Race in the Making of American Literature.* Cambridge: Harvard UP, 1993.

Tate, Claudia. *Domestic Allegories of Political Desire: The Black Heroine's Text at the Turn of the Century.* New York: Oxford UP, 1992.

Terrell, Mary Church. "Lynching from a Negro's Point of View." *North American Review* 178 (June 1904): 853–68.

Townes, Emilie. "Ida B. Wells-Barnett: An Afro-American Prophet." *The Christian Century* 106 (15 March 1989): 285–86.

Truth, Sojourner. *Narrative of Sojourner Truth; A Bondswoman of Olden Time, with a History of Her Labors and Correspondence Drawn from Her "Book of Life."* New York: Oxford UP, 1991.

———. "Speech Delivered to the First Annual Meeting of the American Equal Rights Association." (Rpt. in S. Logan, *With Pen and Voice* 28–29.)

———. "Speech Delivered to the Woman's Rights Convention." (Rpt. in S. Logan, *With Pen and Voice* 26–27.)

Vatz, Richard. "The Myth of the Rhetorical Situation." *Philosophy and Rhetoric* 6 (1973): 154–61.

Walker, David. *David Walker's Appeal, in Four Articles, Together with a Preamble, to The Coloured Citizens of the World.* Ed. Charles M. Wiltze. New York: Hill and Wang, 1965.

Washington, Mary Helen. Foreword. *The Memphis Diary of Ida B. Wells.* Ed. Miriam Decosta-Willis. Boston: Beacon, 1995. ix–xvii.

———. Introduction. *Invented Lives: Narratives of Black Women, 1860–1960.* Ed. Mary Helen Washington. New York: Doubleday, 1987. xv–xxxi.

———. Introduction. *A Voice from the South by a Black Woman of the South.* 1892. New York: Oxford UP, 1988.

Wells, Ida B. *Crusade for Justice: The Autobiography of Ida B. Wells.* Ed. Alfreda Duster. Chicago: U of Chicago P, 1970.

———. "Lynch Law in All Its Phases." *Our Day: A Record and Review of Current Reform* 11 (Jan.–June 1893): 333–47. (Rpt. in S. Logan, *With Pen and Voice* 80–99.)

———. *A Red Record.* 1895. *On Lynchings: Southern Horrors, A Red Record, Mob Rule in New Orleans.* Salem, NH: Ayer, 1990. 1–101.

———. *Southern Horrors: Lynch Law in All Its Phases.* 1892. *On Lynchings: Southern Horrors, A Red Record, Mob Rule in New Orleans.* Salem, NH: Ayer, 1990. 4–24.

Wells-Barnett, Ida B. "Lynch Law in America." *The Arena, a Monthly Review of Social Advance* 23.1 (January 1900): 15–24.

———. *Lynch Law in Georgia.* Chicago: Chicago Colored Citizens, 1899.

———. *Mob Rule in New Orleans.* 1900. *On Lynchings: Southern Horrors, A Red Record, Mob Rule in New Orleans.* Salem, NH: Ayer, 1990. 1–48.

Wesley, Dorothy Porter. "Remond, Sarah Parker." *Black Women in America: An Historical*

Encyclopedia. Vol. 2. Ed. Darlene Clark Hine et al. Bloomington: Indiana UP, 1994. 972–74.

White, Deborah Gray. *Ar'n't I a Woman: Female Slaves in the Plantation South.* New York: Norton, 1985.

Williams, Fannie Barrier. "The Club Movement among Colored Women of America." *A New Negro for a New Century.* 1900. New York: AMS, 1973. 379–405.

———. "The Colored Girl." *The Voice of the Negro* 2 (June 1905): 400–403. (Rpt. in *Invented Lives: Narratives of Black Women, 1860–1960.*) Ed. Mary Helen Washington. New York: Doubleday, 1987. 150–56.

———. "The Intellectual Progress of the Colored Women of the United States since the Emancipation Proclamation" in Sewall 696–711. (Rpt. in Logan, *With Pen and Voice* 106–19.)

———. Letter. *Woman's Era* 1.3 (June 1894): 5.

———. "A Northern Negro's Autobiography." *Bearing Witness: Selections from African-American Autobiography in the Twentieth Century.* Ed. Henry Louis Gates. New York: Pantheon, 1991. 11–22.

———. "Religious Duty to the Negro." World's Parliament of Religions. *The World's Congress of Religions.* Ed. John Wesley Hanson. Chicago: International Publishing, 1894. 893–97.

———. "The Woman's Part in a Man's Business." *The Voice of the Negro.* Nov. 1904: 543–47.

———. "Women in Politics." *Woman's Era* 1.8 (Nov. 1894): 12–13.

Wilmore, Gayraud. *Black Religion and Black Radicalism: An Interpretation of the Religious History of Afro-American People.* 2nd ed. Mary Knoll, NY: Orbis, 1983.

Wilson, Francille Rusan. *The Segregated Scholars: Black Social Scientists and the Creation of Black Labor Studies, 1890–1950.* University Press of Virginia, forthcoming.

Wilson, Louis. "Africa and the Afrocentrists." *Alternatives to Afrocentrism.* Ed. John J. Miller. Washington, DC: Manhattan Institute, 1994. 23–26.

Woman's Era (24 Mar. 1894; 1 May 1894; 1 June 1894; Apr. 1895; Aug. 1895).

Wright, George C. *Life Behind a Veil: Blacks in Louisville, Kentucky, 1865–1930.* Louisiana State UP, 1985.

Yankah, Kwesi. "Proverb Rhetoric and African Judicial Processes: The Untold Story." *Journal of American Folklore* 99 (July–Sept. 1986): 280–303.

Yates, J. Silone. "Kansas City Letter." *Woman's Era* 1.5 (Aug. 1894). 9.

Yellin, Jean Fagan. *Women and Sisters: The Antislavery Feminists in American Culture.* New Haven: Yale UP, 1989.

Young, Robert Alexander. Excerpt from *The Ethiopian Manifesto, Issued in Defence of the Black-man's Rights, in the Scale of Universal Freedom. A Documentary History of the Negro People in the United States.* Vol. 1. Ed. Herbert Aptheker. New York: Citadel, 1951. 90–93.

Index

Shirley Wilson Logan is an associate professor of English at the University of Maryland, where she directs the Professional Writing Program and teaches courses in nineteenth-century rhetoric and African American literature. She is the author of articles on black women's discourse and the editor of *With Pen and Voice: A Critical Anthology of Nineteenth-Century African-American Women.*